CREATING DUAL LANGUAGE
FOR A TRANSFORMED WORLD:
ADMINISTRATORS SPEAK

Virginia P. Collier and Wayne P. Thomas

DUAL LANGUAGE EDUCATION OF NEW MEXICO
ALBUQUERQUE, NM   FUENTE PRESS

DUAL LANGUAGE EDUCATION OF NEW MEXICO
FUENTE PRESS
1309 Fourth St. SW, Suite E
Albuquerque, NM 87102
www.dlenm.org

©2014 by Virginia P. Collier and Wayne P. Thomas

All rights reserved. No part of this book may be reproduced in any form or by any electronic or mechanical means, including information storage and retrieval systems, without permission in writing from the publisher, except by a reviewer, who may quote brief passages in a review, with the exception of reproducible figures, which are identified by the *Thomas and Collier* copyright line and can be photocopied for educational use only.

Library of Congress Control Number: 2014949973

ISBN 978-0-9843169-3-9

DEDICATION

To all visionary

families, administrators, teachers, and policy makers

who are starting, operating, supporting, and sustaining

dual language schools:

Your hard work and dedication are preparing

our students

for their new future

as global citizens.

Table of Contents

Acknowledgments   vii
Introduction   viii
Overview of the Book   x
Prologue: Sustainable Student Success Through Quality Dual Language Programs   xiii
  Dual Language Education Articulates a Powerful Vision of Student Success   xiv
  Dual Language Education Acknowledges the Research   xv
  Core Programmatic Features of Quality Dual Language Education   xv
  Taking the Risk – Becoming Visionary Leaders   xx

Chapter One: Students—Creating and Sustaining Diverse Instructional Communities   1
  All Students and Families Benefit   1
  Inclusion: English to Speakers of Other Languages (ESOL) Students and Students with Special Needs   5
  Native English Speakers and the Lottery   7
  Meeting the Needs of English Learners First   9
  Expanding Dual Language from a Strand to a Schoolwide Program   10
  More Examples of Dual Language Admissions Decisions   13
  Mobility/Attrition: One-way and Two-way Dual Language Are Both Enrichment Models   14
  Conclusion   15

Chapter Two: Planning the Dual Language Program   17
  A Central Office Perspective on Preparing a School District for a Dual Language/Immersion Program   18
  Principals' Perspectives on Preparing for Program Implementation   23
  From Transitional Bilingual Education to Enrichment Dual Language Education   27
  Implementing and Sustaining Dual Language Education: Critical Considerations   39
  Leadership in Dual Language Education   41
  Conclusion   44

CHAPTER THREE: TEACHERS—RECRUITING AND PROFESSIONAL DEVELOPMENT   45
  Recruiting Teaching Staff   45
  Recruiting Bilingual Teachers for Large Dual Language Programs   46
  Staffing Practices   48
  Recruiting Bilingual Teachers in Smaller Dual Language Programs   50
  Regions with Fewer Bilingual Teachers   51
  Professional Development and Instructional Practices   54
  Professional Development Needs Assessment   56
  Developing Professional Learning Communities   57
  Book Study Groups and Professional Conferences   60
  Conclusion   62

CHAPTER FOUR: LEADERSHIP—PROGRAM DESIGN, SCHEDULING, AND BUDGETING   65
  Transforming Educators' Underlying Beliefs   65
  Dual Language as a Fundamental Redesign of Schooling Practices   69
  Program Design: The First Years of Implementation   73
  Program Model Design   75
  Program Expansion to More Elementary Schools   77
  Single School Contexts: Changes in Dual Language Program Designs   79
  Equalizing the Spanish/English Minutes in a 50:50 Program   79
  From 50:50 to 90:10—Deciding to teach all students to read in Spanish first, then in English   80
  Budgeting and Financial Support   84
  Leadership Responses to "Bilingual Concerns"   87
  Conclusion: Dual Language Leadership Skills and Dispositions   90

CHAPTER FIVE: ASSESSMENT—ACCOUNTABILITY AND DUAL LANGUAGE SOLUTIONS   95
  Mandatory Assessments   95
  Program Evaluation   97
  Testing in Both Languages   99
  Student Academic Achievement   100
  Assessment Guidelines for Dual Language Students at East Central ISD   101
  Understanding the "How Long" Research Findings   102
  Aligning Assessments in English and Spanish   105

   Passing the State Tests   106
   Communication Across Administrative Levels in Large School Districts   107
   Language of Assessment   107
   Benchmark Assessments   109
   Districtwide Strategic Planning Initiatives   111
   Assessment and Evaluation for the Future of Dual Language Education   114
   Support Systems for Dual Language Education for the Long Term   114
   Accountability and Dual Language Solutions   116

CHAPTER SIX: PARENTS, PARTNERSHIPS, AND ADVOCACY   119
   Parent Groups in One School   120
   Parent Cross-Cultural Communication and Advocacy   122
   Principal as Parent   123
   Parent Challenges   126
   Parent Involvement   129
   Developing Partnerships   131
   Advocacy   134

CHAPTER SEVEN: SECONDARY DUAL LANGUAGE EDUCATION—MOVING INTO MIDDLE AND HIGH SCHOOL   139
   Creating Secondary Dual Language Programs   139
   The Middle School Expansion of Collinswood Language Academy   140
   Expansion to Intermediate (Grades 4-5) and Middle School (Grades 6-8)   143
   Developing the Secondary Dual Language Program   146
   Planning and Sustaining the Dual Language K-12 Program   151
   Omaha Public Schools High School Dual Language Program   155
   Bilingualism/Biliteracy Seal Legislation   160
   Conclusion   163

EPILOGUE   165

"WE ARE INFINITE"   167

REFERENCES   169

INDEX   176

CONTRIBUTING AUTHORS   178

Acknowledgments

What an amazing collaboration this has been! The book that you are holding in your hands represents the hard work of dozens of dedicated and talented writers and editors. First and foremost is our phenomenal editor of this whole series of books, Dee McMann. She is the most gifted, organized, thoughtful, knowledgeable, resourceful, and gracious writer and editor we have ever encountered in our long professional careers. Although you will not see specific sections authored by Dee, her words are on every page, as she skillfully clarifies concepts and extends points when needed to make the writing crisp and very readable. We thank Dee for her enormous contributions to the field of dual language education through her tireless leadership in producing the publications of Dual Language Education of New Mexico, including *Soleado*, monographs, and this book series. David Rogers, as Executive Director of DLeNM, has also contributed many hours to reading and editing this book, and we thank all the staff of DLeNM for their support in making these books happen.

The 24 contributors to this book have generously poured their hearts and souls into their writing to share with you readers the reality of their everyday decisions in dual language schools. We are grateful to all of these school leaders for taking the time to get down on paper many of the innovative strategies and solutions that they have created in their varied work contexts for families and students and teachers to come together and make dual language programs work well. These dual language administrators' voices add spice and wit and wisdom to our field.

We would also like to acknowledge the larger community of dual language practitioners with whom we have worked in the last 4 years in many school districts and education policy contexts in California, Florida, Illinois, Nebraska, New Mexico, New York, North Carolina, Ohio, Oregon, Tennessee, Texas, Virginia, and Washington. As we have visited your schools and spoken to your colleagues and communities, you have raised interesting questions that expanded our research explorations, helped us improve our explanations of our national research findings, made known to us typical local conditions and needs to which dual language programs must respond, and helped us understand the larger issues that you find most important. The knowledge you have shared helps us to narrate the overall regional and national perspectives that this book, and the two previous books in this series, present.

And, finally, great thanks go to our families and to our friends in central Virginia, always there for caring and support, helping us to envision and co-create this beautifully transforming world.

INTRODUCTION

Bilingualism is an idea whose time has come in the United States. We have finally caught up with the rest of the world! This book illuminates a powerful idea, with strong theoretical and research underpinnings, as presented by experienced school leaders who are working in the real world of U.S. schools. This book is what you need to be an effective education leader. If you are interested in experiencing the benefits of dual language schooling for your community, you need to read this book and learn what these accomplished dual language administrators have to say.

Our first two books in this series were focused on presenting the theoretical foundations and research support for dual language education. This book is very different because it includes the voices of experience working to make all of this happen. These voices are grounded in reality, so keep on reading and don't put the book down—you will find wisdom and clever ideas and real-world solutions, as well as entertainment!

Audiences for this book include principals, school board members, policy makers, central office administrators, parents, community members, teachers, school staff, and anyone interested in the implementation of dual language education. This book answers the questions of why we should provide this type of education for all students, what its potential impact on all groups will be, and what the nitty-gritty of administrators' decision making in dual language programs and schools is actually like.

As the Thomas and Collier analyses have over the past 30 years continued to build enormous research support for the astoundingly positive impact that dual language education is having on students' lives in school, educators have asked the question, "How does this truly work?" What can we do to make sure that our dual language program is as successful as the ones that Thomas and Collier have analyzed? Maybe our school district is different. Do we have the resources and the staff to pull this off? Do we have community input and support? What do we need to think about as we plan and improve our dual language program? How have other dual language educators handled the inevitable stumbling blocks along the way? Can we create a consistently successful, empowering, sustainable dual language program?

To address these sincere questions, we asked a number of highly experienced school and district administrators to write about their successes and challenges as they have implemented dual language education. The voices in this book include principals, central office administrators, dual language coordinators, dual language staff development specialists, state policy makers, dual language high school graduates, dual language researchers, and university professors specializing in dual language administration. The dual language programs described in this book include rural agricultural contexts as well as small and large city school districts in the states of California, the District of Columbia, Illinois, Nebraska, Nevada, New Mexico, North Carolina, Oregon, Texas, and Virginia.

We narrators of this story, Virginia Collier and Wayne Thomas, have worked with many of these authors in their school districts. They have used our theoretical foundations and research findings to help them convince policy makers and fellow administrators to develop and sustain dual language schooling. These collaborative authors have been pioneering implementers of dual language programs, and they have lots to say to you fellow educators. They have addressed many questions in this book, including the following:

- What do you recommend to other dual language administrators?
- What are key issues to consider in the planning stages?
- How does the program progress in the first several years, and what is considered successful implementation?
- After the program has matured, what pitfalls and triumphs may continue to emerge?
- What is your vision for the future of dual language education?

In the next section, our overview of the book provides the details of each chapter.

We, the 26 collaborating authors of this book, hope you will truly enjoy the reading! We have poured our hearts into these messages. We all care about our students, and we want the very best for the families of the communities we serve. We hope that this book will be read thoughtfully and that the messages of hope and collaboration on these pages will resonate with you school leaders of the 21st century, for this is the time to envision new ways of schooling our students. Our time has come!

Ginger and Wayne

Overview of the Book

This third book continues our series on dual language education, published by Dual Language Education of New Mexico's Fuente Press. The first and second books, *Educating English Learners for a Transformed World* (Collier & Thomas, 2009) and *Dual Language Education for a Transformed World* (Thomas & Collier, 2012) present the theoretical and research foundations for why dual language schooling works so incredibly well for all groups of students. This book provides the rich reality of day-to-day life and decision making in dual language schools, as told by experienced dual language administrators.

We authors, Virginia Collier and Wayne Thomas, have conceptualized and organized this book, determined its major topics, and written an interconnecting narrative which is woven throughout the text of this book to provide the context and connections for the contributions from our 24 guest authors. The Collier and Thomas sections are presented in Calibri, a sans serif font which is slightly darker than the Adobe Garamond Pro used for the guest contributors. The guests' text is introduced by a color bar identifying that person and a thinner color bar marking the end of the guest text. In the Collier and Thomas narrative throughout the book, we have added insights and "bigger picture" regional and national perspectives, as well as research summaries that back up the administrative decisions being described.

The Prologue, *Sustainable Student Success Through Quality Dual Language Programs,* begins with a vision of the educational future that we are creating now through dual language education. Guest author Francisca Sánchez describes the overall goals of dual language programs; the core programmatic features and empowered pedagogy; the challenging and relevant curriculum, instructional resources, and comprehensive assessment that need to be in place; the high-quality professional preparation; the powerful family and community engagement that is present; and the advocacy-oriented leadership required as we expand dual language education contexts throughout the U.S. and the world.

Chapter One, *Students—Creating and Sustaining Diverse Instructional Communities,* focuses on the wide variety of students who choose to enroll in dual language programs and the amazing benefits that result from the intercultural and socioeconomic mix of students. Our guest authors from California, Illinois, North Carolina, Texas, and Virginia share many stories of their experiences assisting families with the decision to commit to dual language schooling for their children. English learners benefit the most and must be assured that they have guaranteed admission. At the same time, native English speakers benefit too, including students with special needs and students of low-income background.

Chapter Two, *Planning the Dual Language Program*, provides planning advice from administrators in small school districts developing a strand in one dual language school in a region with no dual language schools nearby, as well as those in large urban contexts with districtwide plans for dual language. Our guest authors from Illinois, North Carolina, Nevada, Texas, and Virginia advise taking 1 or more years to plan the program before starting implementation, and they narrate their own experiences with obstacles, challenges, and triumphs in the first stages of implementation. All authors have strong advice and rationale regarding many decisions unique to dual language schooling.

Chapter Three, *Teachers—Recruiting and Professional Development*, addresses the challenges of recruiting highly qualified bilingual teachers for both large and small school districts, including those in regions with fewer certified bilingual teachers. Whatever their local context, these leaders have found it necessary to take out-of-the-ordinary steps to find and recruit the bilingual teachers that they need to make their programs successful. Once teachers are recruited, professional development becomes an ongoing need for all staff because dual language programs require enhanced teaching and full understanding of the program's goals and strategies. Our guest experts from Illinois, North Carolina, Texas, and Virginia provide practical suggestions for staffing practices as well as strategies for regular support of the staff through professional development.

Chapter Four, *Leadership—Program Design, Scheduling, Budgeting*, gets into more specifics after the dual language program is in place. These include strategies for sustaining the program for the long-term; transforming educators' belief systems; surviving the first years of implementation; expanding the dual language program; and modifying the program model as needed. The authors also discuss budgeting issues, leadership challenges, and overall leadership skills that are required for administering dual language programs. Guest contributors' voices in this chapter come from California, Illinois, New Mexico, North Carolina, Texas, and Virginia.

Chapter Five, *Assessment—Accountability and Dual Language Solutions*, addresses the many assessment issues that interact with dual language program decision making. In particular, mandated assessment requirements can provide benefits and opportunities, as well as disadvantages and impediments, to successful dual language program implementation. Experienced guest experts from California, Illinois, North Carolina, Oregon, Texas, and Virginia provide insights as to how assessment decisions can improve the quality of program implementation and set the context for an effective long-term program evaluation. The guest contributors discuss the special assessment requirements of dual language programs and the various types of tests that best meet a dual language program's assessment needs. Finally, we authors emphasize that a K-12, systemic, districtwide approach to assessment decision making is highly advantageous and even necessary for addressing the long-term educational needs of both English learners and native English speakers.

Chapter Six, *Parents, Partnerships, and Advocacy*, describes the very important roles that parents play in assuring a successful dual language program. Parent involvement, especially in the forms described by the guest experts from California, North Carolina, Texas, and Virginia, is a most important research-validated resource for dual language programs that increases instructional effectiveness, builds community support, and bridges cross-cultural understanding. Engaged parents, from all cultural groups in the school, become crucial advocates and valuable partners with dual language educators. Experienced parents are also important sources of information and advice to newly-arrived immigrant families. Keeping communication open and flowing with all parent groups is a key element in assuring program success. Finally, we discuss how dual language programs can benefit from strategic partnerships with community organizations and sister schools in other school districts or even in other countries. Such efforts can greatly enhance advocacy and support for highly effective dual language schools at the local, state, national, and international levels.

Chapter Seven, *Secondary Dual Language Education—Moving into Middle and High School*, provides a valuable set of guidelines for school districts to reap the full K-12 benefits of dual language education. Secondary dual language programs are still few in number, and they represent an expanding frontier for U.S. bilingual educators. Our guest experts from Nebraska, North Carolina, New Mexico, Oregon, and Texas offer specific descriptions of how they have met the unique challenges that they and their students face in the middle and high school years. They address secondary-related issues of dual language curriculum, course planning, increased cognitive demand of instruction, higher language proficiency levels, subject areas and electives, and bilingual personnel requirements. In addition, we hear from an honors graduate of an exemplary dual language program about student ownership of the program. Finally, we describe the national importance of current legislative efforts in 17 states to create a seal of bilingualism/biliteracy for the diplomas of graduates who have demonstrated high levels of curricular mastery and deep academic proficiency in both of their languages of instruction.

The Epilogue concludes with visions of the near future for dual language education and ends with a beautiful poem by Francisca Sánchez, "We Are Infinite."

Prologue:
Sustainable Student Success Through Quality Dual Language Programs

Our book begins with a vision of the future. The author of this prologue, Francisca Sánchez, has served in several roles as an educational leader at the central administrative level in large school districts in California. She has, from the beginning, led our field to new heights, new awareness, and new visions by writing and speaking about transforming our schools. This inspired prologue examines the visionary range of possibilities that we can create as we expand dual language education experiences for all students throughout the United States and the world.

Many administrators, while immersed in the daily decision making, lose sight of the bigger picture. So when you are down and less clear about where you are and what steps to take next, it is important to take time to come back to this prologue and be inspired by what we are creating when we envision our new schools of the 21st century. Don't get discouraged by those who are blocking the way. Instead, keep the inspiration that leads to creative thinking.

Throughout the chapters of this book, you will read about the obstacles and challenges that our collaborating authors—all of whom have served as principals and administrators directing dual language programs—have had to face. Life as a school leader is not easy when you are guiding educators and communities into a new way of conceptualizing what school is all about. But our authors have also demonstrated their persistence and hard work and included effective solutions for resolving the problems and challenges that they have faced in implementing dual language programs. You will also read of their successes. This prologue provides the dream, the overview, the goals, the vision, the bigger picture of our future as dual language educators. It sets the stage, so that we can align our goals, face the challenges, and know where we are headed as we guide the transformation of our schools, creating equitable and sustainable contexts for lifelong learning.

AUTHOR: FRANCISCA SÁNCHEZ— PRESIDENT OF THE CALIFORNIA ASSOCIATION FOR BILINGUAL EDUCATION

Dual Language Education Articulates a Powerful Vision of Student Success

I believe that through the work we are doing in dual language education, we represent one of the most powerful leadership efforts for transforming our schools and changing the world for the better. Unfortunately, for far too long, mainstream educators have not been able to successfully articulate a powerful vision of student success that puts multilingualism front and center. As a result, our children and youth, even those who are successful in the current system, are ill prepared to participate in powerful ways in our global, 21st century society. In too many ways, their voices have been silenced.

Yet, in the world of dual language education, we are poised to adopt a new and very powerful vision of success that will guide our work on behalf of all students in our care. Our students will have the confidence, capability, and information needed to make positive choices for their future and will have demonstrated strength and competence in all areas needed for full participation in the 21st century economic, political, cultural, and intellectual life of our nation and global society. In addition to academic preparation, these areas include college and career readiness; mastery of advanced literacies and multimedia, multilingual, and multicultural skills; innovation, creativity, and solution-seeking competencies; social, environmental, and civic responsibility; technological fluency; and strength of body, mind, and character. And at the heart of our dual language classes are our intentions regarding language learning:

- Celebrate, respect, and appreciate our language diversity.
- Build a broad array of language/literacy, cross-cultural, and communication skills.
- Assert the legitimacy of students' native languages and dialects, protect rights to language, and systemically use students' languages, cultures, experiences, and skills.
- Create a foundation for new learning and success across the curriculum and beyond to the 21st century world.
- End the eradication and marginalization of languages other than English by countering unequal status.

(*From Laurie Olsen and the PROMISE Initiative in Southern California*)

Who benefits when students achieve proficient bilingualism/multilingualism?		
Students	**Families/Communities**	**The World**
• Healthy identity formation • Enhanced cognitive flexibility • Enhanced communication skills • Enhanced metalinguistic awareness • Expanded capacity to think divergently • Greater creativity • Healthier minds	• Increased family cohesion • Enhanced communication • Smarter citizens: 　•Strong identity and confidence in their abilities 　• More flexible and creative thinkers 　• Better problem-solvers and communicators 　• More skilled at working across differences	• Greater economic opportunities • Increased scientific/cultural creativity and knowledge development • More effective international collaboration and understanding • Enhanced communication among diverse populations

Dual Language Education Acknowledges the Research

It's important to embrace the body of research going back decades confirming that when students can achieve proficient bilingualism or multilingualism, not only do students themselves benefit in powerful, life-changing, and multiple ways, but their families and communities benefit as well (Olsen & Jaramillo, 1999; Olsen, Bhattacharya, Chow, Jaramillo, Tobiassen, & Solorio, 2001; Thomas & Collier, 2002, 2012). And it doesn't stop there. Those benefits accrue to our society and our world, transforming the way that human beings relate to each other across all their differences.

Core Programmatic Features of Quality Dual Language Education

In order to make our vision and these commitments a reality in the lives of our children and youth, we know we must ensure a set of core features that will serve as programmatic guidelines for the development or reform of any of our dual language education programs. I'll touch on each of these features, which include enriched and affirming learning environments, empowering pedagogy, challenging and relevant curriculum, high-quality instructional resources, valid and comprehensive assessment, high-quality professional preparation and support, powerful family and community engagement, and advocacy-oriented administrative and leadership systems.

Enriched and affirming learning environments. At the heart of dual language education programs is a change in the sociocultural context of schooling for students. Quality dual language education programs create safe, nonthreatening, affirming, and enriched environments for participatory and inclusive learning where it is the norm for students to interact, collaborate, communicate, and negotiate meaning with their peers; experience education that is gifted and talented rather than remedial; utilize and fully develop their languages and cultures; speak their truths and have their voices heard and reflected in the whole of the school community; and share equitably in the allocation of power and resources.

Dual language learning environments promote the following characteristics:

- **Community,** so that students feel they belong and are able to establish positive relationships with other students, teachers, and other adults. In short, they feel connected to the classroom and the school.
- **Self determination,** so that students' identities are affirmed, rather than eradicated. Students are encouraged to be self-aware, to reflect, to be responsive to those around them and to take responsibility for their own learning, including speaking out when what's happening in classrooms is not meeting their needs.
- **Trust and respect,** so that students can develop empathy for others and a certain generosity of spirit, where every student can experience dignity, where there is no room for selfishness, humiliation, or mean-spiritedness.
- **Democracy,** so students can be involved in both decision making and problem solving, so they are intrinsically motivated, so they see themselves—and are seen—as competent and able to make change, and so they learn to advocate on their own behalf and on behalf of others.

These environments support the development of the necessary skills for students to become academically competent, multilingual, multicultural, proactive, moral, and socially responsive members of a democratic society.

Empowering pedagogy. Dual language education changes how we teach students. Quality dual language education programs use culturally and linguistically responsive pedagogies that focus on students' experiences, interests, and "needs to know" in order to maximize learning, actively access and develop student voice, and provide opportunities for leadership. That means providing complex, hands-on learning experiences in low threat/high challenge contexts, as well as opportunities for active processing. Students benefit from instructional pedagogy that helps them link new knowledge with prior knowledge and that provides them with opportunities to bring their lives into the classroom. In classrooms that are responsive to all students, there is a dynamic student/teacher collaboration around generating the inquiry that forms the basis of diverse students' new learnings and that stimulates dialogue and reflection.

Dual language programs also make sure that students develop autonomy as learners, acquiring the social, cognitive, linguistic, and metacognitive learning strategies that help them figure out how to be better learners of both content and language—and how to be better knowledge creators as well. Given that our dual language programs go beyond an instrumental purpose to a transformative focus on reading the *world* as well as reading the *word* (Freire, 1970), this definitely involves bringing students' lives into the classroom and examining issues of social justice which have daily impact on their communities.

Challenging and relevant curriculum. Quality dual language education programs engage students in challenging and relevant curriculum that's well-articulated and age-appropriate; that purposefully builds bilingualism, biliteracy, and multiculturalism; and that is cognitively complex, coherent, relevant, and challenging. Part of this is intentionally planning for the triple curriculum: language, content, and culture. In addition, Cummins (2000) identifies two equally critical features—maximum cognitive engagement and maximum student identity investment. In other words, this is an extremely personal enterprise, and students must know that who they are matters and is supported by their teachers and other students. The academic curriculum and pedagogy must

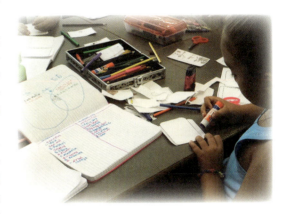

focus students on (1) meaning, making input comprehensible and developing critical literacy in both the subject matter and in language; (2) the two instructional languages, including language forms and uses across the academic language of the different disciplines; and (3) using language to generate new content area knowledge, create literature and art, and act on social realities. High levels of biliteracy development lead to increased knowledge of the world and more mastery of language forms, conventions, and uses—including language transfer and teaching to similarities and differences across students' two languages. Biliteracy development helps students clarify and organize their thinking, solve problems, and gain access to the rich cultural, historical, and literary traditions of the partner language group. Additionally, it helps students become critical consumers, users, evaluators, and creators of knowledge and information, as well as autonomous learners.

Dual language programs often organize the curriculum thematically, since themes have several advantages over other ways of organizing curricular content. Not only are they meaningful from the students' perspective, especially when students can participate in their selection and development, but they also potentially provide dual language learners with active learning and interactive literacy situations; varied social contexts for different uses of language; heterogeneous language and ability groupings; functional and authentic language use; teacher-mediated literacy instruction; use of topic-related literature and content-area print materials; print experiences based on students' experiences, interests, and needs; linking of new knowledge with prior knowledge; natural integration of other disciplines; and critical investigation that stimulates dialogue and reflection.

High-quality instructional resources. Quality dual language education programs utilize high-quality standards-aligned instructional resources that provide equitable access for English learners to core curriculum and academic language in English and the partner language in the classroom, school, and community. These resources include electronic, digital, and technological resources, as well as other traditional materials and human resources. They provide authentic models of the vast array of academic language uses. And they expand parents' ability to communicate with teachers, to actively engage in their children's schooling, and to participate meaningfully in decision making. Dual language programs take care that these resources represent the partner languages and cultures authentically.

Valid and comprehensive assessment. Quality dual language education programs build and implement valid and comprehensive assessment systems in both instructional languages, designed to promote reflective practice and data-informed planning in order to improve academic, linguistic, cognitive, and sociocultural outcomes for all students. They include multiple measures, are ongoing, include teacher observations and judgments, and provide clear analyses of actual student work and performance. Assessment helps dual language schools and communities know with certainty how every student is doing. There are structures available for classroom teachers to observe and assess students' progress on a daily basis and then apply the results of those assessments to their teaching. There are reasonable benchmarks that allow teachers and students themselves to know how close they are to meeting the identified goals and standards. There are ways of triangulating data so that judgments about student achievement and progress are not dependent on any single indicator. At the heart of these types of assessment systems are three fundamental decisions: What do we want our students to learn in each area of the triple curriculum (language, content, culture)? What evidence will we accept to verify their learning? What will we do if they don't learn what we've decided should be mastered?

High-quality professional preparation and support. Quality dual language education programs provide coherent, comprehensive, and ongoing professional preparation and support programs based on well-defined standards of practice. The bilingual teachers chosen must be academically proficient in the language(s) of instruction and fully certified to teach the content areas of their assigned classrooms. Without a doubt, teacher quality and preparation matter. Neither is there any doubt that students of color, students of poverty, and English learners are much more likely to be assigned novice or underprepared teachers. Dual language programs provide opportunities for teachers to join with colleagues in professional learning communities where they support each other in developing a common, clear vision of what good teaching is for language learners and establishing well-defined standards of practice and performance that are explicit in what they should know and be able to do to meet the diverse needs of their students. Dual language educators themselves help create and enact systems for teachers and other staff to develop high levels of personal and professional efficacy, accountability, responsibility, and advocacy on behalf of students.

Powerful family and community engagement. Quality dual language education programs implement strong family and community engagement programs that build leadership capacity and also value and draw upon community funds of knowledge to inform, support, and enhance teaching and learning for both English learners and native English speakers. Dual language programs recognize that when families, educators, and communities all work together, schools get better and students have a better chance of getting the high-quality education they need and deserve. In dual language programs, strong family and community engagement programs help families establish home environments that support learning for their children and provide information and ideas to families about how to help their children with homework as well as other curriculum-related activities. They work toward establishing more effective forms of school-to-home and home-to-school communications about school programs, student progress, and family and community resources and help recruit and organize family/community support and assistance in the school. But most important of all, dual language programs include parents in school decisions and actively promote the development of parent/community leaders and representatives who can advocate more effectively for marginalized students. They create structures to identify and integrate community resources and services to strengthen programs and practices for these students.

Advocacy-oriented administrative and leadership systems. Quality dual language education programs provide advocacy-oriented administration and leadership that institute system-wide mechanisms to focus all stakeholders on the diverse needs and assets of language learners. These administrative and leadership systems structure, organize, coordinate, and integrate programs and services to respond systemically to language learner needs and to leverage available resources most powerfully. In dual language programs, issues of data, communication, accountability, and equity are addressed, and programs and services for students are effectively coordinated and administered.

Taking the Risk — Becoming Visionary Leaders

Our students are depending on us. As dual language educators, we have a special calling. Our words can be a call to action because our lives are testimonies, and witnessing and representing are critical in this global universe that is our home. With our words turned into action, we can help our students grow and give shape to the dreams that some of them may not even know are theirs yet. Our students can gather strength and wisdom from us; we can inspire them to give full voice to the talents that live in them and to take action to achieve a future worth living. Our students can make sea changes of difference in the world. This future is a dream that belongs to all of us.

CREATING DUAL LANGUAGE SCHOOLS FOR A TRANSFORMED WORLD: ADMINISTRATORS SPEAK

Virginia P. Collier and Wayne P. Thomas

DUAL LANGUAGE EDUCATION OF NEW MEXICO
ALBUQUERQUE, NM

FUENTE PRESS

Chapter One: Students—Creating and Sustaining Diverse Instructional Communities

Author: Erin Bostick Mason, Adjunct Professor—California State University, San Bernardino, and former Program Manager, Dual Language/English Learner Services—San Bernardino County Superintendent of Schools, San Bernardino, California

All Students and Families Benefit

I believe in the vision of dual language education. Now, how can I explain this vision to others so they will join me in a successful journey toward creating bilingual, biliterate, multicultural graduates? How do I explain who belongs in this program and why it is needed, especially if our population is labeled "at-risk"? Do we need middle class, native English-speaking students to make this work?

Over the last 16 years, I have joined a wave of educators, families, and community leaders who appreciate that our communities are rich multilingual and multicultural environments. We realize that everyone benefits when public school systems embrace the full range of the cultural and linguistic capital of the students. Furthermore, the benefits of multicultural and multilingual proficiency are not far-off aspirations for our students, somewhere in their distant future. Instead, they are highly valuable, urgently needed life skills in our neighborhoods, as well as academic assets in the daily lives of our students and their families today. Indeed, the populations we often consider most at-risk are those who are most in need of and those who are best positioned to apply these skills immediately. While some communities look at dual language education primarily as a means to prepare students for college and career, there are many neighborhoods where the ability to communicate across languages and cultures unlocks daily access to curriculum and instruction, as well as builds ground-breaking friendships among children and families that cross traditional community boundaries. The ability to speak one another's language creates relationships between children that reshape their sense of identity and builds bonds one family at a time. Dual language education can prevent the cultural conflicts and linguistic isolation that fuel stereotypes, gang violence, and xenophobia.

In addition to academic achievement data, we need to look at sociocultural data to measure the need for and the success of our programs. Interviewing parents about changes they see in their children's attitudes towards different cultural, ethnic or linguistic groups can give valuable insight. One African American mother told me she was horrified to realize in the first week of kindergarten that her daughter thought she shouldn't be friends with "that Mexican girl" in her class. While reflecting on the daughter's comment, the mother realized they hadn't had any family friends who were of Mexican heritage or who were Spanish speaking. The daughter must have internalized this as an unspoken rule in her community and family. In turn, the classmate of Mexican heritage told her teacher she refused to sit next to "that Black girl" during rug time. Both families realized their children had already drawn conclusions based on skin tone and language as a result of the cultural/linguistic separation they witnessed in the community. Their first month of kindergarten unearthed and tested these 5-year-olds' assumptions about their identity and the social boundaries in our communities.

As a program facilitator, I looked for ways to create social gatherings where parents could discuss these observations and these experiences with me and with each other. We included teachers as well. We used this anecdotal evidence along with attitude surveys from the students to measure multicultural proficiency, changes in identity, and the development of friendships during the year. I even informally relied on what I termed "the birthday party test" to see how often and how many of our students were socializing outside of school together at birthday parties and other community events. By the end of kindergarten, the two girls who initially refused to sit together were literally best friends. The friendship lasted, and by fifth grade, they had hosted joint birthday parties together in their homes. Other parents often reported their students speaking in their second language to community members at the supermarket, the bank, or the doctor's office.

Many of the African American children in the program were often asked if they were Cuban or Dominican because community members found it surprising to hear African American children speaking with native Spanish accents in a neighborhood that had traditionally been divided between English-speaking African American and Spanish-speaking Hispanic populations.

Dual language programs can transform individuals and neighborhoods from within while accelerating achievement for our most at-risk culturally and linguistically diverse children, as well as for native English-speaking students. Historically, many programs across the nation were started by small groups of passionate, engaged, knowledgeable community and school members who knew how to navigate the decision-making structure of the school system. In many cases, those with the institutional power to move the vision forward within the system have been middle class, native English speakers who knew how to formally advocate for their children. As a result, many programs host a balance of middle class, Caucasian, native English-speaking students and speakers of the partner language who may represent lower-income populations, immigrant or first generation families, or others who have often been less familiar with and empowered by our school systems.

In fact, many school and community members erroneously assume that in order for dual language programs to succeed, there must be middle class, native English-speaking students. It is often an unspoken assumption that dual language programs need at least some portion of Caucasian students to succeed. However, in recent years, we have seen the birth of many programs in which all or most of the students represent populations traditionally considered minorities, at-risk, low-income, or under-achieving. They are witnessing the same research-based success any fully implemented program will see in the long term. Since dual language is by design a culturally-responsive approach with culturally-relevant curriculum and instruction, it builds on the students' strengths and accelerates achievement. The model works! A program may serve a balance of Hispanic English-dominant and Hispanic Spanish-dominant students, most of whom may represent low-income families. Other programs host African American students (some of whom speak varieties of non-standard English) and immigrant or first-generation native speakers of the partner language such as Korean or Chinese. Dual language classrooms strive for a linguistic balance, not an economic balance, and actually benefit all socioeconomic and cultural communities.

In addition, many communities are demanding access to dual language for all of their students, both those in English-only education and those who qualify for special education services. Parents are challenging the system and proving that dual language can be for all by requesting the same dual language program opportunities for their children with special needs as for their children without special needs. One Hispanic family explained to me that all their children live under the same roof, where Spanish is the home language. So why shouldn't their third daughter with Down Syndrome attend the same dual language program the two older girls without special needs attend? Another African American mom explained that her children live in this diverse neighborhood where Spanish, English, and Vietnamese are spoken. So when her son qualified for special education services for a learning disability, she did not want to pull him out of dual language. His neighborhood hadn't changed and neither had the need for multilingual, multicultural skills. The research of Fred Genesee and others (Genesee, 1987; Genesee, Paradis, & Crago, 2004; Lindholm-Leary, 2001, 2005; Thomas & Collier, 2014) uncovers the full range of options for students with special needs in dual language programs. Based on this research, administrators need to have individual discussions with each family to discuss the most appropriate instructional options, program contexts, and realistic outcomes for students. Research does not support automatically exiting students with special needs. Once again, we need to redesign the system so special education staff and dual language staff are cross-trained and work together to implement research-based strategies.

These programs are groundbreaking because they challenge our deepest assumptions about who belongs in dual language education. Dual language administrators need to facilitate these discussions. It is our duty to provide access to information, build relationships, and foster an inclusive identity. We are taking on systemic reform in the greatest sense of the term when we implement a dual language program. Because of the fundamental power shift in a 90:10 or 50:50 dual language program, those considered at-risk are actually accelerated and students' perceived deficits become strengths. At the most basic level, the deficit label of being "limited English proficient" becomes the asset-oriented label "Spanish dominant," "native Korean speaker," "Russian proficient," or "emerging bilingual." Dual language is *by design* a systemic intervention that accelerates learning and closes the achievement gap for those who are most vulnerable in an English-only system.

Research support. All student groups gain in dual language classes. The longitudinal research on academic achievement clearly demonstrates all student groups benefit from schooling through two languages (Genesee, Lindholm-Leary, Saunders, & Christian, 2006; Genesee, Paradis, & Crago, 2004; Lindholm-Leary, 2001; Thomas & Collier, 1997, 2002, 2009, 2012, 2014; Thomas, Collier, & Collier, 2010). In the summaries of our North Carolina research findings (Thomas & Collier, 2012, 2014), we illustrate that all groups participating in two-way dual language classes—English learners, Latinos proficient in English, Caucasians, African Americans, students of low-income background as measured by free and reduced lunch, and students with special needs—score significantly higher than their counterparts attending the monolingual English curriculum. This pattern repeats itself throughout elementary and middle school participation in dual language classes, with most dual language students scoring as much as a grade level ahead of their peers not in dual language. The gains for English learners and African Americans attending dual language are especially strong. In other words, this program brings huge advantages for all groups while at the same time addressing the needs of historically underserved groups of students. All students benefit immensely!

AUTHOR: DR. MARJORIE L. MYERS, PRINCIPAL—KEY SCHOOL~ESCUELA KEY, ARLINGTON PUBLIC SCHOOLS, ARLINGTON, VIRGINIA

Inclusion: English to Speakers of Other Languages (ESOL) Students and Students with Special Needs

In 1995, when I was hired as principal of Francis Scott Key School-Escuela Key, a two-way dual language/Spanish immersion school, I was told there were four programs in the building, and I must not mix them up. These programs included the dual language/immersion program; a Primary Montessori program for 3-, 4-, and 5-year-old children; a special education program; and an English to Speakers of Other Languages (ESOL) program. I was specifically instructed not to include the children with special needs or the English learners (primarily the new arrivals) in the dual language/immersion program.

That lasted about a month. As I watched the small groups of about ten children at each grade level in small pullout classrooms work with the same teacher all day long in English, it just didn't feel right. I asked the dual language/immersion teachers if they could include the special education students or the ESOL kids when they did certain activities. Then I asked that these students be allowed to attend class with them on occasion. The dual language teachers tried, but the rooms were small at that time with about 25 children crowded into each one. Adding additional children was not feasible that first year.

For the second year, I asked the Director of Special Education if I could add the children to the dual language/immersion classrooms and attempt inclusion at the school. He told me other schools used their special education teachers for inclusion contexts, and I certainly could do the same thing. Then, as I met with staff, it came up that although our upper-grade children with special needs and our English learners may have Spanish spoken at home, they had never had any instruction in Spanish. The students certainly did not know how to read or write in Spanish. So, for the first year of inclusion, we included kindergarten through second-grade special education and ESOL students into the dual language/immersion classrooms while the upper-grade students with special needs remained apart and self-contained.

Chapter One: Creating and Sustaining Diverse Instructional Communities

Once that group of third graders graduated, all of the children at Key School were included in the regular dual language/immersion program, and the program became a schoolwide model. A few years later a teacher recommended we look at the way we placed students into the classes for the subsequent years. She said something to the effect of "Think of the students as A, B, C, D, E, F, G ... it breaks down to A being gifted, B potentially gifted, C average, D resource special education, E self-contained special education, F advanced English learners ready to be classified as proficient, G new arrival ESOL, etc. One team would have every other group. The first team might have A, C, E and G groups, and the second team the B, D, F kids." This concept for class assignments has helped us by filling every class with a range of students and no team is the high team or the low team. This process has made it easier to assign the resource reading, ESOL, and special education teachers, and it has insured that all children are included in dual language/immersion at Key School.

Research support for dual language inclusion. There is no question that English learners must be included in the dual language program. In fact, they are the group that most benefit from this form of schooling (Collier & Thomas, 2009; Thomas & Collier, 2012). This program best integrates English learners with English-proficient students and places the two groups in more equal status, using the linguistic resources both groups bring to the classroom. For example, in a Spanish-English program, the Spanish-proficient students lend crucial peer support for natural second language acquisition to develop among the non-Spanish speakers when the instruction is in Spanish, and likewise, the English-proficient students serve that same role when the instruction is in English. All other programs for English learners are less efficient in helping these students reach grade-level achievement in their second language. Some English-only programs do not ever allow English learners to reach grade-level achievement in English because they don't allow the acceleration needed to catch up to the constantly advancing native English speakers. The acceleration is stimulated by supporting students' grade-level work in native language while acquiring the second language, which is one of the major goals of a dual language program for both language groups.

Inclusion of beginning ESL (English as a second language, a term used interchangeably with ESOL) students from the first year of the program works very well, as long as the dual language teachers have been well trained in second language acquisition methodology for mixed groups of students. Including the newly arriving ESL students in the upper grades presents a challenge for programs. These students also benefit strongly from attending the dual language classes, especially for the instruction in their native language. In fact, if they arrive with strong formal schooling in their home language, they can be a great resource for the school. Older ESL new arrivals do need special assistance from ESL teachers in the initial stages of English language acquisition, so the program in the upper grades should include ESL staff who provide focused instruction during a portion of the English instructional time.

How about students with special needs? The research evidence is mounting that these students benefit so much from schooling through two languages that it is very worthwhile to provide them the opportunity to enroll in dual language classes if the family and child are supportive of this idea. In the Thomas, Collier, and Collier (2010) as well as the Thomas and Collier (2014) research findings in the U.S., we confirmed Genesee's work in Canada (Genesee, 1987; Genesee, Paradis, & Crago, 2004) as well as Lindholm-Leary and Howard's research in the U.S. (Howard, 2003; Lindholm-Leary, 2001, 2005; Lindholm-Leary & Howard, 2008). Students with exceptionalities outscore their comparison group being schooled monolingually, when followed longitudinally. Dual language schooling does not harm these students. If they are happy and thriving in the dual language class, it is the best placement they can have.

> AUTHORS: IRIS GONZÁLEZ ORNELAS, BILINGUAL/ESL/DUAL LANGUAGE PROGRAM COORDINATOR, AND MANUEL ENRIQUE ORNELAS, FORMER MIDDLE SCHOOL PRINCIPAL—EAST CENTRAL INDEPENDENT SCHOOL DISTRICT, SAN ANTONIO, TEXAS

Native English Speakers and the Lottery

One of our very first challenges in East Central Independent School District during our planning year was convincing English-speaking parents to allow their children to participate in this enriched educational program. Interested parents attended sessions on the program benefits, structure, critical components, and the stages of second language acquisition. Parents from other school districts were invited to share their personal experiences of having their children in the program. Even though many parents expressed interest, many chose not to have their kindergarten student participate the first year. The district had approved two kindergarten dual language classrooms, yet we were only able to fill one class. During the first year, we showcased the dual language class at every opportunity—PTA meetings, board meetings, etc. The second year, we had so many English-speaking parents interested in having their children in the program that a second kindergarten dual language class was added and the lottery system had to be used.

A lottery is often used for admission of native English speakers to dual language classes when the program experiences maximum enrollment space for that demographic portion of the classes. By using a fair and carefully managed lottery system, the decisions for admission should be equitable for potential participants.

We learned some lessons with the lottery system. Initially, we held two required information sessions for parents to understand the program and for us to explain the reason for using the lottery system. We did mention that if they wanted their child in the program, the information sessions were mandatory. We felt parents needed to understand the commitment to the program, the rigor, the stages of second language acquisition, and all the challenges their child could experience throughout the years in the program.

But in the second year, we failed to carefully inform parents regarding the process of the lottery system for student selection. After the second parent information session, we mentioned to the parents that the lottery system was going to be held. Only those students whose names were called out would be eligible to participate in the program. At the end of the session that evening, we had crying children and parents. Some parents couldn't understand the limited slots available for English-speaking students. What they did understand is that if their child did not enter the program in kindergarten, they would have missed a lifetime opportunity. Seeing the parent interest and demand for this educational opportunity and not being able to provide it was difficult for us. Over the years since then, we have made the selection process very clear to parents.

The lottery is the only system used to select English-speaking students for the program. Our program does not screen students for disabilities or academic deficiencies. Once the student is in the program and we find that the student needs additional support, we provide services according to the student's needs within the program. This was another significant lesson. In the initial years of our program, a few parents wanted to pull their child out as soon as they were informed that their child qualified for special education or showed signs of dyslexia. Immediately, they assumed learning in two languages was causing their child's learning problem or disability. Now, as part of the parent orientation sessions, we inform parents that this enriched educational program will not cause dyslexia or any learning disability. Instead, parents are informed that students with special needs enrolled in dual language classes have been found to do as well as or even better than those students with special needs who are schooled monolingually.

Meeting the Needs of English Learners First

All the collaborating authors of this book have discussed the increasing demands by native English-speaking families for their children's participation in the dual language program. This is a positive trend, as the U.S. population becomes increasingly less isolated and more interested in multilingualism for their children. At the same time, most dual language directors recognize they must first serve the most "at-risk" populations. With English learners at the top of the list of those needing dual language programs (given that they have the largest "gap" to close in second language academic achievement), it is crucial that at least half of each dual language class be reserved for these students, when the partner language is the English learners' heritage language.

But several challenges come along with the pressure from English-speaking parents to enroll their children in dual language classes. Finding the qualified bilingual teachers and the high quality curricular resources are continuing concerns as the program expands. Another is the need to continue to serve the families who prefer English-only instruction, usually done as a strand within the school. In urban areas, a nearby school is often close enough that two schools can partner, with one providing a schoolwide dual language program and the other providing English-only instruction for parents who prefer that choice. After many years of dual language implementation, a few school districts have chosen to implement dual language districtwide. The Woodburn, Oregon, public schools have done this by arranging "English plus" tracks for the few parents who do not want their children to receive their schooling through two languages, while the large majority of their students receive their schooling through either Spanish-English or Russian-English (the main heritage languages of the community).

The following example illustrates the thinking process of one principal as she faces the growing need for expanding her school's dual language strands into a schoolwide model, and the challenges regarding admission of English speaking students to keep the balance in a two-way program.

AUTHOR: DR. EMILY BIVINS, FORMER PRINCIPAL—CARRBORO ELEMENTARY SCHOOL, AND CURRENT PRINCIPAL—COLEGIO FRANK PORTER GRAHAM BILINGÜE, CHAPEL HILL-CARRBORO CITY SCHOOL DISTRICT, CHAPEL HILL, NORTH CAROLINA

Expanding Dual Language from a Strand to a Schoolwide Program

The most pressing issue for our two-way dual language program at Carrboro Elementary School in Chapel Hill, North Carolina, has become a political hot button—expansion into the full school vs. remaining a school within a school. We have one to two English-only classrooms and two to three dual language classrooms at each grade level. Our dual language program operates as a school within a school and can serve up to 48 English speakers and up to 24 Spanish speakers within three classes, as illustrated in Table 1.1. All Spanish speakers attending this neighborhood school have the opportunity to join the dual language program at any grade level. The school started as a 50:50 dual language model, but after several years of implementation, we added a 90:10 class, which is available for the families who prefer that their children receive a strong reading foundation in Spanish before moving into formal English literacy in second grade.

We have been tracking enrollment and demand for the program within our school for several years. With about 40 students in English-only classes in K-2, 30 to 35 English speakers are on or have been on the waiting list for dual language, thus we currently have demand for a schoolwide dual language program with our current population. Of the students not enrolling, some are speakers of

other languages and refugees from Asia whose parents are concerned about the acquisition of a third language. They are willing to enroll their children in Spanish-English dual language if we recommend it, but we have not done so at this time. New parents have expressed interest followed by frustration to know they are number 35 on a waiting list. There are a few families who just don't want dual language for their children—maybe because of special needs concerns, or they're just not interested. Our challenge has been what to do to provide access to the dual language program within our school, as well as to meet the needs of families who are choosing not to participate.

Table 1.1

Grade Level	# of English Speakers	# of Spanish Speakers
Kindergarten 50:50 2 classes	24	24
Kindergarten 90:10 1 class	up to 24	any overflow
First Grade 50:50 2 classes	24	24
First Grade 80:20 1 class	up to 24	any overflow
Second Grade 50:50 2 classes	up to 24	up to 24
Second Grade 70:30 1 class	up to 24	any overflow
Third Grade 50:50 3 classes	up to 24	up to 24
Fourth Grade 50:50 3 classes	up to 24	up to 24
Fifth Grade 50:50 3 classes	up to 24	up to 24

New English speakers not admitted after Grade 1; New Spanish speakers admitted Grades K-5.

Given all these challenges, why would I want to advocate for dual language or a change in our school? The research is pretty clear. Dual language is the only approach that closes the achievement gap for our ESL students by more than 50% over time (Thomas & Collier, 1997, 2002, 2009, 2012, 2014). I also believe that multilingualism and cross-cultural competence are critical 21st century skills. If we are truly preparing children in North Carolina for the world of tomorrow, we only have to look at our current demographics and birthrate patterns to see that multilingual skills and cross-cultural competence in particular are going to be needed. In addition, critical thinking, literary and mathematical fluency, collaboration, and problem solving will be essential. Thus, our school district moved ahead to provide more access to dual language education. My first thought when thinking beyond my school was the other 300 Spanish speakers in other elementary schools who do not have access to dual language instruction. My next thought was for all students having access to this option.

Since school boundaries and students' designated assignments are district-based decisions, a solution/proposal for moving to a schoolwide dual language model has been a focus of the district Dual Language Advisory Committee's work. This group has looked beyond our school to consider expanding access for students across the district. Surveys were done, community information meetings took place, and board discussions were held. One solution was to have a sister school concept with a neighboring elementary school. Our school would receive additional Spanish speakers and some English speakers to enroll our school at full capacity for 50:50 dual language classes, starting in kindergarten and "growing" through Grade 5. Another possibility was a magnet model, and yet another solution was a schoolwide dual language program with current enrollment, shifting the program model to 90:10 for some classes and allowing those not interested to opt out and transfer to another elementary school. This process has involved data analyses to prove dual language works here, even though the national and international research was presented. In order to address concerns with community partners and board members, we have also shared research and voices from teachers, students, and parents—all advocating for dual language instruction. We challenged the naysayers to find research that countered the benefits of dual language instruction. No one has brought me anything yet. While I will admit I am not politically savvy and probably don't know how to navigate those waters well, I think we provided answers and responses to every question that came from parents, the community, and the board of education.

Finally, because of the popularity of the dual language program among English-speaking parents and the growing needs among Spanish-speaking families, the Chapel Hill-Carrboro City school district decided to expand this program. Beginning in School Year 2014, Dr. Bivins was selected to become the principal of their first schoolwide magnet at Colegio Frank Porter Graham Bilingüe. This two-way Spanish-English dual language school works to enroll an equitable balance of Spanish and English speakers. Other Chapel Hill schools continue with Spanish-English strands, and Glenwood Elementary has a long-running Mandarin Chinese-English strand.

More Examples of Dual Language Admissions Decisions

Dr. Myers describes the Arlington Public Schools' experience with balancing admissions and with serving the neighborhood children once a schoolwide dual language program is in place.

AUTHOR: DR. MARJORIE L. MYERS, PRINCIPAL—KEY SCHOOL~ESCUELA KEY, ARLINGTON PUBLIC SCHOOLS, ARLINGTON, VIRGINIA

Key School became a full schoolwide dual language program in School Year 1996 when I was hired. Unfortunately, not every school has the necessary support from the school board and the superintendent to take this step. The first priority for admission to Key School in kindergarten is to neighborhood children who want to be in dual language/immersion. If they do not, there is a second school about one mile away, Arlington Science Focus School, that serves the non-immersion children from the neighborhood boundary area. The second priority goes to siblings of current students in our school. We try to take all siblings so that once a family commits to being a bilingual family, all of the children in the household have the opportunity to join Key and have the same educational program. Two other schools serving this neighborhood accept transfers from Key School and Science Focus School, to balance diversity among the four schools.

When Claremont Immersion School was opened because Key could not handle the demand for dual language/immersion in the county, it was created not as a neighborhood school, but as a cluster school. There were two schools close to one another that had a dual language/immersion strand. When Claremont opened, the strands from the two schools were combined to make Claremont a full schoolwide immersion/dual language school like Key. Then, any parent who was in the neighborhoods of the original schools with the strands was given a priority for admission to Claremont. When space is available for extra admissions in Key and Claremont, students from the remaining 22 schools in the county may apply.

Both Key and Claremont attract many new families to Arlington, so they can take advantage of this incredible opportunity to have children grow up bilingually. Together we serve more than 1200 children each year.

Mobility/Attrition: One-way and Two-way Dual Language Are Both Enrichment Models

One more major issue with student admission decisions is mobility. Families move for many reasons, and newly arriving immigrants are just getting established and often go through several changes of housing in the initial stages of resettlement. Also, in large metropolitan areas, native English speakers may not represent a significant portion of the demographics within the school boundaries. These directors of a large dual language program in Elgin, Illinois, describe their decision making regarding mobility and maintaining class size.

AUTHORS: WILMA VALERO, DIRECTOR OF EDUCATIONAL SERVICES FOR ENGLISH LANGUAGE LEARNERS, AND PATRICIA MAKISHIMA, COORDINATOR OF DUAL LANGUAGE EDUCATION—SCHOOL DISTRICT U-46, ELGIN, ILLINOIS

The fluctuation of dual language enrollment at times makes it difficult to maintain the required linguistic balance in a two-way dual language classroom. As central office administrators, within our marketing piece, we need to have a "check and balance" of enrollment numbers/student count that reflects the fiscal responsibility that is part of staffing for the following school year. One challenge we face is the high mobility rate of students. This means from the date that parents sign up for the program to the actual start of the school year, some students move out of the school boundaries, out of the district, or out of the country, which has an impact on the two-way dual language numbers, and thus the linguistic balance might be compromised.

Making data projections requires that we establish criteria, procedures, and deadlines to guide our decisions, rather than basing projections on our love for the program and students. However, we must not forget to focus on the ultimate goal of this program: Students will become bilingual, biliterate, and bicultural citizens. This program is designed for English learners, and research shows it is the only program to close the achievement gap for these students. So, even if we do not have the linguistic balance to implement a two-way dual language program, the same instructional program should be replicated in a one-way dual language program, providing our students the opportunity to be in a program where their language and culture count as an asset for further academic success.

Conclusion

AUTHOR: DR. EMILY BIVINS, PRINCIPAL—COLEGIO FRANK PORTER GRAHAM BILINGÜE, CHAPEL HILL-CARRBORO CITY SCHOOL DISTRICT, CHAPEL HILL, NORTH CAROLINA

Dual language is an amazing program that has benefits for all students beyond the acquisition of a second language. It requires passion and resilience because so many challenges will come. Every job and every program in public education has challenges. If we are going to problem solve and work hard, why not do it for programs that will really serve *all children* well and prepare all of our students for the 21st century?

Chapter Two:
Planning the Dual Language Program

Dual language programs are started for many different reasons. Sometimes one principal has a long-term vision, and with patience and determination, this vision eventually becomes reality. Year after year, central administrative staff assigned to the directors' positions for services to English learners, immigrants, and refugees may track the number of students they serve, their language and country backgrounds, their test scores and other data, and conclude that they want more effective programs for their students. State mandates sometimes require programs that are less effective than dual language, and the superintendent and other instructional leaders take a leap of faith by implementing these mandates more effectively through enrichment dual language education. Other times, parents may be the initiators of the idea. They have heard about dual language implementation in other school districts, and they want their own children to have the experience of developing deep multilingual proficiency and cross-cultural competence. Parents understand that these experiences come from starting in the early years, using the school curriculum and the diversity of their own community as a means of naturally acquiring these crucial 21st century skills.

Once the decision has been made, and it's a "Go," many who have worked so hard to get the program approved by the school board want to start right away (especially the parents!). But all of the 25 experienced dual language administrators who are authors in this book caution new implementers of dual language to take considerable time to plan the program carefully before leaping into full implementation. Most advise 1 full year of planning, and some even say 2 years are needed in challenging political contexts where English-only proponents are outspoken. The timeframe for planning and implementation can be influenced by student enrollment and by the amount of outreach and advocacy needed to educate families whose children qualify for or can benefit from the program. The planning also includes establishing the process for recruiting and hiring bilingual staff and providing immediate opportunities for professional development. This professional development helps to ensure that the entire staff has clarity about instructional methodology in a second language context and that appropriate, high-quality curricular materials are chosen for both languages. All administrators, teachers, and support staff need to be trained, so they understand what dual language classes are doing and why. This includes those who are not teaching in the dual language strands because dual language program implementation can be sabotaged by those not implementing the program or by other non-supportive administrative personnel.

Yes, there is much to think about and plan. In this chapter, we will share implementation stories from those who started in small, isolated contexts, as well as those who work in large urban school districts with huge numbers of students in dual language programs. We will start with the tale of a small city school district in central Virginia in the Shenandoah Valley, where no other dual language program exists within 100 miles in all directions and the only form of support for English learners had been English as a Second Language (ESL) classes.

> AUTHOR: WANDA HAMILTON, FORMER SUPERVISOR FOR ESL, FOREIGN LANGUAGE, ENGLISH LANGUAGE ARTS, AND TITLE I—HARRISONBURG CITY PUBLIC SCHOOLS, HARRISONBURG, VIRGINIA

A Central Office Perspective on Preparing a School District for a Dual Language/Immersion Program

As the English learner population in a school district grows, programs must adjust and change to meet new needs and challenges. It is imperative that the central office be involved with each school's program, working with school teams to make program adjustments and recommendations based on their demographics, teacher strengths and weaknesses, student needs, and data. As a school district moves from a 12% English learner population to 40%, many changes should be made internally to meet students' needs. Central office personnel must work effectively with schools to determine budgeting needs, staff development, personnel, and program descriptions.

In our school district, the central office administrators of Harrisonburg City Public Schools have worked hard to coordinate programs for all students across schools. Change continues to happen each year as our population and demographics change. We have re-evaluated our programs yearly, based on our numbers and data, attempting to meet the needs of our growing and changing English learner population. Supervisors, ESL specialists, and school administrators all participate in this yearly re-evaluation of all school programs.

In 2004, with a growing ESL population reaching about 31% of the total student population, Harrisonburg City Public Schools (HCPS) invited Professors Wayne Thomas and Virginia Collier to work with our superintendent, school board, and administration to begin mapping out the process to develop an effective ESL program based on their longitudinal research data and work across the country. During this process, we looked at where we were and where we wanted our programs to be in 10 years, both instructionally and financially. At this time, it was important to look at the types of programs that were being used around the country and to become familiar with their advantages and disadvantages. It was also important to identify a program that fit our population and demographic needs.

One reality for Harrisonburg City Public Schools was that we needed to move from a pull-out to a push-in model, both for effective instruction and for cost effectiveness. For example, ongoing study of research by our ESL advisory team indicated that teaching ESL through the content areas is more effective than pulling students out of a mainstream classroom to work on English as a subject by itself (Echevarría, Short, & Powers, 2006; Echevarría, Vogt, & Short, 2008; Thomas & Collier, 1997, 2002).

Collier and Thomas also infused excitement into our future plans about the possibilities of a dual language immersion school or program, which then became a long-range goal for our district. HCPS needed to decide the types of data that would be valuable for us to collect and use to evaluate whether our programs were effective over a period of time. We began the process of setting up an extensive English learner database that would provide district- and school-level longitudinal data for our students in Grades K-12.

The central office ESL supervisor served as a facilitator of planning meetings with administration to decide what our priorities should be. At this time, we decided to begin moving to a push-in content-based instruction model at the elementary level. We also were fortunate to be chosen by the U.S. Department of Education to participate in a pilot program with the Center for Applied Linguistics (CAL) to train two Sheltered Instruction Observation Protocol (SIOP) Model coaches per school in Grades K-12. This was a year-long pilot course for all teachers, both mainstream and ESL; the program also included our secondary schools in the process of training teachers in best practices for English learners, especially in the content areas.

Our ESL population continued to grow, and within just a few more years, all of our elementary schools were over 40% English learners. Sixty percent of these students were still at levels 1 and 2 of our locally developed English language proficiency measures, which included the Stanford English Language Proficiency (SELP) test, reading levels based on the Qualitative Reading Inventory (QRI), the IDEA Proficiency Test (IPT) for oral assessment, plus a writing sample. HCPS set up Language Enrichment for Academic Excellence (LEAP) classes for our level 1 and 2 students in Grades 2-5. The objective was to accelerate their progress through levels 1 and 2 and provide a stronger English language foundation integrated into all content areas. Our goal was to give students the tools to be more successful in the mainstream classroom. Over 2 years, there were fewer English learners at levels 1 and 2, but these advanced ESL students still needed more cluster grouping for instruction within mainstream classrooms. This practice has been extended in the last 2 years into modified language arts classes at the middle schools to bridge students from newcomer classrooms to the mainstream classroom. Newcomer classrooms in Grades 3 through 8 provide foundational English language learning to help students transition to a mainstream setting.

Another outcome of the planning process was continued conversations with one principal, Gary Painter, on how to move to a dual language/immersion school. Harrisonburg soon realized that it does take commitment from the central office, superintendent, school board, and community to move in such a different direction. If our school system were to take this step, it also required a committed administrator, with a supportive Foreign Language/ESL supervisor and superintendent, who were all convinced that the dual language/immersion model was the next step. The dual language journey began with one principal, the encouragement and support of the supervisor, and education of the school board, parents, and community. There were some pilot programs using first language support and one-way immersion for native English speakers as bilingual teachers were hired. It did not happen overnight, but these steps were a commitment and a process of learning and communication.

HCPS is only in our fourth year of two-way dual language implementation in School Year 2014, but it has been a smooth and rewarding 4 years. We did our work upfront and took a full year to plan the program once it had been approved by the school board. Yet there were many obstacles as Harrisonburg worked to move toward a dual immersion approach. It took 5 years to overcome them and be able to commit and actually begin the process.

Our first obstacle that stopped us in our tracks was the lack of teachers who were native bilingual speakers. We spent quite a few years going to recruitment fairs and networking to find the teachers to staff one grade level. We still do not have what we need and are constantly recruiting bilingual teachers, including the possibility of looking at the international teacher programs. Again, this becomes an important partnership between the HCPS Central Office Human Resources Department, the Foreign Language/ESL supervisor, and the principal.

The second obstacle was that there were no other dual language/immersion schools in Central Virginia for sharing and training purposes. Therefore, we became involved with Arlington, Virginia, public schools in the DC metro area, where we began visits to Key Elementary and then later, Claremont. Our visits included Harrisonburg's administration, central office staff, and teachers. This gave us a foundation for building our program, using discussions at many levels on how we wanted our program to function. Although these visits helped, Harrisonburg still had no one in the system or at James Madison University (our local state university) who had actually worked in or been associated with a dual immersion school. However, through consultations with Collier and Thomas, discussions with Arlington dual language educators, and reading many books on bilingual education, we proceeded with planning. Many teachers also provided a plethora of ideas as to what a dual immersion school might look like.

A third obstacle we encountered as the planning process progressed was that the district needed to know if a dual immersion strand within a school would be accepted and supported by our parents and community. It was important to have the support of both our Spanish- and English-speaking populations. We worked through parents and community organizations to get input. Our home-school liaison was a huge help in talking with the Hispanic population, and the principal gave presentations to our preschool families since the program would begin in kindergarten. The most interest appeared to be from middle-class White families, with some hesitancy from our Hispanic population. At this point Harrisonburg committed to a 50:50 model in kindergarten with 50% of each instructional day in Spanish and 50% in English.

Budget has not been a problem because our program has not added classrooms but replaced classrooms with a different program. We have needed to add Spanish materials and texts, which HCPS added to their adoption process. Title I and III funds have been used to support components of the program. This has been a function at the central office level to help provide financial startup support.

Our big breakthrough was the building of a new elementary school, with the principal being the advocate for the new building to serve as the dual immersion school. The first year the school was open became the true planning year, using all the information collected over the past couple of years. Bilingual staff had been hired by the principal in the years prior to the program startup, as positions became available, so that the bilingual staff were in place at the new school and fully involved in the planning process. This process included trips to Arlington; a trip to Albuquerque, New Mexico; textbook and materials meetings; as well as meeting with central office. Presentations were made to the school board, at parent meetings, and at community meetings. This planning year was essential to laying the foundation needed to launch the program, which began in kindergarten the following year.

The dual immersion program is now being offered in Grades K-4 at Smithland Elementary for School Year 2015. Drs. Collier and Thomas joined us in the spring of the first year to evaluate what had been started in terms of instruction, data

collection, and program set up. It was a full-day meeting with the ESL supervisor, school administration, dual immersion teachers, and resource staff. There were many discussions about instructional balance of the two languages, teacher resource allocations, materials chosen, teacher proficiency in each instructional language, and as a result, some changes were made for the following year.

From my central office position as a supervisor, it has been exciting to watch the progress as the dual immersion program develops. The teachers have gained confidence in their understanding of how the program should be implemented. The progress of the students has been remarkable in terms of their learning of both languages. The excitement of administration, teachers, and students is also a product of the successes that the dual immersion program brings to the school. Within the first 2 years of implementation, discussions had already begun about how the middle school program might be developed, as the first group will soon be entering Skyline Middle School (Grades 5-8) as bilingual learners. At this stage, we will see the true impact of bilingual education on our students in Harrisonburg. As of School Year 2012, this program had been so successful that the principals of all the other elementary schools in HCPS began to consider the possibility of expanding the dual language classes to other HCPS schools. Keister Elementary began their dual immersion program in School Year 2014, and Waterman Elementary will start their dual immersion classes this coming year, 2014-2015.

Principals' Perspectives on Preparing for Program Implementation

AUTHOR: GARY L. PAINTER, PRINCIPAL—SMITHLAND ELEMENTARY SCHOOL, HARRISONBURG CITY PUBLIC SCHOOLS, HARRISONBURG, VIRGINIA

Yes, I'm the principal who was so impressed with Drs. Thomas and Collier's idea of starting a dual language/immersion school in Harrisonburg. After their presentation, my teachers and I spent the next few years reading articles and books on dual language programs in the U.S. Trips to visit schools in Arlington, Virginia (Key and Claremont), and Chapel Hill, North Carolina (Carrboro Elementary), gave teachers opportunities to observe students and teachers in longstanding dual language programs. Principals and teachers in these schools were professional and passionate about their programs and willing to answer questions and provide support.

Recruiting, hiring, and retaining quality dual language teachers are high priorities before beginning program implementation. I formed relationships with the local universities, attended teacher recruitment fairs, and made my plans known with the local community. After years of recruiting, we had hired a team of 13 educators with proficiency in Spanish and English to implement the first dual language program in the Shenandoah Valley. These included classroom teachers, ESL teachers, a reading specialist, a music teacher, a parent specialist, and paraprofessionals.

I presented the proposal for a two-way dual language immersion program at my elementary school to the HCPS School Board during two meetings in November 2009. School board members favored the idea and wanted detailed cost figures to implement a program. To provide staff training, curricular materials, and classroom supplies, we found that we needed additional funds of $14,000 per year beyond the standard curricular and resource expenditures of the English-only classes. The board voted to support the implementation of a bilingual program because it aligned with the school division goal for an elementary foreign language program. During an interview with the local newspaper, HCPS School Board member Kerri Wilson said, "I really felt like this was a big bang for the buck. It's a tremendous opportunity for these children."

And so the dual language immersion program in Harrisonburg City Public Schools was launched, the first of its kind in the Shenandoah Valley and in central Virginia—not an easy sell to a community that had been solidly Southern, mostly English-speaking, and somewhat skeptical about the newly-arriving immigrants, even though they needed the help with labor for the manufacturing and farming sectors of the economy. The diversity of the community includes Mennonites and immigrants/refugees from Russia, but the largest language group is Spanish-speaking immigrants, who are well served by the dual language program now that the Latino community has gradually embraced the significance of the program. More and more English-speaking parents have also begun to see the advantages for their children, and thus the principals of the remaining elementary schools are beginning to consider implementing dual language strands in their schools.

Another perspective on the first years of implementation comes from an experienced and committed dual language principal who started her principalship years ago with no knowledge of the field of dual language education in a school with a relatively new dual language strand. She presents the first six years of her experiences and the lessons learned from leaping in when little planning for the program had taken place at the central administrative level.

AUTHOR: DR. EMILY BIVINS, FORMER PRINCIPAL—CARRBORO ELEMENTARY SCHOOL, AND CURRENT PRINCIPAL—COLEGIO FRANK PORTER GRAHAM BILINGÜE, CHAPEL HILL-CARRBORO CITY SCHOOL DISTRICT, CHAPEL HILL, NORTH CAROLINA

Have you ever felt so small that your entire world might fit on the end of a pencil? I never really considered that my world was small until I became the principal at Carrboro Elementary School in Chapel Hill, North Carolina, 8 years ago. Our dual language program began as a 50:50 two-way Spanish-English program 12 years ago. At that time, I was the Director of Elementary Education and Professional Development at the central office. Dual language was a special program, and other central office staff were not integrated into the planning and implementation process beyond an awareness level. It was not until I became principal that I learned a lot about dual language. Since then my journey has taken me on many paths—instructional leader, parent educator/advocate, parent, and political advocate.

As an instructional leader, I had assumed that dual language instruction was like any other classroom except taught in another language. I never considered that at least half of the students in each class are second language learners and that instruction needs to be different. My first year at Carrboro (I was assistant principal 9 years ago), I began planning with two teachers who were new to our school and teaching a 1-2 split—one in English, the other in Spanish. These teachers had not been dual language teachers before, were not ESL-certified, and did not have much experience with our district approach to instruction—balanced literacy, cognitively guided math instruction, inquiry-based learning, and culturally responsive practices. You might be thinking, "Why did you hire them?" In my naïveté, they both spoke Spanish, and I assumed the rest would come. What a learning year that was for me!

I guided those teachers through hours of planning based on our school district's instructional framework, observed their teaching, analyzed data with them and problem solved. With the help of those teachers, I had a clear picture of what was needed to support instruction and the type of teachers and professional development needed. When I became principal, I immediately sought the help of others. Our central office, while very supportive, did not know what to do to help, but other schools and programs opened their doors, and a network began to develop. That year we dealt with things like teaching literacy in both languages, time allocation, and basic instructional resources. We read research and planned, and I thought we were well on our way by the end of the year. At least we were vastly farther along than we were, but we had so much to learn. At this point, our program was 4 years old.

That summer I attended the Illinois Resource Center's Trainer of Trainers professional development for dual language. It was at that moment my world began to shrink. I felt like the only monolingual in the room, and for the first time in my life, I realized that was a problem. I learned a lot about leadership for dual language, policy, standards, and pedagogy. I also realized how far our program had to go. That fall, we took our first team to Dual U ("University"), a professional development opportunity offered at that time by the Illinois Resource Center in collaboration with the Center for Applied Linguistics. That was the first real professional learning our teachers had about dual language pedagogy. Administrators gathered to talk, to brainstorm, and to share ideas about policy change, resource acquisition, and effective support for our teachers.

It was so refreshing to know I was not alone in my journey. Well-established programs struggled with the same things brand-new programs struggled with, and we were all able to have a shared body of knowledge and expertise. I was on fire when we drove home. However, to say my teachers were blazing is an understatement. They were talking and planning a mile a minute. We finally had an action plan based on standards, common language, and research about dual language instruction. We strongly recommend that you plan and evaluate your program frequently using the *Guiding Principles for Dual Language Education* (Howard, Sugarman, Christian, Lindholm-Leary, & Rogers, 2007). This document can be found on the Center for Applied Linguistics (CAL) website at *http://www.cal.org/twi/guidingprinciples.htm.*

In Years 5 and 6, our action plan for dual language had short- and long-range goals centering on three primary areas that were challenges for us—professional development, resources, and assessment. For the next 2 years, we worked on these issues. Teachers formed study groups and affiliated with local universities to become certified in ESL (our state does not currently have bilingual certification). Each year, another cohort attended Dual U (contact the Illinois Resource Center, *http://www.thecenterweb.org/irc/,* for current professional development opportunities), and we began to have commonality about our approach to dual language instruction. Teachers were scaffolding for all linguistically diverse students and providing more experiential learning opportunities.

Teachers really began to talk about how to bridge instruction across English and Spanish classrooms and content. We gathered every funding source available to support the purchase of materials—state and local instructional funds, Title I, Title III, our PTA, local grants, and parent fundraisers. We added to classroom libraries, take-home books, teacher instructional resources, media center collections, and textbooks. We sought recommendations from other programs, teachers we had hired from other places (what did they use before they came to us?), and what we could find through various vendors. The quantity and quality of our resources improved vastly during that time period.

The story of Chapel Hill's dual language program continues to unfold, as this small program serving as a strand within a couple of schools has gradually expanded. The program started with one school (Carrboro Elementary) offering a 50:50 Spanish-English program, while in a separate school (Glenwood Elementary) 50:50 Mandarin Chinese-English classes were provided. The program has been implemented grade by grade for Grades K-5, with both language programs continuing at the feeder middle school (McDougle Middle) through Grades 6-8. The English-speaking parents in this university community are now demanding bilingual classes for all their children, and Latino parents have also gradually become advocates as they have caught on to the power of this program for their own children. When we get to the parent chapter, Dr. Bivins has more interesting stories to tell.

In these first sections of this chapter, Wanda Hamilton, Gary Painter, and Emily Bivins have provided us with some key insights about the early planning and implementation of dual language programs in relatively small city contexts where bilingual schooling is very new to the community. They have shared with frankness the obstacles and triumphs they faced, so administrators reading this can learn from the lessons they experienced.

From Transitional Bilingual Education to Enrichment Dual Language Education

Now let's move to the state of Texas to experience the dual language planning process for large school districts that have been implementing a state-mandated bilingual program for English learners in Grades K-5 since the early 1970s. Enforced by state legislation, transitional bilingual education services in Texas are required where there are at least 20 ESL students of one language background in the same grade. These programs, only for English learners, use the students' primary language to teach literacy and most subjects of the school curriculum while the students are acquiring the English language, with a gradual transition to English-only instruction within a few years' time. These bilingual programs have existed in Texas for four decades, so there are many bilingual teachers certified to teach in these bilingual classes, providing a potential resource for dual language classes as schools choose to enrich their model of bilingual schooling. At the same time, transitional bilingual teachers need to be trained for a very, very different way of teaching.

This is only one of many potential stumbling blocks to implementing dual language in states with a history of mandated transitional bilingual education. The most formidable challenge can sometimes be the English-only voices of some administrators, school board members, and the community because some oppose many forms of bilingual schooling. The history and experience with bilingual education in Texas serve bilingual program directors well as they work to make schools more effective with enrichment models of dual language education. But at the same time, this history and experience can create challenges with those who want to maintain the status quo, as well as with those who want to eliminate bilingual programming altogether.

The next author describes the complicated preparations needed in the first stages of planning at the central administrative level to guide large urban school districts from transitional bilingual education to more effective dual language models of enrichment bilingual schooling.

AUTHOR: DORA TORRES-MORÓN, LANGUAGE AND LITERACY EXECUTIVE DIRECTOR—DALLAS INDEPENDENT SCHOOL DISTRICT, DALLAS, TEXAS

The information, scenarios, and recommendations presented here are based on my personal experiences as the director of a dual language program, as well as the language and literacy executive director in two different inner-city school systems in north Texas. Irving Independent School District has an enrollment of 35,000 students with 39% (13,000) English learners and 85% poverty rate, as measured by those qualifying for free and reduced lunch. The second district, where I am currently employed, is Dallas Independent School District (ISD), with an enrollment of 164,000 students, where 41% (65,000) are English learners and 87% qualify for free and reduced lunch. The focus of these two districts has been to promote the language proficiency and academic achievement of both English learners and students seeking to learn a second language as enrichment, with the overall district goal of college and career readiness. It is important to note the overall dual language program intent. The goal of the dual language program in both school districts is to provide literacy and content instruction through two languages to promote bilingualism and biliteracy, grade-level academic achievement, and multicultural competence for all students.

In Dallas ISD, there are two dual language programs implemented simultaneously:

- Two-way dual language/immersion program in which approximately half of the students are native speakers of the partner language and approximately half of the students are native speakers of English; and
- One-way dual language/immersion program in which all of the students are native Spanish speakers learning English as a second language.

In Irving ISD, there was also a transitional bilingual program, where all students who are native speakers of Spanish learn enough English to exit the program and then transition into all English classes as early as third grade. This model was offered as an additional parent option.

Increasing opportunities to succeed. When looking to increase opportunities for at-risk students to succeed, districts continuously search for a magic bullet that will meet that need. However, in my experiences as an educator, it takes much more than just one magic bullet. It really does take extra effort and an entire village to raise a child. The formula begins with dedicated and knowledgeable teachers and administrators, parents and a community prepared to work as partners, and a comprehensive district plan. A school, or even an entire school district, cannot accomplish this enormous task alone. When a district is building a plan for improvement, a variety of essential stakeholders must be included in the planning.

Especially significant is the support of top-level management; this is crucial to the success of the program.

Building collaborative relationships. Successful schools make a concerted and purposeful effort to build collaborative relationships with parents and empower the surrounding community where they all come together as a team to address the goals within the campus and district plan. The shared work of families and community does not just happen; it takes explicit and strategic planning and intervention by the campus and district leaders. It is up to us as school and district leaders working together to find ways to include and support parents of every child in the school. School and district leaders consistently plan together and seek ways to develop collaborative relationships.

Creating a culture of caring. It is critical that campus and district leaders work as a team and provide a common vision for the kind of classrooms that are necessary for student success. This vision needs to be shared by all stakeholders, from the cafeteria staff to the parents and community to the students and teachers in the classroom. Schools need a cohesive district and schoolwide shared vision; clearly written and measurable goals defining their expectations; and a strong commitment

shared by students, parents, teachers, and administrators. Relationships are crucial for school improvement. In order to create program efficacy for our children, we must develop student-centered classrooms. A student-centered classroom is one that is safe for language learners and promotes continuous learning and risk taking. To provide the needed change, sustained staff development and parent and student involvement are fundamental. Teachers, administrators, and parents need the tools to be able to create the optimal learning environment for all students.

Sharing a common vision, values, and goals creates a respectful and responsive school culture in which the belief that all children can learn not only leads to a high-performing school, but also contributes to a high-performing community by strengthening the entire family in the process. It may be difficult to believe, but the dual language program can be the vehicle to reach that goal. The whole culture of the school seems to change when so many people come together towards one goal!

Communication. Implementing a dual language program requires immense planning, more than you would anticipate. However, the more time spent in planning, researching, and discussing the details of the program, the smoother the implementation will be. One entire year, if not two, is needed in order to discuss every detail before making final decisions. Setting the mindset of continuous improvement is also part of the planning process. The most vital component of the planning process is communication. One cannot over-communicate! The lack of communication with all stakeholders can compromise all of your good intentions. Implementing a dual language program is political and controversial in nature; therefore, identifying all stakeholders from the beginning and bringing them to the table is essential. I highly recommend bringing someone from your communications department into the planning process to develop a communication plan along with a pronounced promotional plan that alerts the entire community. This is something I wish I had done in the beginning.

The communication plan should state the purpose of implementing a dual language program, the goals of the program, and the research behind dual language. It is also important to state whom the program will serve, and when and how students will be selected. In addition, offer several opportunities for the community, including the business community, to ask questions and to find out more about the program. This can be done through your parent meetings, brochures, information on the district website, a letter sent home, or through social media. Use as many of your communication resources as possible, and use them several times over!

As obvious as it sounds, a major goal of a dual language program is to develop deep proficiency in two instructional languages, one of which is English; but if the goal has not been effectively communicated to all stakeholders, be prepared to get push-backs, such as, "Students need to be able to speak English; we live in America." The key to developing your advocates is to make sure everyone knows this dual language goal from the start! Address language acquisition that includes a PK-12 dual language program in which the goal is an additive model, versus a subtractive one (Lambert, 1975; see Collier & Thomas, 2009, pp. 39-40) with the clear message that bilingualism is valued. This communication plan can include these steps:

- Decide upfront to whom and how this message will be communicated.
- Plan when, what, and how you will communicate to all stakeholders.
- Describe the benefits of implementing a dual language program, from college readiness to economic value:
    - Developing cultural competency prepares students for cross-linguistic and cross-cultural encounters as part of their responsibility as global citizens.
    - Students will be able to compete globally.

- Dual language education provides an opportunity for *all* children to learn another language and develop cultural competency. (When naysayers learn that dual language is not for a specific group, they more readily accept the program.)

Even when you think you have let everyone know, you will still have someone say they didn't know about the program. It's very disappointing to parents when they miss out on this opportunity because they didn't hear about it.

Continue to communicate the successes of your program throughout the first year of implementation and in the years that follow. I highly recommend inviting the community to visit the program as one of the best ways to do that. The director or representatives can also present at community events or state and national conferences, as well as providing information and training to your local school district staff. These communication strategies are just the beginning stages of designing a well-implemented program, but a very important foundation for the success of your dual language program!

Experienced bilingual educators can learn from the voice of this gifted central office administrator who took on the challenges of directing two huge metropolitan school districts' programs for linguistically and culturally diverse students. As described above, the political climate and the ups and downs of support throughout the district can always be challenging when transformative programs are put in place and begin to have an impact on hundreds of thousands of students! What a responsibility this program development is, and yet the bilingual educators who have moved into the role of implementing this greatly enriched model of bilingual schooling called "dual language" have taken the leadership role with courage and conviction that it will lead to their students' success, after years of disappointments and setbacks. And as the authors of this book repeat over and over, this program is for all students, not just English learners.

The following authors from East Central Independent School District in San Antonio, Texas, describe their school district's response to the idea of enriching their bilingual support programs for Latino students. The authors then introduce their school district's first stages of the implementation process that led to a successful two-way 90:10 dual language education with both native English speakers and native Spanish speakers schooled together in an integrated model through the students' two languages of their community.

Chapter Two: Planning the Dual Language Program

> AUTHORS: IRIS GONZÁLEZ ORNELAS, BILINGUAL/ESL/DUAL LANGUAGE PROGRAM COORDINATOR, AND MANUEL ENRIQUE ORNELAS, FORMER MIDDLE SCHOOL PRINCIPAL—EAST CENTRAL INDEPENDENT SCHOOL DISTRICT, SAN ANTONIO, TEXAS

Background. In my first year as a bilingual teacher at Highland Elementary, I asked what type of bilingual program I was to implement with my third-grade class. I did not get a clear answer. I soon started investigating my students' language proficiency levels and assessed their comprehension skills in English and Spanish. The students spoke mostly English, even though their language proficiency levels indicated that they were not yet proficient in English. The students also spoke Spanish, but they had not been taught to read or write in Spanish. They had been taught some English phonics, and some refused to read or speak Spanish. They had a strong negative attitude towards their Hispanic culture.

During this year, when I taught science or math concepts, I found myself conducting lessons in Spanish so students could understand the material. Even the students who refused to speak Spanish seemed to understand concepts better when taught in Spanish. Some parents requested conferences with me after the first week of school. They could not understand why I was teaching their children in Spanish. I kept trying to look for the best way to serve my students. It would have been so much more effective if they could have learned to read and write in Spanish first. At district-level bilingual meetings, I realized that in the other schools my students came from, bilingual education meant teaching in English and clarifying in Spanish when necessary. Only a few overachieving students had figured out that they could read in Spanish, even though they had been taught primarily in English since preschool.

I saw the great need for a more effective bilingual education program that included cultural awareness. In my former school district, I had been a member of a dual language task force. This group was assigned to gather information and research on the dual language model that the district planned to implement. As I thought about meeting the needs of the students in my new school district, I concluded that the 90:10 two-way dual language immersion model would be the most effective.

The assistant principal of my school was easily convinced. He had been an assistant principal at the Dual Language Magnet School in San Antonio, Texas, and over the years had attended professional development sessions on dual language at conferences such as the National Association for Bilingual Education (NABE), Texas Association for Bilingual Education (TABE), San Antonio Area Association for Bilingual Education (SAAABE) and La Cosecha (Dual Language Education of New Mexico). He had also visited model dual language schools in El Paso and New

Mexico. The challenge was going to be presenting the idea to the school principal and the district superintendent.

As we initiated the dual language education conversations with the principal, bilingual education coordinator, and the superintendent, we realized we needed to provide research for all stakeholders. Some were more receptive than others, but they all agreed to learn more about the program. Local university professors, as well as experts in the field of bilingual education, were invited to present to district administrators, teachers, parents, and community members. After several meetings and collegial conversations on the program benefits, the superintendent gave approval to draft an implementation plan to start a 90:10 two-way dual language immersion program. He stated that if we were going forward with dual language, we needed to do it with the best and most effective program according to research. This was a dream come true. We were surprised at the district administration's decision! Another deciding factor taken into account was the opportunity for English-speaking students to become bilingual/biliterate.

We started drafting the implementation plan, which included a year of professional development for all bilingual teachers at the first campus, focusing intense training on Pre-K and kindergarten teachers. All the bilingual teachers at Highland Elementary were excited with the news of implementing a two-way dual language program. We could not wait until the following year. In addition, my son was starting kindergarten that year. Since he had attended the Dual Language Magnet School in Pre-K, he was a perfect candidate for our new dual language program. Based on all those facts, we decided to start a two-way dual language program during the "planning year." However, at the end of the year, the principal changed that decision and pulled out all the English-speaking students and placed them in mainstream English classrooms the following year. Only one Latina fluent in English remained in the class because the mother did not allow the principal to remove her daughter from the program. By ninth grade, that first dual language class was taking Spanish V and Algebra taught in Spanish.

The phase-in process. The central office administrators of East Central ISD created a dual language task force with its main purpose to draft the phase-in plan as well as to plan professional development. We met once a month to discuss the plan, debrief the staff at our planned dual language schools, organize visits to other districts, discuss our learning at conferences, and anything else that could help us with designing our program.

The first step was to identify the bilingual teachers and conduct a book study. Teachers for the program were carefully selected. I searched for teachers who were proficient in academic Spanish and had experience teaching in a two-way immersion program or late-exit model. *Dual Language Instruction: A Handbook for Enriched Education* (Cloud, Genesee, & Hamayan, 2000) was selected for the book study during the planning year. This handbook allowed us to gain knowledge of the critical components of a two-way immersion program. The selected teachers met weekly to have collegial conversations over each chapter.

The professional development sessions were also strategically selected. Teachers attended the following conferences: SAAABE, TABE, NABE, and La Cosecha. Experts in the field of bilingual education were also invited to the school district to present to the district administrators and dual language teachers. Invited experts included Rosa Molina, Virginia Collier, Wayne Thomas, Stephen Krashen, Kathy Escamilla, Katherine Lindholm-Leary, Else Hamayan, Margarita Calderón, Howard Smith, David Rogers, David Briseño, and Elena Izquierdo. Today, we continue to invite experts in the field to our district and continue to send administrators/teachers to attend conferences focusing on dual language education.

A challenge we experienced during our first years of implementation was from the campus staff not actually implementing dual language. Many teachers not directly involved in the dual language program had mixed feelings and emotions regarding our program. We held individual conferences with these teachers to clarify misconceptions and presented informational sessions to the campus staff, including the office staff. We created and distributed program brochures among all campus staff and made them readily available for community members. As the program has expanded and the students have achieved at high levels academically and become leaders in the school community, this concern among non-dual language teachers has lessened.

But Texas is not the only state that has struggled with this transformation from remedial models of bilingual schooling to enrichment models. In the following section, we listen to advice from bilingual educators in Illinois, where state-mandated legislation is also in place for implementing transitional bilingual education and other support services for English learners. In Elgin, Illinois, located in the metropolitan area of Chicago, the following authors serve in the central office administration as directors of all programs for English learners, including the newly implemented dual language program, in the large School District U-46.

> AUTHORS: WILMA VALERO, DIRECTOR OF EDUCATIONAL SERVICES FOR ENGLISH LANGUAGE LEARNERS, AND PATRICIA MAKISHIMA, COORDINATOR OF DUAL LANGUAGE EDUCATION—SCHOOL DISTRICT U-46, ELGIN, ILLINOIS

For several years, we have been having conversations about second language acquisition—talking, analyzing, and even presenting research on second language acquisition best practices and the reality in School District U-46. There are numerous concepts and names of programs for bilingual/ESL education, and every concept is interpreted differently across the nation, even across districts that share the same state regulations and terminology—late-exit, early-exit, heritage program, pull-out, push-in, language resource, native language instruction, sheltered English instruction, and so on. All these concepts and labels were developed in the attempt to address the needs of the growing population of second language learners.

National demographics in the latest U.S. Census clearly establish the sense of urgency for educators to develop equitable learning opportunities for the fastest growing demographic groups in our schools. That is the challenge of bilingual education, without even mentioning the sociopolitical connotation that bilingual education and immigrant students brings to the forefront. As educators, we're very clear that our main role is to empower all our students, independently of their immigrant status. But while this role should be acknowledged as an automatic expectation among educators working with English learners, it often is not. Instead, the mainstream instructional practices are intended to remove the rich layers related to our students' language and culture.

For several years, our district's practice was the traditional transitional bilingual education program with its main purpose being for second language students to acquire English proficiency and for students to be able to move into the mainstream general education classes. As district administrators, we were struggling with that notion, since we were aware of the existing best practices and the importance of developing, maintaining, and instructing students in their native language as they acquired English. We knew that it was the right thing to do! But how would we bring on board the decision-making stakeholders?

The data didn't lie: English learners in our district were falling behind, with the achievement gap growing wider. The data was consistent around us and nationwide. However, when we looked at schools with the same demographics that had dual language programs across the nation, we could see that English learners were no longer behind. Instead, as dual language students, they were making gains and significant progress.

With a knowledgeable leader having a background in bilingual education, we didn't have to look anywhere else for the answer. The vision of our superintendent led the district to embrace the linguistic and heritage strengths of all our students to make our dream a reality. A saying from the California Association for Bilingual Education described our goal clearly: "No students have to lose a language to learn another language!" Great beginnings require great vision! This was the beginning of the expansion of the dual language program in our district. Our next challenge was to develop an integrated districtwide system that provides achievement along with equity and social justice—and not just in one school.

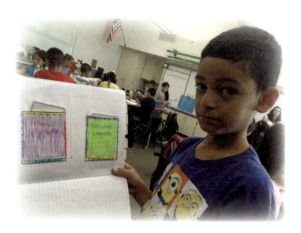

Implementation 101. Administrators leading this effort need the stakeholders' valuable input and buy-in to develop an effective implementation plan. The district leadership, in collaboration with the district's board of education, should appoint a committee with representation of all stakeholders. This committee, which includes administrators leading the re-design of programs for English learners, must count on the representation and expertise of different district and community members. Having this support ensures that all components of the district's demographics, with their vision and goals for all student populations served, will lead to development of the best instructional programs.

One of the non-negotiable charges of your committee is to conduct a feasibility study that provides the crucial data for the future development of the dual language programs in the district. When we talk about crucial data, we're referring to the following:

- the legal and theoretical framework,
- demographics (including, but not limited to, ethnicity by school site),
- academic and linguistic student performance,
- building capacity,
- teacher certification and state-required endorsements for bilingual education,
- instructional and financial resources,
- assessment framework,
- contractual language, and
- design of the instructional days that can sustain the dual language program model adopted for the district.

Once all data has been presented and analyzed by the committee, committee members must allocate time to look at the research that best fits the district's demographics, visit dual language sites in different districts, conduct interviews with program directors and teachers, and have courageous conversations regarding the instructional program model that best fits the district's profile. With this information, your committee will make a well-informed decision regarding the development or expansion of dual language programs. The ultimate goal is to provide students with an educational program that will allow them to succeed in a global society.

Multi-tasking as administrators—"Be the change you want to see in the world." (Mahatma Gandhi) As an administrator, in the midst of the hectic and dynamic planning and early implementation stages of the dual language program, you must give yourself time to step back and look at the implementation as a whole picture, as a blueprint, always keeping in mind your ultimate goal. Reflecting on your practice—reviewing, revisiting, redoing—results in a better instructional program. Along the way, you should look carefully at every single detail, value all stakeholders' input, and learn from parents and practitioners, so you can continue to improve the dual language program in your district.

The journey of implementing a dual language program in a large school district is a huge responsibility. Knowing the significant weight of your assigned task, you can embrace this challenge with pride, while also knowing there are multiple components embedded in this endeavor that might be outside your comfort zone. However, you must claim ownership of all components since successful implementation requires that you look at the instructional program as a whole, validate the expertise of your colleagues, and transform those individual, but crucial, pixels into a clear overall vision. Once you have this vision, it is time to develop your program's blueprint.

This blueprint should encompass pivotal areas to be addressed in the implementation or transition of the current bilingual program model into a dual language program, including non-negotiables. Within these non-negotiables, you must ensure that the district's instructional core, as well as the financial capacity, can support this implementation plan. You must develop a system checkup to ensure that a strong foundation is in place for the program to be developed and sustained within the district's internal and external resources. Once the pivotal areas are identified, an overall implementation timeline of the dual language program can identify the sense of urgency in each particular area in order to scaffold a consistent and meaningful support system that addresses the program needs.

Compliance. At all times, the program implementation must follow state and federal guidelines related to the population that is entitled to receive language services. Compliance procedures ensure not only that your program reflects the legal framework, but also that English learners are placed in the right instructional program.

Having clear procedures for the identification, assessment, and placement of students is critical. These consistent procedures must be followed districtwide. A monitoring system should be in place to determine if the program is implemented with fidelity and to identify areas of improvement. Clear roles must be defined among administrators and staff at the district and school levels in order to develop and sustain consistent practices that are based on the federal and state regulations.

District/school culture. As educators, it is not only our professional responsibility, but also a moral one, to empower our student population. Being aware of the increasing growth of the Latino and other language minority communities and knowing your student population, you can be certain that fostering the acquisition of at least two languages will empower your community and will better serve your students.

However, it goes beyond languages. Student and community cultures encompass traditions, celebrations, and belief systems. As district/building administrators, we must foster, nurture, and celebrate the tapestry of all students' cultures. This will result in a welcoming environment that promotes learning and collaboration between the school and the community. It is by our actions that we develop district/school culture in an inclusive environment where primary language is an asset and not a disability. For some detractors, fostering multilingualism and multiculturalism is a disadvantage. As the district voice, you must be prepared with valuable and current data that addresses the instructional impact of the program. The dual language program is the only program for English learners that fully closes the achievement gap (Collier & Thomas, 2009; Thomas & Collier, 2012). At the same time, the dual language program provides the opportunity for other students to become bilingual, biliterate, and bicultural in order to compete in this modern economy.

Ah, yes, you guessed it. Dual language educators are passionate! We want all of our students to succeed. The last section of this chapter on the first stages of implementation of dual language programs is another passionate plea from two professors in the southwest U.S. who are trainers of dual language administrators. They make the case for the special importance of serving not only English learners through dual language programs, but also linguistically and culturally diverse students who have not been well served by U.S. schools, even though they might be classified as English proficient. This section presents the rationale, the foundation, and the cornerstone for dual language education as you present your case to your school board and upper administration to serve your English learners well.

AUTHORS: DR. ELENA IZQUIERDO, ASSOCIATE PROFESSOR—UNIVERSITY OF TEXAS AT EL PASO, AND DR. TRACY SPIES, ASSISTANT PROFESSOR—UNIVERSITY OF NEVADA, LAS VEGAS

Implementing and Sustaining Dual Language Education: Critical Considerations

The fastest growing segment of the school-age population in the United States is English language learners (ELLs). (Elsewhere in this book we use the shorter term "English learner.") "English language learner" refers to students whose first language is not English, who are at various levels of proficiency in their English language learning, and who require instructional support in order to fully access the academic curriculum to succeed in their schooling (Rivera, Collum, Schafer, & Sia, 2006). Districts all around the U.S. are faced with this demographic explosion. California, Florida, Illinois, New York, and Texas, referred to as the Mega-States, now serve more than half, or 2.9 million, of the nation's English language learners (National Center for Education Statistics, 2013). However, other states have been experiencing rapid and large increases in their English language learner population, including South Carolina, North Carolina, Tennessee, and Indiana (Lazarín, 2006). Likewise, according to the most recent data released from the U.S. Census, the most commonly spoken language by this group of students is Spanish (National Clearinghouse for English Language Acquisition, 2011b). Yet, nationally, and in almost every state, the Hispanic-White achievement gap has not closed.

The nation's public school system has never been in such distress over the achievement and graduation rates of English language learners. Educators and policymakers watch these demographics changing and continue to survey ways to address the achievement gaps. While this is a paramount challenge for schools, it is a dual challenge for the students to increase their proficiency in English while learning cognitively challenging content and skills in English in order to be promoted and ultimately graduate. Schools are faced with meeting state assessment accountability requirements, which include the academic and linguistic achievement of English language learners, and the heated discussion revolves around whether these students learn English more effectively through bilingual education or immersion in English-only instruction (Izquierdo, 2011).

Currently, English language learners receive a variety of bilingual instructional programs that include some use of the students' first language in transitional models and the goal of acquiring English through English as a Second Language methodology and/or sheltered instructional approaches. Extensive research of the various program models implemented across the country has indicated the use of students' first language as a major factor in making academic progress (Lindholm-Leary & Borsato 2006; Thomas & Collier, 1997, 2002, 2012). Research concludes that well-designed, long-term bilingual programs best promote the cognitive and academic development necessary for academic success. The non-English-proficient child continues cognitive and grade-level content development in a known language while acquiring English. Concepts transfer while the child develops English literacy across the content areas—*the premise of bilingual education.*

Many question bilingual education because they fail to understand the role the first language plays in second language education and the benefits of becoming bilingual. It is not just about learning English. It is also about preparing students—*all students*—for the global imperative. Speaking more than one language is a global obligation, and in the field of bilingual education, the most effective programs are those that strongly promote both languages. Two-way dual language is a form of bilingual education in which students develop biliteracy and high academic content in two languages. But even more importantly, it is an enrichment model in bilingual education. It brings English language learners and native English speakers together in a classroom where their curriculum is delivered and learned in two languages.

As multiple regions of the country become predominantly Hispanic in language and culture (National Clearinghouse for English Language Acquisition, 2011b), the nation as a whole becomes more bilingual and bicultural. Speaking two or more languages has become not only a necessity, but a national asset.

As the research consistently highlights the academic and linguistic gains of English language learners in dual language programs, more states are implementing two-way dual language programs to meet the needs of this increasing population. In 2010, 227 districts encompassing 422 schools registered on the national directory as having two-way dual language programs (Center for Applied Linguistics, 2010). The total number of schools with dual language programs has more than doubled since 1997 when only 197 programs were in place. Additionally, districts are committing to long-term program services by implementing dual language programs through high school. In 2010, there were 332 reported elementary programs, 74 middle school programs, and 15 high school programs (Center for Applied Linguistics, 2010). In addition, many more programs already begun are ready to add their names to these lists. The growth in dual language programs is impressive, and it is clear that more school leaders see its value in educating English language learners.

Research findings on dual language education have shown the potential of this type of education for increasing results on student outcomes and closing achievement gaps for English language learners (Collier & Thomas, 2004, 2009; Thomas & Collier, 2012). This has contributed to an increase in dual language programs, including transitional models of bilingual education evolving into one-way and two-way dual language models. Simultaneously, the research shows these as promising programs that lead to linguistic and academic achievement and cultural competence for all students. Sustaining this education reform toward dual language programs requires thoughtful planning and implementation on the part of school and district leaders.

Leadership in Dual Language Education

Leadership is involved at every level in establishing the groundwork, promoting, and ensuring the sustainability of dual language programs. The total school context is a critical factor, and administrators and other school staff must commit to a comprehensive plan for dual language education. Equally important is the cultivation of a common language of responsibility and commitment when parents, teachers, administrators, and other community members come together to plan and develop a program that expects a rigorous curriculum delivered and learned in two languages and embraces the value of knowing more than one language.

Leadership develops a collaborative school culture and facilitates the groundwork which includes planning before implementation. These planning steps should include reading and discussing the available research on dual language, conducting site visits to other dual language programs that have experienced success, attending professional development opportunities on dual language, and including parents and other key district leaders in all of these gatherings.

Just as important is the leadership needed to engage in regular dialogue with school and district officials regarding the goals and guidelines for this type of program, with the expectation that the program is an integral component of the district offerings and has the resources and curriculum supports needed for its implementation and sustainability. These resources and supports include specific program guidelines for staffing, assessment policies, and educational materials. District leaders have a responsibility in guiding this responsive school reform from a remedial focus to an enrichment model of education.

While this is an unquestionable responsibility for schools, significant obstacles at the local school and district levels, such as curriculum and assessment policies, can challenge the success of the program. In addition, other variables that contribute to the day-to-day obstacles of quality implementation of dual programs are the lack of teachers, staff, and administrators who have an understanding of dual language education. They need to understand second language acquisition; second language literacy; making instruction comprehensible in first and second languages through the various content areas; and the affective, linguistic, cognitive, and sociocultural components critical to dual language education (Izquierdo, 2012). The total school context is a critical factor influencing academic achievement.

Administrators and other school staff must commit to providing a school climate that values cultural and linguistic diversity and views it as a resource and not a problem. This climate is especially needed in schools where the demographics highlight a growing number of English language learners. In other words, perceptions about what is essential to establishing the school culture model of education reform can alleviate or aggravate the stigma of social segregation that older programs create. Dual language for all is a major cultural shift in thinking. School leaders need to understand the urgency of developing new visions of this shift among their faculty and staff, as well as district level administrators.

District-level administrators are tasked with making decisions based on the needs and outcomes of students districtwide as a single body. These decisions are typically based on formative and summative quantitative assessment data, analyzing outcomes for English language learners as a whole. However, in states such as Texas, within one school district, these students are sometimes served in a variety of programs such as dual language, transitional bilingual, or ESL. Each program has distinctly different philosophies, goals, and objectives in regard to student outcomes; thus it becomes important to measure English language learners' progress by the type of program they are attending, so the most effective programs can be expanded to serve as many students as possible. Furthermore, to measure program effectiveness, dual language programs must utilize multiple measures in assessing linguistic progress in both languages in order to more accurately assess a student's academic progress in both languages. The role of the student's first and second language literacies across all subject areas requires thoughtful consideration for instruction, assessment practices, curriculum, and staffing.

Some administrators emphasize the urgency for students to transition to English; however, the focus on English prevents the use of the first language to the degree needed to attain high levels of literacy in either first or second language.

> ELLs are in fact *emergent bilinguals*. That is, through school, and through acquiring English, these children become *bilingual*, able to continue to function in their home language as well as in English—their new language and that of school. When officials and educators ignore the bilingualism that these children can and must develop through schooling in the United States, they perpetuate inequities in the education of these children. That is, they discount the home languages and cultural understandings of these children and assume that their educational needs are the same as a monolingual child (García & Kleifgen, 2010, p.2).

In dual language education, the notion of students as emergent bilinguals is a major paradigm shift. Biliteracy is a goal of dual language education. Biliteracy development is achieved through the two languages where literacy skills required for academic success transfer and apply from one language to the other language. The interdependent roles of first and second languages are pivotal to both the development of biliteracy and to its influence on academic language and academic achievement. This interdependent use of the first and second languages relies on the informed and intentional design of instruction, assessment, curriculum, and staffing for dual language education.

Conclusion

AUTHOR: DORA TORRES-MORÓN, LANGUAGE AND LITERACY EXECUTIVE DIRECTOR—DALLAS INDEPENDENT SCHOOL DISTRICT, DALLAS, TEXAS

Dual language allows all of our children to have the opportunity to learn another language and develop cultural and linguistic competency, and it provides an important value in transforming the experiences of teachers, administrators, parents, and the community as a whole. An additional benefit of implementing a dual language program is the positive campus culture that is created when students, teachers, parents, and the community work together toward the goal of bilingualism. Students and families learn to respect each other's language and culture by learning more about how languages and cultures work. The more they learn about how and why people do things in different parts of the world, the more their curiosity grows. In the end, we find we are more similar than we are different. After all, we are all part of the larger human race!

Chapter Three: Teachers—Recruiting and Professional Development

Recruiting Teaching Staff

The administrators in the last chapter made it quite clear that a crucial first step is recruiting highly qualified teachers before the dual language program begins. Let's look at this in more detail. Of course every principal wants the most effective teachers and staff. You are envisioning such an outstanding team for your school—full of enthusiasm and experience, knowledgeable and caring, deeply proficient in the two languages of instruction, confident and capable, and fully certified across all the curricular subjects they will teach. Oh my! Where will you find these teachers, and who does the hiring? And will you be able to hire the new bilingual staff in a cost-effective way? Will the school district and the human resources department be able to support your continuing needs for effective bilingual and English partner teachers for many years to come?

If you are working in a region that is new to bilingual schooling, you may initially find it challenging to recruit the needed bilingual staff. Principal Gary Painter advises forming relationships with the local universities, attending teacher recruitment fairs, and making your needs known to the local community. He did this for several years before the dual language program started at his school by hiring bilingual staff as positions opened and by hiring qualified candidates when they were available. This includes watching for opportunities to hire paraprofessionals within your local immigrant community who were teachers in their home country. With support from a teacher education program at the university, these teachers can enroll in the coursework needed to complete U.S. teacher certification standards, especially if a source of tuition assistance is provided by the university or by the school district.

In this chapter, we will first address some of the teacher recruitment issues in large school districts with a constant flow of new arrivals coming from countries outside the U.S. States with a history of large numbers of immigrants, as well as states in the southwest U.S. with a history of Latino-heritage and indigenous-heritage families, have a pool of potential bilingual teachers, some of whom have already been teaching in transitional bilingual and English as a second language (ESL) programs for many years. Secondly, we will address the needs of smaller districts that are relatively new to bilingual schooling and how they differ from larger, urban districts. But many of the issues regarding staffing and sustaining the dual language program in the long term are the same in both large and small contexts.

Recruiting Bilingual Teachers for Large Dual Language Programs

The states with a history of large numbers of newly arriving immigrants have experienced many different forms of schooling for English learners. Most of these states, such as New York, New Jersey, Florida, Illinois, Texas, and California, have experimented with varying forms of bilingual schooling; therefore, they have a pool of experienced and certified bilingual teachers. In large urban areas in these states, the hiring policies and practices can be quite complex. The authors of the next two sections provide a few examples of some issues that dual language administrators face when recruiting bilingual teachers for their large dual language programs in urban areas.

> AUTHORS: WILMA VALERO, DIRECTOR OF EDUCATIONAL SERVICES FOR ENGLISH LANGUAGE LEARNERS, AND PATRICIA MAKISHIMA, COORDINATOR OF DUAL LANGUAGE EDUCATION—SCHOOL DISTRICT U-46, ELGIN, ILLINOIS

Certification. Teacher effectiveness is the most important factor in a student's academic and linguistic success. As an administrator of a dual language program, you have to work closely with Human Resources to develop a comprehensive and strategic recruitment plan. This plan should also identify state-approved teacher certification programs that have proven to be rigorous and in alignment with your district mission and vision. It is the role of human resources to have procedures and assessments in place to determine that the teacher candidate has mastered partner language proficiency. Likewise, mastery in English is required for those who will be providing the English portion of the curriculum. In some cases, even though teachers pass a basic language proficiency test, this level of proficiency is not enough to develop bilingual, biliterate students. It is extremely important that the teachers have mastered the linguistic features and nuances of both languages. In addition, if a dual language class is self-contained with only one teacher, the bilingual teacher must have deep academic proficiency in both languages of instruction, across the curriculum. If a team teaching approach pairs one teacher proficient in the partner language with an English-speaking teacher, both teachers need to have enough fluency in their second language to communicate in depth with each other as they plan for each teaching day.

We have to add that the candidate must have cultural empathy; in other words, the teacher candidate must be a believer in the importance of bilingualism, with the language and cultural sensibility that promotes learning. It is very important for the district to have a bank of qualified candidates who meet state and district certification requirements, as well as language proficiency, within the high expectations required for the position. During the interview process, it is also essential that dual language practitioners be part of the interview committee.

Staffing. Staffing must follow certification requirements for your state. Multigrade dual language classrooms should be avoided to the extent possible, since language allocation will vary across grade levels. Based on your school population, you will need to estimate the number of full-time educators needed according to the expected growth of the dual language program. We highly recommend that you develop a recruitment action plan to address the needs of the dual language program. For example, offering early contracts can ensure the availability of highly-qualified staff. Some districts offer a bonus for high-needs areas such as dual language. And there is always a great need for certified bilingual special education staff to support identified students.

Districts should develop partnerships with higher education institutions in order to develop grants to support "grow your own future teachers" initiatives. By doing this, we ensure the bilingual staff within our district have the opportunity to be part of a program that they are invested in, and in many cases, these individuals are also active leaders in the community. In the same way, general education teachers can be given opportunities to serve the English learner population when holding an ESL endorsement. Due to the substantial increase of linguistically- and culturally-diverse students in many communities across the U.S., it is essential that teachers be well qualified to teach these students. Even though some of your teachers may not be assigned to a dual language classroom, chances are  that a large number of the students whom they serve are English learners. As a responsible manager, you must ensure that the district's financial investment in providing monetary assistance to the teachers will result in their commitment to stay with your district in good standing for a minimum number of years, to be determined in a formal agreement.

Chapter Three: Teachers—Recruiting and Professional Development

AUTHORS: DR. ELENA IZQUIERDO, ASSOCIATE PROFESSOR—UNIVERSITY OF TEXAS AT EL PASO, AND DR. TRACY SPIES, ASSISTANT PROFESSOR—UNIVERSITY OF NEVADA, LAS VEGAS

Staffing Practices

Hiring policies and staffing practices at the district level should ensure that each classroom is staffed with the most qualified educator. The shortage of bilingual teachers is a concern for many districts, especially districts with larger percentages of English learners. Many times, in an effort to create equity in hiring bilingual teachers across campuses, policies are created that inadvertently hinder acquiring the most qualified teachers for dual language classrooms. Furthermore, these competent teachers need to be happy and fully supported at their campuses to ensure that they commit to the dual language program for the long term. The following scenario demonstrates how one district's hiring policies and practices made if difficult for each campus principal to place dual language teachers in the appropriate setting.

In an effort to combat the bilingual teacher shortage and to create equity and fairness in filling bilingual positions across campuses, the district's human resource administrators established personnel policies in the hiring and placing of bilingual teachers. Bilingual teachers were hired in masses at the central office level. A team of campus principals and district level administrators interviewed the teachers. Teachers were not interviewed based on meeting the needs of a specific campus or language program. Interviews focused on generic pedagogy, plans for parental involvement, collaboration, and meeting student needs. If selected, the teachers went into a pool. As principals had openings in their schools, the next available candidate was placed on that campus.

High-quality dual language teachers have a unique set of skills and beliefs that set them apart from teachers in traditional bilingual programs. Dual language teachers believe that first and second languages are equally important and treat both as such in the curriculum. They understand that during both the Spanish and English instructional time, they have students with varying levels of proficiency in the language of instruction, and they use second language teaching methodologies to make the material meaningful to all students. These teachers also value the cultural component of dual language and know how to build and foster relationships between the different cultures represented in the classroom. They have a high level of enthusiasm for the program, which in turn supports the recruitment and retention of students. Additionally, dual language programs are typically more rigorous and time intensive than traditional bilingual programs. When teachers who do not understand dual language or its goals are placed into dual language positions without the appropriate training, programs suffer.

How did leadership address this issue? One of the concerned campus principals addressed this hiring practice carefully with central office so as not to alienate peers, as this policy was put in place to support the difficulty principals were having in finding dual language teachers who were a match for their programs. The principal met with the human resources director and explained the difference between a transitional bilingual teacher, an ESL teacher, and a dual language teacher. They worked collaboratively to modify hiring practices to include consideration of dual language campuses. Together they reviewed the interview questions and added questions that would give the team insight into a teacher's potential to work in a dual language classroom. Instead of placing all qualified teachers into one pool, the hiring committee recommended teachers to either the transitional bilingual teacher pool or the dual language teacher pool.

While the policy of a bilingual teacher pool was not reversed, the campus principal was able to provide insight as to how policy might be modified to better support dual language campuses. In an effort to avoid inappropriate classroom placements and ensure the best match of teachers with instructional programs and grade levels, principals would reexamine all teacher/classroom placements on the campus. Looking globally at their staffing, under the former policy, dynamic teachers with flexibility in their instructional settings would often have to be reassigned to different grade levels or programs to accommodate a more appropriate placement of the teachers from the hiring pool. While these decisions were made with the best interests of students in mind, continuous reassignment of teachers placed undue stress on the entire instructional program at each school. The new policy better supported teacher placements on dual language campuses.

This example from a very large urban school district demonstrates the importance of thoughtful principal decisions regarding the hiring process as dual language teachers are chosen. Getting it "right" the first time also involves close coordination with the central office human resources staff. Careful planning before the program starts must involve many levels of district administrators working together.

Recruiting Bilingual Teachers in Smaller Dual Language Programs

Our next author comes from a smaller school district that started their program with a dual language strand in two schools. The dual language program now has twelfth-grade graduates and, as of School Year 2013, has expanded into one schoolwide magnet as well as strands within several of the other public elementary schools. Dr. Bivins addresses the important issue of achieving linguistic balance among bilingual staff when choosing the teachers who will provide support for the "specials" (music, art, physical education, etc.) as well as the special needs of students.

> AUTHOR: DR. EMILY BIVINS, FORMER PRINCIPAL—CARRBORO ELEMENTARY SCHOOL, AND CURRENT PRINCIPAL—COLEGIO FRANK PORTER GRAHAM BILINGÜE, CHAPEL HILL-CARRBORO CITY SCHOOL DISTRICT, CHAPEL HILL, NORTH CAROLINA

Another challenge has been how to hire the bilingual personnel to ensure all students' needs are being met and in the correct language. For many years our dual language strand at Carrboro Elementary did not have bilingual resources in gifted education, speech and language, occupational therapy, and specials (art, music, physical education). We were able to hire bilingual staff for counseling, cultural enrichment, special education and reading. Our Response to Intervention (RTI) team had to modify protocol because of language and resources and often struggled with not having the right type or quality of assessment for Spanish or the number of resources that are available in English. Thus, we were forced to make decisions that might not have been the best we could make for our kids, but we had to make do with the available resources. More and more staff suggested it would be easier if we were a full dual language school to avoid parallel conversations about dual language and English-only. With a schoolwide dual language program, we would also feel more pressure to "grow our own" or only hire bilingual staff. In our community, this could be a challenge, but it is one I think we are ready to tackle and seems like the next step for our program.

And that is exactly what happened the year after Dr. Bivins wrote these words. She is now principal of the schoolwide program in Chapel Hill. She recommends that principals make hiring decisions based on the actual needs of the program. For example, an English-speaking music teacher may be available, but if a Spanish-speaking teacher is needed to achieve the linguistic balance in the program, it is important to find a way to make that happen. There are creative ways to acquire bilingual staff, but the human resources office must support this journey. Also, it requires being sensitive to staff who may be displaced because personnel needs shift.

Regions with Fewer Bilingual Teachers

Now let us move into contexts where very little dual language schooling has taken place in the past, but the word has gotten around that dual language is a best-kept secret that now needs to expand. Some regions of the U.S., having little previous experience with bilingual schooling, expanded dual language schooling with statewide initiatives supported from the governor's office and the state board (e.g., North Carolina, Utah, and Delaware). These initiatives sometimes lead school administrators to look for a teaching pool outside the U.S. until their programs mature enough to "grow their own" bilingual teachers from graduates of their programs. An example of the process that a principal must go through when recruiting international faculty comes from Collinswood Language Academy in Charlotte, North Carolina. Begun in 1997, this very successful two-way dual language Spanish-English public school chose to expand their schoolwide program in 2010 from Grades K-5 to Grades K-8.

AUTHOR: NICOLETTE GRANT, PRINCIPAL—COLLINSWOOD LANGUAGE ACADEMY, CHARLOTTE-MECKLENBURG SCHOOL DISTRICT, CHARLOTTE, NORTH CAROLINA

From 2008-2010, our planning years for the new middle school extension at Collinswood, I vigorously began the hunt for the best teachers to join our staff for Grades 6-8. After searching for middle school bilingual teachers available locally, I involved current staff members in the reviewing of applications and résumés and conducting phone interviews with teaching candidates from Visiting International Faculty (VIF is a private corporation that assists with recruitment of teachers from other countries). We then conducted face-to-face interviews and made the final selection of new staff members. When our new staff arrived in August, my strong and dedicated Parent Teacher Association members and international staff welcomed our new international teachers with open arms. They invited them to stay in their homes while drivers' licenses, cell phones, apartments, cars, and furnishings were secured. I also assigned an experienced teacher as a mentor to each new staff member to help the new arrival in the process of adjusting to living in Charlotte or in the United States for the first time.

Many of the bilingual teachers in North Carolina have been recruited from other countries during the first decade of implementation of these two-way dual language and immersion programs, with the goal of NC school districts to eventually "grow their own" bilingual teachers as these programs produce graduates. Principal Nicolette Grant says that her school is so successful because of the cross-national diversity of the staff. She tries to have every Latin American

Chapter Three: Teachers—Recruiting and Professional Development

country and Spain represented among her staff, so students get cross-national experiences in cultural perspectives, plus many varied "ways of knowing" across all curricular subjects. The students are also exposed to many regional variations of standard Spanish.

But there are numerous challenges that can come with recruiting international faculty. In addition to the support systems needed when the faculty members first arrive, legal paperwork must be in place, and the new teachers need time to adjust to the different systems for living and teaching in the U.S. If an outside organization is used to recruit the teachers and provide the initial support for visas and housing, this can be a considerable expense to the school district. Sometimes the teachers are very homesick, and they choose not to stay for the full length of their visa arrangements (usually 3-5 years). Rural contexts may be especially challenging if the teacher comes from an urban environment in the country of origin and misses the conveniences of urban living, or vice versa. Dual language program directors, who have spent an extraordinary amount of time and energy providing the needed staff development to help international teachers adjust to teaching practices in the U.S., feel very disheartened when they lose good bilingual teaching staff who decide to return to their country earlier than planned.

AUTHOR: DR. MARJORIE MYERS, PRINCIPAL—KEY SCHOOL~ESCUELA KEY, ARLINGTON PUBLIC SCHOOLS, ARLINGTON, VIRGINIA

For years I was able to sponsor teachers for the H1B visas that could then become green cards, and the teachers could become U.S. citizens. Since that time, due to changes in the immigration laws and procedures for legal fees, I have not been able to hire any more native Spanish speakers from abroad. This has changed the dynamics of the school. Now the Spanish-speaking staff is more commonly from Puerto Rico, or they grew up in the U.S. Those who have grown up here present themselves differently than someone from Colombia or Peru who brings the full cultural experience of another country along with the language to the school. I miss the H1B teachers. Fortunately, most of those who received their visas have either stayed with us or moved up to positions of authority in this school system or others.

When I started at Key School in 1995, I was told to hire Spanish-speaking teachers for the Spanish side of the day, and English-speaking teachers for the English side. Unfortunately, I began to realize that if everyone didn't have at least a conversational ability in the other language, the two language groups would not integrate very well. The Spanish-speaking teachers were isolated from the English-only-speaking teachers. So I began to hire staff that had abilities in both languages. I also had some preconceived notions that teachers should teach only in their first language About 4 years into this principalship, I was presented with a very strong candidate from El Salvador. She had moved to the area with her new husband and was looking for a teaching position. I interviewed her in Spanish but didn't have an opening at the time. Later that week, I received a call from the central office and was asked to reconsider my decision. The argument was that this teacher had been educated at Escuela Americana in El Salvador and had taught there. In fact, she was fluent enough in English to teach on the English side of the day. She became my first teacher to teach in her second language. About the same time, I hired a native English speaker who had grown up in Miami and spent a year in Spain to be a second-grade Spanish teacher. She is now one of my art teachers and teaches exclusively in Spanish.

By hiring bilingual staff, I have been able to have a more unified staff. The more everyone understands one another, the better it is for the program and for the children. This has been one of my better decisions. I highly recommend that everyone on staff either be bilingual or have some connection to the Spanish-speaking world. One of my former English as a Second Language (ESOL) teachers didn't speak Spanish, but he had traveled all over the world. He was a lovely addition to the staff because he had traveled to many countries in South America, so he was a cultural asset for our school.

I am also an advocate for inclusion in the mainstream for all students, regardless of special needs or language abilities, but in order for this to be productive and appropriate for students, I need to hire staff with multiple certification endorsements. Some of my best classroom teachers are certified as either special education teachers or ESOL teachers. Every teacher at my school, including the special education and ESOL staff, must be certified in elementary education. For years my Spanish-speaking teachers were only certified in K-12 Spanish, but with NCLB, they were required to get the elementary education certification. That has made good teachers better teachers.

Professional Development and Instructional Practices

Along with recruiting the dual language teaching staff, a professional development plan is an essential element of the planning year(s) as well as an ongoing need for all staff. The following sections describe both the initial steps in professional development when the dual language program is just beginning, as well as the ongoing process of bringing staff together to resolve concerns and develop evolving teaching strategies as the program matures.

> AUTHOR: DORA TORRES-MORÓN, LANGUAGE AND LITERACY EXECUTIVE DIRECTOR—DALLAS INDEPENDENT SCHOOL DISTRICT, DALLAS, TEXAS

Professional development is the cornerstone of successful schools. By providing all staff with access to the knowledge, skills, and behaviors to be successful in the dual language classroom, we help to ensure successful students. Professional development should include not only the latest research and best practices, but also the "non-negotiables" that every classroom should follow (e.g., separation of languages, content word walls in both languages, guided reading centers, literacy centers, program fidelity, and the use of language acquisition strategies such as building background knowledge, providing comprehensible input, the use of graphic organizers, etc.). Consistency and fidelity of program implementation will ensure that teachers and students master biliteracy in listening, speaking, reading, and writing.

As part of professional development, it's also important to address how teachers will use data to make instructional decisions that will highly impact student achievement. Consider the following questions:

- Which data are important to use? How do teachers develop instructional plans for each student that include reading level in both languages, strengths, weaknesses and areas of concern?

- How and when do teachers set goals for each student: by mid-October, by the end of December, by mid-February, by early April or mid-May? Who will oversee and follow up on progress monitoring of both languages and how?

- How and when do teachers track and monitor required intervention plans (reading intervention groups, computer-based literacy programs, tutoring, any additional assistance the student receives)? Who oversees the intervention component and how?

- Is it clear that the teacher is planning instruction using the data from diagnostic tools to deliver effective instructional lessons? What does that look like? Who is responsible for overseeing accountability?

All of these questions and concerns need to be addressed before program implementation begins. The staff needs to know how to measure success and what it will look like. This includes formalizing clear goals and establishing benchmarks to measure the program's progress toward realizing the goals.

Be sure to provide professional development that includes working with diverse populations, English language acquisition, and building academic language in both languages. Promote the usage of language through disciplinary literacy, which is based on the premise that "students can develop deep conceptual knowledge in each discipline by using the habits of reading, writing, talking, and thinking which the discipline values and uses" (McConachie, Hall, Resnick, Ravi, Bill, Bintz, & Taylor, 2006, p. 8).

Campus and district administration—and don't forget to invite school board members—should be included in professional development opportunities. This is a must in assisting with program implementation fidelity and having everyone on the same page. It is beneficial to provide administrators with periodic leadership professional development institutes that include updates on the latest research on dual language regarding administrative decision making and implementation practices. An effective leader serves the chief role of spokesperson for the program. In addition, an effective leader takes responsibility for developing, planning, implementing, and assuring that the model is implemented with fidelity.

When teachers do not have background knowledge in bilingual theory or dual language education, they risk making poor program structure, curriculum, and instructional strategy choices, which can lead to low student performance and the perception that bilingual education does not work (Clark, Flores, Riojas-Cortez, & Smith, 2002). One cannot assume that because a teacher has a bilingual credential that s/he has current knowledge of the dual language program and understands or supports it. Every teacher should participate in the professional development opportunities. All teachers need to understand the school or district model in order to promote more successful student outcomes.

Having a specific professional development plan for every teacher and administrator is extremely helpful. This sets clear expectations. Dallas ISD has done an excellent job of communicating the professional development plan, the dual language model, and the system to audit the program expectations. This increases accountability, which leads to increased student achievement.

It is also imperative that all teachers participate in the professional development plan, whether they are directly involved in teaching in the dual language program or not. Everyone on campus needs to completely understand the framework of the program, the process of first and second language acquisition, and how to provide opportunities to develop academic language in both program languages.

> AUTHORS: WILMA VALERO, DIRECTOR OF EDUCATIONAL SERVICES FOR ENGLISH LANGUAGE LEARNERS, AND PATRICIA MAKISHIMA, COORDINATOR OF DUAL LANGUAGE EDUCATION—SCHOOL DISTRICT U-46, ELGIN, ILLINOIS

Professional Development Needs Assessment

By conducting a needs assessment for your dual language program, you are identifying the extent and nature of your teachers', administrators', and other stakeholders' needs. You can provide support in the necessary areas in order to impact the instructional core of your program. This assessment is a valuable tool to inform you throughout the implementation process. As an example of language acquisition issues, the needs assessment should measure the knowledge of the teachers and administrators in the areas of second language acquisition strategies, developmentally appropriate practices in both languages, teaching literacy in both languages, sheltered language instruction, the non-negotiables of dual language, as well as assessment in both languages—with all of these language categories applied to each subject across the curriculum. Background information collected by the needs assessment can include the level of experience of teachers by grade level, educational background, and their expertise in dual language and bilingual education. The *Guiding Principles for Dual Language Education* (Howard, Sugarman, Christian, Lindholm-Leary, & Rogers, 2007) provides a very comprehensive system for monitoring and assessing this and all other dimensions of the program.

Based on the results of the needs assessments, the administrators will be able to build a professional development action plan that supports the stakeholders involved. This professional development plan should be available to teachers and administrators at the beginning of the school year in order for planning at the building level to happen. The professional development plan should be in unison with the initiatives at the district level so a seamless, invisible line crosses all departments. Each professional development session should scaffold the upcoming ones and build on the knowledge acquired by the participants.

With each succeeding year of the dual language program, the goals of the professional development sessions will be based on your implementation timeline. For example, in the first year of implementation, if you are starting the program with kindergarten and first grade, your professional development program will address the language and content allocation plans, as well as specific dual language instructional strategies and the expected daily classroom routines. The teaching of literacy in both languages must be addressed and can be very different for each language, due to the linguistic features of each particular language.

As you phase in the dual language program grade by grade, in addition to the initial implementation plans above, the professional development plan must address the needs of the new teachers, developing their foundational second language knowledge, dual language instructional principles, the rigor and relevance of the instructional time in the partner language, curriculum essentials, and planning for instructional resources. These professional development sessions must also provide opportunities for teachers to develop professional learning communities (PLCs) within and beyond their grade level. Without doubt, this kind of interaction is a crucial element that develops effective teachers who are fearless advocates of the program. Overall, the professional development sessions should empower teachers and administrators, elevate the status of the partner language(s) districtwide, and create a shared vision of graduates who are bilingual, biliterate, and culturally competent.

AUTHOR: DR. EMILY BIVINS, FORMER PRINCIPAL—CARRBORO ELEMENTARY SCHOOL, AND CURRENT PRINCIPAL—COLEGIO FRANK PORTER GRAHAM BILINGÜE, CHAPEL HILL-CARRBORO CITY SCHOOL DISTRICT, CHAPEL HILL, NORTH CAROLINA

Developing Professional Learning Communities

Our PLC model is based on the DuFour (2004) model where teachers work in teams to establish norms for their work, decide essential standards, create common assessments, analyze data, and plan support for struggling and advanced students. Since Carrboro Elementary, my former principalship, is a school within a school having about half of the classes in the dual language strand and the other half English only, teachers had worked in a parallel situation. They talked about instruction, standards, assessments, and interventions/enrichments, but they never knew what to do with the differences in language. For example, in Grade 1, one of the essential skills is sight word recognition. For English-only classrooms, this involves students recognizing the sight word list similar to the way a kindergartner would recognize letters. We tried mirroring this in Spanish, and while helpful in giving kids a word bank, it did not add to comprehension or understanding, particularly for English speakers. Dual language students needed contextualized vocabulary. At that time, I did not know how to help the teachers and would say things like, "Just do the best you can and continue meeting as a team."

Teachers are amazing people. They continued meeting and realized as they struggled through some of these issues that there were more commonalities than differences and that they each had expertise to share with one another. Some PLCs figured it out, and others watched to see what they did. The agreement was that sometimes things were different (like conventions in writing), and they worked separately on these issues. They were explicit with their students about the differences rather than assuming that 5-, 6-, and 7-year-olds were inferring and compartmentalizing the differences. Where there were commonalities across the two languages, the teachers enhanced the work they were doing, shared resources and strategies, and became more deliberate about assessments and common expectations of all students. The PLCs serve an important role across the two programs in the school, but in these PLCs, the teachers continuously identified concerns that need to be addressed differently, as well as commonly, across the two languages. From our experiences with PLCs, we recommend that all teachers work together in teams, even when they are teaching in another language. Good teaching and learning are essential in every classroom, regardless of the language of instruction.

Our instructional journey at Carrboro Elementary has now taken us through 12 years of dual language in our school. In both Carrboro and my current school, we continue to work on resources for teachers, adding native Spanish books and additional resources that have been published since we began the program (e.g., Fountas & Pinnell now has a K-2 Spanish literacy assessment that mirrors our English assessment). Teachers are still receiving professional development and time to work on unit planning and strategies taught by Illinois Resource Center staff. Our district has hired a dual language coach who advises teachers. We have continued to work on personnel hiring, especially with resource positions.

The new goals for Carrboro Elementary are based on our data—the achievement gap between White and Latino students. We don't see this achievement gap when the skill is taught in Spanish, so we need to understand what's happening in our English instruction and create the bridge across languages to ensure that our Spanish-dominant speakers are also able to achieve at high levels in both languages.

We also have an ESL population of Burmese/Karen refugees in our English-only classrooms. We made the decision to provide comprehensive professional development, coaching, and monitoring to ensure that every teacher is using the Sheltered Instruction Observation Protocol (SIOP). SIOP is providing a common language and structure for every teacher in the school to talk about lesson plans, comprehensibility, vocabulary, and other facets of instruction.

We began with several teams of teachers attending various training sessions offered by the North Carolina Department of Public Instruction. We developed a school-based team and are implementing SIOP consistently in every classroom, using strategies that integrate language and content, every instructional minute. These strategies have helped every child in the school—dual language, ESL, exceptional children, low-income—everyone. This has done more to support students in dual language and English-only classrooms than anything we have done before. Teachers are also beginning to talk about the Common Core and how the transition into Common Core will force all teachers into unit planning (very similar to what our dual language teachers learned at Illinois Resource Center training sessions) and careful attention to process, not just content. The transition to common core is our next big hurdle!

Author: Dr. Marjorie Myers, Principal—Key School~Escuela Key, Arlington Public Schools, Arlington, Virginia

I am often asked what we do for professional development at Key School. The truth is that most of our staff development is similar to that of the rest of our school district, which often transcends the dual language/immersion model. Of course we have to put our lens on this district professional development and modify it for our situation.

Due to my desire to have everyone know everything, I generally keep our teachers together for the majority of each staff development session. Only when the training is done in Spanish do I look for something comparable for the English teachers to do so that they will benefit from the time together. For example, this year the Math department implemented Instructional Discourse in Spanish. The English teachers received training on the same strategies, resulting in Instructional Discourse strategies across the curriculum. This has been a very powerful initiative and plays well in a school where every single child is a second language learner. We have also spent 4 years on SIOP training, and after a great presentation by Dr. Roy Lyster of McGill University about how to combine language and content in instruction, we agreed that this was needed on the English side as well as the Spanish side.

Book Study Groups and Professional Conferences

Many school districts with dual language programs that are just beginning, as well as experienced, mature programs have organized ongoing professional development book study groups for their teachers and administrators. Among the books frequently chosen for study are the following:

- Colin Baker, *Foundations of Bilingual Education and Bilingualism* (5th ed.), Multilingual Matters, 2011;

- Colin Baker & Nancy Hornberger (Eds.), *An Introductory Reader to the Writings of Jim Cummins*, Multilingual Matters, 2001;

- Ellen Bialystok, *Bilingualism in Development: Language, Literacy, & Cognition*, Cambridge University Press, 2001;

- Nancy Cloud, Fred Genesee, & Else Hamayan, *Dual Language Instruction: A Handbook for Enriched Education*, Heinle, 2000;

- Virginia Collier, *Promoting Academic Success for ESL Students: Understanding Second Language Acquisition for School*, Bastos Books, 1995;

- Virginia Collier & Wayne Thomas, *Creating Dual Language Schools for a Transformed World: Administrators Speak*, Dual Language Education of New Mexico/Fuente Press, 2014;

- Virginia Collier & Wayne Thomas, *Educating English Learners for a Transformed World*, Dual Language Education of New Mexico/Fuente Press, 2009;

- Virginia Collier & Wayne Thomas, *La educación de los estudiantes de inglés para un mundo en constante transformación*, Dual Language Education of New Mexico/Fuente Press, 2013;

- Jim Cummins, *Language, Power and Pedagogy: Bilingual Children in the Crossfire*, Multilingual Matters, 2000;

- Ester de Jong, *Foundations for Multilingualism in Education: From Principles to Practice*, Caslon, 2011;

- Jana Echevarría, MaryEllen Vogt, & Deborah Short, *Making Content Comprehensible for English Language Learners: The SIOP Model* (3rd ed.), Allyn & Bacon, 2008;

- Kathy Escamilla, Susan Hopewell, & Sandra Butvilofsky, *Biliteracy from the Start: Literacy Squared in Action*, Caslon, 2013;

- Yvonne Freeman & David Freeman, *Teaching Reading and Writing in Spanish and English in Bilingual and Dual Language Classrooms* (2nd ed.), Heinemann, 2006;

- Yvonne Freeman & David Freeman, *La enseñanza de la lectura y la escritura en español e inglés en salones de clases bilingües y de doble inmersión* (2nd ed.), Heinemann, 2007;

- Yvonne Freeman, David Freeman, & Sandra Mercuri, *Dual Language Essentials for Teachers and Administrators*, Heinemann, 2005;

- François Grosjean, *Bilingual: Life and Reality*, Harvard University Press, 2010;

- Elizabeth Howard & Julie Sugarman, *Realizing the Vision of Two-way Immersion: Fostering Effective Programs and Classroom*, Delta Systems, 2007;

- Kathryn Lindholm-Leary, *Dual Language Education*, Multilingual Matters, 2001; and

- Wayne Thomas & Virginia Collier, *Dual Language Education for a Transformed World*, Dual Language Education of New Mexico/Fuente Press, 2012.

For those who are just beginning to develop your first dual language program and needing help with finding information and resources, our authors recommend attending professional conferences and networking with other dual language educators. These conferences and networks serve the needs of experienced dual language educators too, as every program needs continuous professional development as well as incentives to reignite the fire of your seasoned teachers and staff.

Author: Gary Painter, Principal—Smithland Elementary, Harrisonburg City Public Schools, Harrisonburg, Virginia

Once the school board approved our dual language program, they supported a professional development opportunity in December 2009 by sending our future dual language teachers and staff to a program retreat led by Dual Language Education of New Mexico. There were many benefits from attending La Siembra (the Seed), designed for new program planning. This program retreat helped build our team and provided time to plan, prepare, and design a dual language program for Smithland. Our group was introduced to tools (self-assessments, checklists, action plans, etc.) and processes, and we learned how to apply them in our program. After attending the retreat, as the principal of the first dual language program in the Shenandoah Valley of Virginia, I found it easier to lead meetings and provide program information to parent groups and college classes. We were also introduced to *Soleado*, a free quarterly publication of Dual Language Education of New Mexico (DLeNM), which has become an important reference for our program. It provides dual language schools with current topics in the field. Most important, the retreat allowed our staff to network with other dual language educators across the country who were also in the beginning stages of implementing dual language.

DLeNM also sponsors El Enriquecer retreats for experienced and mature dual language programs, providing for self-evaluation and reflection. All of the collaborating authors of this book encourage networking with other dual language educators throughout the U.S. as one of the most powerful forms of ongoing professional development. This can happen at local, regional, and national professional conferences and summer institutes, as well as through visits to each others' dual language programs.

The largest and most popular national conference focused exclusively on dual language education is La Cosecha, sponsored by Dual Language Education of New Mexico. Dual language educators from over 30 states gather together each year in November in either Albuquerque or Santa Fe to learn the very latest innovations in dual language schooling. A second conference focused exclusively on dual language is sponsored by the Association of Two-Way and Dual Language Education (ATDLE). This was formerly known as the Two-way CABE conference, started two decades ago by the California Association for Bilingual Education, and it takes place every summer in July in a California city. The National Association for Bilingual Education (NABE) Annual Conference, with its focus mainly on English learners, sponsors sessions for all models of bilingual and ESL schooling, including dual language education. The Illinois Resource Center provides professional development for dual language educators, as well. In Chapter 5, we will look at partnerships with universities and colleges as another important support system for professional development of dual language educators.

Conclusion

Clearly the greatest challenge for dual language administrators in the U.S. at the present time is recruiting and retaining highly qualified bilingual staff. Dual language programs are spreading very rapidly, even in states that have not encouraged bilingualism in the recent past. Rapidly changing student demographics, along with the increasing popularity of these programs for native English speaking families, has accentuated our shortage of certified bilingual teachers, and many universities are not yet geared up to provide the needed coursework. In the 1970s, Title VII funds from the federal government's Elementary and Secondary Education Act were an important source of funding for certifying bilingual teachers and for educators to pursue doctoral degrees to prepare future faculty specialized in bilingual education. If this type of funding were renewed, it would significantly invigorate the pipeline for preparing highly qualified bilingual teachers.

In the meantime, school districts must take the major responsibility for ongoing professional development by building collaborative relationships with local universities and sponsoring coursework needed by dual language teachers, as well as working with organizations such as DLeNM, IRC, and CAL that provide professional development training conducted by very experienced dual language educators. Teachers can also learn from the experience and expertise of their colleagues. Opportunities to visit each others' classrooms and build networks and professional learning communities, both within and across schools, support the exchange of ideas for innovative teaching and provide teachers with an active role in their own professional development.

Dual language education is the mainstream, general curriculum, taught through two languages. Students and families have the right to expect the highest standards in teacher preparation and professional development because it is the quality and fidelity of dual language implementation, both instructional and programmatic, that create success and engagement for students and teachers alike. Sustained, relevant, contextualized professional development gives teachers the knowledge, experience, and support to become confident, committed, and highly effective dual language educators. In the long run, teachers say dual language is the most rewarding teaching assignment imaginable.

Chapter Three: Teachers—Recruiting and Professional Development

Chapter Four:
Leadership—Program Design, Scheduling, and Budgeting

Author: Edward Tabet-Cubero, Deputy Director—Dual Language Education of New Mexico, Albuquerque, New Mexico

Transforming Educators' Underlying Beliefs

From the first days of implementation of a dual language program, most dual language leaders focus their leadership initiatives on the pressing concerns of administrators, such as program design, classroom instruction, scheduling and curriculum alignment, budgeting, assessment, and community engagement. While this chapter now turns to some of these topics, we are going to start this discussion with a foundational concern that, if ignored, can lead to future dismantling of the dual language program. Often neglected is the need to first address the underlying beliefs of educators who implement these programs—beliefs about the communities in which they teach, about the programs, and most importantly, about the students themselves.

Skilled leaders may address beliefs about programs through the sharing of data such as "The Graph" (English Learners' Long-Term K-12 Achievement in Normal Curve Equivalents [NCEs] on Standardized Tests in English Reading Compared Across Seven Program Models) from Collier and Thomas (2009; Thomas & Collier, 2012), but they typically do not take the time to address issues like teachers' belief systems. Efforts to infuse high expectations into the system are often cursory, rather than reflective, and typically play out in the form of mission statements with idealistic language such as "ensuring that all students learn at high levels." Unfortunately, these processes rarely challenge educators to reflect on whether or not they really believe that *every* child in their school can learn at high levels or that they themselves possess the skills to ensure this happens.

In *Failure Is Not an Option,* Alan Blankstein (2012) writes:

> Beliefs about low-performing students often vary among teachers. A small number of classroom teachers often account for the majority of those students who are referred to the principal's office. At the same time, other teachers are able to succeed with those same students. This is generally not a case of the student's becoming more intelligent or a better person once he or she reaches the classroom of the successful teacher. It has more to do with the varying belief systems in operation within the school. (p. 99)

As educators, we all have stories in our minds about students—their intellect, behavior, values, etc., as well as stories about our own abilities to teach them. Inevitably, these become intertwined with the larger narrative about students of color, which is frequently based in deficit thinking. This thinking is reinforced when staff are repeatedly presented with achievement gap data that seems to affirm the myths about children of color—that they cannot learn at high levels because they come from impoverished homes, because their families do not value education, and so on. A primary role of instructional leaders is to challenge these assumptions and myths by developing counter-stories that highlight possibilities of achievement and success. The following strategies, with examples from my own leadership experience, provide some possible sources of counter-stories for leaders.

Put a face on the data. When I was assistant principal at a predominantly Hispanic, English language learner (ELL), chronically underperforming middle school, the first-year principal and I were charged with leading the school through NCLB-mandated restructuring. There were two prevailing stories as to why these students could not learn at high levels: (1) they were immigrants, and (2) they faced seemingly insurmountable challenges of poverty.

To counter these justifications for low expectations, the principal and I began to collect data to challenge assumptions. We reviewed the cumulative folders of all 671 students to see where they were born. We shared with staff the fact that two thirds of our students were born in the U.S. and began kindergarten in our district. With that information, the staff could no longer bemoan the "fact" that students could not learn at high levels because they were immigrants. Addressing the same notion about the one third of our students who *were* immigrants took more time.

Another strategy the principal employed was to have staff tour the local neighborhood in school buses, as most teachers did not live in the community. Looking out at the run-down homes and apartments could have reinforced the prevailing narrative about students' lack of ability to learn because of poverty. However, every few blocks we would stop, point out a dilapidated house or apartment, and share a counter-story about the child who lived there—of children identified as gifted, students scoring in the 97th percentile on state tests, and so on. Block after block, we'd stop and offer a success story, creating a new narrative of possibilities in the minds of our teachers.

Every data set we analyzed offered a similar opportunity. Our school leadership team completed in-depth reviews of current students' files, beginning in kindergarten. They analyzed assessment and grading information, looked at pictures in order to put a real face to the data, and noted teachers' comments. To the team's dismay, most of the report cards included years of negative, discouraging comments. Teachers on the leadership team challenged the entire staff to include comments that would lead to a higher sense of self-efficacy for students, ultimately offering the possibility of a more positive academic identity.

Provide students with a variety of identity options to try out. During my first year as principal of a predominantly Hispanic, ELL, and Title I elementary school, we faced a definite gang issue. Two classes of third-grade boys identified with the city's two predominant gangs. One class dressed down all in red and the other in blue. We had daily tagging on school walls, and a 9-year-old brought a BB gun to school, threatening "rivals" on the playground. Although not formally "jumped in" to these gangs, the students were already limiting their possible self-identities to south-side and north-side gangbangers. Some members of the staff requested that the police department come in and take a "scared straight" approach with students and families. Although we did take the time to talk about gang awareness with students, the issue ran much deeper. These third graders did not see many options for possible identities, so they stuck with what they saw as high status in the community—red and blue.

Two years later, we had no tagging or wearing of gang colors at school. When talking one day with an educational assistant, I asked what he thought led to the change, and he replied, "It's all about the Ducks and the Beavers ... ever since you began requiring third through fifth-grade classes to participate in a college field trip, students have identified with the Ducks and the Beavers (two state university mascots). Now, when they're talking trash on the soccer field or arguing in the lunch line, it's about whether they're a Duck or a Beaver instead of a Norteño or Sureño." Those third-grade boys needed other identities to "try on" and, thankfully, they selected academic ones. The field trips were part of a larger school-wide focus on attending college. Each class adopted a college, teachers and students wore their favorite college gear on Fridays, and we highlighted colleges in assemblies and daily announcements—all with the goal of students seeing themselves as college bound and families embracing that vision.

Engage parents from an asset perspective. In high poverty schools with majority-minority student populations, staff members often approach their work with parents from a deficit perspective. When I became district Migrant Programs Director, several school leaders suggested that monthly migrant parent meetings focus on gang and drug prevention, parenting training based on a deficit perspective, immigration, etc. Although some of those topics may have been relevant, we chose instead to focus on academic topics such as college readiness, state assessments, school budgeting, bilingual enrichment programs, and gifted identification. For example, we looked at the fact that Hispanics and English learners were far less likely to be identified as "gifted," and parents learned the process for gifted identification. Sharing their thoughts with the director of gifted education, they ultimately influenced changes in the identification process.

Similarly, at our annual back-to-school nights, we would share schoolwide data disaggregated by subgroups, then explain the cut scores for proficiency on state tests and encourage parents to ask teachers about their children's current level of performance and the teachers' plans to get them to the next level. We quickly discovered it was not that parents did not care about their children's education; they simply needed tools to access the system and advocate effectively for their children.

One of the simplest, most powerful strategies for changing the narrative that minority parents don't value education is simply to ask them about their hopes and expectations for their children. I have yet to meet a parent who didn't say that their child's education was a top priority. Sharing these hopes and expectations with staff has proven motivational, helping them to see they share a common goal with the students' parents. Making sure those goals are clearly understood by all is critical.

Clarify goals for dual language enrichment education. A final key strategy for dual language instructional leaders is maintaining clarity on the explicit purpose and goals of our dual language programs. Deficit language in the field often finds its way into narratives about program models. Consider the terms used to describe our students, such as "Limited English Proficient," or even "English Language Learner." While somewhat more positive, English language learner or, ELL, still implies a student deficit. If not challenged, this thinking can negatively suggest students are lacking something and require remediation when, in fact, they are actually quite gifted and being enriched. They are not only learning two languages; they are learning academic content *in* two languages. Perhaps a more accurate, asset-based description is the term "emergent bilinguals" (Escamilla, Hopewell, & Butvilofsky, 2013; Garcia, Kleifgen, & Falchi, 2008). This term demonstrates an understanding that these students do not possess a deficit. Rather, they are on the road to becoming linguistically and academically proficient bilinguals—precisely the goal of dual language enrichment education.

Admit it or not, we all hold narratives about the children we serve—narratives based in either asset- or deficit-thinking. In the book *Courageous Conversations About Race,* Singleton and Linton (2006) state, "Rather than blaming factors external to schools for causing the racial achievement gap, educators should address the critical factors within their control that influence student achievement …. Closing the racial achievement gap begins with an examination of self rather than of other" (p. 73). It is the responsibility of the instructional leader to challenge staff to engage in such self-reflection, ensuring that deficit beliefs are kept in check and educators are focused on developing the many assets students of color possess. Despite the myriad issues competing for our time as instructional leaders, we must consider the adage "you sometimes have to go slow in order to go fast," and create the time to address the "soft" topic of teachers' belief systems.

Dual Language as a Fundamental Redesign of Schooling Practices

In reflecting on our perceptions and beliefs regarding the students we serve, the inherent structure of a dual language program also brings many questions to the table. This is a new and different way to organize classrooms and teaching staff that requires creativity on the part of administrators in response to well-intentioned reforms that do not align with our vision and do not support all of our diverse students. Students are challenged to learn to work together, across socioeconomic and ethnolinguistic backgrounds, to come to respect and value each other's strengths and weaknesses, and to help each other grow and learn through diverse ways of approaching the curriculum. A British friend visiting two-way dual language classes, somewhat tongue-in-cheek, termed the mix of students "a tidy bit of social engineering." Teachers, as well, are challenged in many ways as they respond to the standards movement and find themselves caught between their innovative teaching ideas and the pressure to follow rules and regulations that do not seem to make sense for meeting the needs of their students. The current expansion of dual language education to many states in the U.S. is very new and challenging because it requires a change in thinking. And it is taking place in the midst of a recent U.S. history of English-only perspectives, which still prevail within many communities, including within current education reforms propelled by many federal and state initiatives. The next author reflects on this complexity and how dual language educators can, from the beginning of the program, take the steps needed to sustain this school innovation, as dual language education is an amazingly powerful model of school reform (Collier & Thomas, 2004).

AUTHOR: ERIN BOSTICK MASON, ADJUNCT PROFESSOR—CALIFORNIA STATE UNIVERSITY, SAN BERNARDINO, AND FORMER PROGRAM MANAGER, DUAL LANGUAGE/ENGLISH LEARNER SERVICES—SAN BERNARDINO COUNTY SUPERINTENDENT OF SCHOOLS, SAN BERNARDINO, CALIFORNIA

How can I find support to help us all last through this long-term process of systemic reform? What if our program is the only one in the district/county/region? How do I avoid feeling like a dual language island in a monolingual sea?

Networks are an essential foundation of support in this process. For those who share the vision of bilingualism, biliteracy, and multiculturalism for their school and community and feel a sense of immediacy, the process of building a fully implemented dual language/immersion program may be both exhilarating and frustrating. Those who commit to starting a new program, strengthening an existing program, or re-invigorating an established one will need a network of support and access to both the most optimal research-based techniques and information on the practical steps to take along the way. Most of all, they will require perseverance during the long journey towards redesigning a system.

As we know from organizational theory, school systems are like webs. Any change to the system affects other parts of the system. Implementing a dual language/immersion program requires intentional and informed changes to *every* part of the existing system. It is a fundamental redesign of many of the current practices in public education in the United States. Resistance to change can come from a system even when everyone involved *supports* the change effort because dual language/immersion requires changes to institutions, policies, and practices, and it uncovers many unspoken assumptions in our communities and schools. Even when everyone involved agrees with the bilingual, biliterate, multicultural vision for students, it still takes a long-term effort to reconstruct the system to reflect the vision. Furthermore, the system includes people and institutions that may appear far removed from the school. For example, many communities start charter schools in order to create a more supportive environment for dual language/immersion education. However, even with this local freedom, leaders and stakeholders will need to navigate and leverage change at the regional, state, and national levels. State testing may be available only in English. Accountability systems may be based only on those high-stakes English test scores. Teacher credentialing may not include any way to identify academic proficiency in the partner language for teaching candidates. Instructional materials may not be readily available in the partner language, or teaching practices may be fundamentally different in the partner language and culture, especially in the cases of some indigenous language programs.

Public school systems in the United States are, by and large, designed as English-only learning environments and create monolingual graduates. They are designed with acculturation and assimilation as the primary goals. Traditionally, when we talk about academic achievement, we are defining and limiting our goals to achievement in one language. Each part of the system is focused on English, including assessment, accountability, curriculum and instruction, family and community engagement, teacher preparation, professional development, and instructional materials. Therefore, when a teacher, administrator, parent, community leader, or student comes to me and asks how to start a dual language program or why we don't have more of them, the answer has to address each part of the system. Starting a dual language program is a systemic action. It requires actively and purposefully redesigning the system, and for this reason, it is more challenging than many may expect and creates an impact on the whole system in return.

As administrators, we are charged with working *on* the system, not *in* the system. That is to say, it is our job to identify the ways in which the system is leading us toward our goals and address the ways in which it is hindering them. Schools can leverage an incredible amount of change at the local level due to the direct impact site decisions have on daily instruction, school and community life, and neighborhood relationships. At the same time, stakeholders will need to marshal broader support beyond the school site for the vision as well as foster an understanding of the optimal changes needed and the progressive steps that can be taken toward those ultimate goals. Relationships between the school, district, region (county, parish, etc), state, and national education agencies are essential to the full implementation of dual language education programs. Organizational theory tells us that relationships, identity, and access to information are the foundations of any organization. As we redesign systems to build bilingualism, biliteracy, and multiculturalism, stakeholders need to build relationships across all parts of the system. This means horizontally at the local level between school staff, programs, students, families, community, and business partners. It also means vertically between site, district, regional, state, and national agencies. This may sound incredibly daunting. However, it is a process that begins by building one relationship at a time.

Chapter Four: Leadership—Program Design, Scheduling, Budgeting

The process is greatly accelerated and improved by participating in support networks whenever possible. This is why dual language education networks play such an integral role in the planning, implementation, and evaluation of programs. In many ways, dual language education networks can serve the same purpose as a professional learning community or a community of practice. They are needed at all levels of the system and in a range of configurations. Many of the dual language/immersion programs exist as a strand within a school. If some of the classes in each grade level are dual language and the rest are part of the English-only program, it can be very isolating for those stakeholders who are in the dual immersion program. If you are the only kindergarten dual language teacher, the only principal of a dual language program, or the only Director of District English Learner Programs who has a dual language/immersion program in your area, it can be very difficult to navigate the English-only system and redesign it where needed. Networks such as California Association for Bilingual Education's Two-Way CABE, Dual Language Education of New Mexico, New Mexico Association for Bilingual Education, Texas Association for Bilingual Education, National Association for Bilingual Education, and other state and national organizations can be effective support systems. In many areas, regional networks are poised to best meet the needs of the stakeholders in all parts of the system.

Over the last 16 years, I have facilitated several networks. If you do not already have one, I encourage you to start one. How broad should the network be? Broad enough to encompass grade-alike and job-alike partners, as well as vertical partners in your regional system. It is especially powerful to host one another on each others' school campuses and engage in walkthroughs of the classrooms. When we began hosting our bi-county Two-Way Immersion Network in southern California on school campuses and touring classes, participation increased from about 25 members to 120 members. Even in tough budget times, schools registered in record numbers. Most recently, we had the participation of nine school districts plus independent charter schools. They jumped at the opportunity to break out of the isolation, tour classrooms, discuss pivotal research, and address common obstacles. Advocacy and common solutions naturally grew from these network sessions. Then with the explosion of social networking forums, teachers and administrators found it easier than in the past to stay in touch between network meetings. The relationships grew, and the network nourished them. In many areas, administrators at the site, district, or state level may move every few years. The leadership structure must be designed to outlive any one individual's participation. We need to institutionalize the process of planning, implementing, and strengthening dual language education programs. Networks are one way to do that.

Program Design: The First Years of Implementation

Now that we have reflected on the students we serve and the kind of challenging redesign of schools that dual language calls for, let's get down to the nitty-gritty of program design by listening to the voices of some experienced dual language administrators who have been through the implementation process. In this third book of our series, we assume that readers have studied the basic knowledge of program design presented in our second book, *Dual Language Education for a Transformed World* (Thomas & Collier, 2012), which is an essential companion to this volume. For example, it is crucial to understand in depth the difference between two-way and one-way programs, as well as 90:10 and 50:50 models of dual language, which are well defined in the second and third chapters of that book. The fourth chapter presents an overview of some instructional practices in dual language classrooms, and the remaining chapters provide the in-depth research foundation for understanding why dual language is such a powerful model for school reform. We are not repeating that information here, but instead we're assuming that readers understand those basic concepts. If you are unclear, be sure to refer to the second book in this series.

The next authors provide overviews of dual language program design from the point of view of large urban school districts that have had an ongoing history of transitional bilingual classes provided for English learners. The process of program design for this type of context includes substantial professional development for experienced bilingual educators to open their eyes to new ways of schooling their students. No longer are the English learners transferred to English-only classes as quickly as possible. Instead, the teachers must challenge students academically to work at grade level in all subjects in both of their languages because all students in these dual language classes are preparing to use both languages in their adult lives, professionally as well as personally. In addition, the bilingual educators serving these new dual language classes are teaching very heterogeneous classes that include English learners, native English speakers, students who speak both languages, and English-proficient students whose heritage language is the partner language of the program. If teachers' former assignments were in a transitional bilingual program, their classes typically consisted of more homogeneous groups of the same language background.

AUTHOR: DORA TORRES-MORÓN, LANGUAGE AND LITERACY EXECUTIVE DIRECTOR—DALLAS INDEPENDENT SCHOOL DISTRICT, DALLAS, TEXAS

The planning and designing of a dual language program requires more time than you initially allow for. It is important to address each item with detail and ample time. Not only must the entire campus be in agreement, but the district, school board, and community will also play a significant role in the decision making. As the director in the Irving Independent School District dual language program, I've learned it is essential to plan a program that will be implemented districtwide, instead of having different program models throughout the district.

As the result of a program evaluation provided by one of the local university partners, Southern Methodist University (SMU), we learned that several models were in place in the district because every campus had been encouraged to create their own model. This variety of program models created a lack of uniformity, a struggle to provide consistent professional development across the district, and a challenge for students who moved from one campus to another. With a high poverty rate, students were very mobile. In order to remain consistent, a district model was needed that remained the same if students transferred. In response to the program evaluation, a task force was created to begin identifying specific characteristics from a variety of dual language models. After consulting and working closely with SMU, regional, and national dual language experts, we came up with a model we could all work with. A dual language logo was even developed! An application process was established, along with a checklist of what to consider, such as professional development that included consideration of both special education and gifted and talented students.

The *Guiding Principles for Dual Language Education* (Howard, Sugarman, Christian, Lindholm-Leary, & Rogers, 2007) is an excellent tool for planning and implementing a dual language program. There is a vast amount of research for review, and this guide will assist districts in making decisions for your district.

We highly recommend developing a partnership with an institution of higher learning to address the following areas:

- guiding best practice for selecting a model and design to meet the identified needs of your district,
- developing an evaluation plan on how the dual language program will be evaluated to assure the program is meeting the needs of all students,
- developing a data management system for tracking student data over time,
- assisting with professional development, and
- assisting with development of an action plan that includes program descriptions, teacher and student selection, and a timeline with checklist.

We also strongly recommend setting up a dual language task force or a professional learning community (PLC) and networking with other dual language programs. This task force/PLC can be responsible for reviewing the research, addressing campus needs and concerns, and discussing how to carry out tasks such as the application process, board approval, program descriptions, teacher and student selection, etc. Irving ISD was fortunate to find someone from another district (Ysleta ISD in El Paso, Texas) who had implemented a dual language program in her district; we learned from her vast knowledge and experiences. She even arranged for a team to visit the district and see firsthand how the program was implemented. All of us learned from the district's experiences, and the visit was extremely valuable.

After implementing our dual language program through eighth grade, with our students approaching their high school years, another field trip was arranged for teachers, principals, and dual language specialists to visit a high school that had implemented their dual language program for over a decade—Pharr-San Juan Alamo High School in the lower Río Grande Valley in south Texas. Again, this experience proved to be instrumental, not only for the lessons learned, but also for energizing our group by witnessing program success.

Program administrators must keep context in mind as they think about the design, implementation, or refinement of their own program. What may work in one area or district may not work in a different region, due to changing demographics and culture, but the overall impact of addressing questions through the experience of visiting other dual language schools is irreplaceable!

> AUTHORS: WILMA VALERO, DIRECTOR OF EDUCATIONAL SERVICES FOR ENGLISH LANGUAGE LEARNERS, AND PATRICIA MAKISHIMA, COORDINATOR OF DUAL LANGUAGE EDUCATION—SCHOOL DISTRICT U-46, ELGIN, ILLINOIS

Program Model Design

The design of your program model (90:10, or 80:20, or 50:50; one-way or two-way; and in which partner languages?) is the backbone of your program. It is the concrete image for the community and the trigger for courageous conversations. When adopting a program model, one must intentionally collect and analyze the data from the academic achievement and language development of your students as the starting point. The program model design adopted by the school district must reflect and respond to student demographics, current research, and recommendations from stakeholders. It is a moral responsibility that student demographics not be the deterrent to implementing a dual language program.

In cases where English learners are the majority of the student population, that should be seen as an asset. Knowing that these students will benefit most from being in the dual language program is a driving force in your decision-making process. We cannot forget that dual language programs were first designed to serve our English learners more effectively.

Under no circumstances should a program model design be chosen and implemented from the top down. The stakeholders must be given opportunities to analyze and to discuss data by reviewing current research on programs that work with the targeted population of students. By doing this, the involved stakeholders will claim ownership of the program and advocate for the implementation and sustainability of this program. These stakeholders represent the diversity of the district and the community, such as parents and community leaders. Going through this process establishes an ongoing communication between the district and the community.

District curricular framework. An effective dual language program must not be developed in isolation. It reflects the high expectations for all students in all curricular areas. District benchmarks for literacy and content knowledge represent these same high expectations for all students, and the curriculum implemented must be the same in all programs across the district. A balanced literacy framework will provide guidance to practitioners and parents about the essential elements of reading and writing expected for each grade level. The effectiveness of your instructional program will depend on the confidence of the teachers, not only with their expertise in the content/grade level, but also the process of teaching and learning through the two instructional languages.

The non-negotiables for the dual language core must be followed with fidelity to ensure the success of the program. We sometimes see well-intended programs without a strong foundation labeled "dual language;" these programs are not effective due to a watered-down curriculum, in which the rigor of teaching through the partner language is not evident. Second language teaching methodologies that scaffold grade-level expectations in every lesson across all content areas must be embedded in dual language teachers' instructional practices.

Dual language curriculum alignment plan. A critical and important piece of the dual language mosaic is the curriculum alignment plan. This plan is an alignment of the existing district curriculum in the areas of literacy, science, social studies, math, and ESL/partner second language. This plan provides a clear blueprint of the language of instruction allocated for each of these content areas by grade level. This document should be developed in collaboration with building administrators, curriculum and instruction staff, and teachers. It is a living document and should be revised annually in order to reflect changes and adjustments to the district curriculum and language allocation. Sample dual language schedules reflect the curricular plan for the district and help administrators identify the non-negotiable practices within teachers' daily classroom routines. The development of the rationale for ESL and the partner second language practices will provide teachers, parents, and administrators with both the theory and the instructional strategies that support the acquisition and development of a second language, including linguistic competence, practices, and perspectives within the cultural context.

> AUTHORS: IRIS GONZÁLEZ ORNELAS, BILINGUAL/ESL/DUAL LANGUAGE PROGRAM COORDINATOR, AND MANUEL ENRIQUE ORNELAS, FORMER MIDDLE SCHOOL PRINCIPAL—EAST CENTRAL INDEPENDENT SCHOOL DISTRICT, SAN ANTONIO, TEXAS

Program Expansion to More Elementary Schools

Three years after we started the program at our pilot school, two additional elementary principals in our district became interested in starting a dual language program. At this time, it became necessary to have written guidelines and procedures in place. The dual language task force met and drafted the East Central Two-Way Dual Language Guidelines. This document outlines the research behind our program, eligibility criteria to participate (including the lottery system as the selection process for native English speakers), percentage of Spanish/English instruction per grade level/subject matter, phase-in and staff development plan to expand the program through Grade 12, commitment letter, and instructional materials relevant to the program. As part of the district's dual language program expansion, Iris became the Bilingual Education/ESL Coordinator and has served in this position for the last 7 years.

Ten years later, all five elementary campuses, the two intermediate schools, two middle schools, and the high school are implementing the district dual language program and/or phasing it in at each grade level. Working collaboratively with the district dual language teachers and a reading consultant and using the district-adopted general curriculum, we initially created an interdisciplinary dual language guide for Grades K-5, followed by one for the middle school grades. In this document (see Table 4.1, page 78), you will find the Texas Essential Knowledge and Skills (TEKS) for Spanish language arts are common or transferable within the two languages, as well as non-transferable English Language Arts TEKS for teachers to address during English language development time. Also in this guide are interdisciplinary science, math, and social studies connections to the language arts objectives.

Table 4.1

90:10 Dual Language Instructional Schedule: East Central ISD, San Antonio, Texas

Grade Level	Students	Time	Spanish Instruction Subject Areas (SSL)	Time	English Instruction Subject Areas (ESL)
PK	Spanish Speakers & English Speakers	90%	Language Arts Mathematics Social Studies Science	10%	English Language Development (ELD) through the content areas: Science, SS, Math
Kindergarten	Spanish Speakers & English Speakers	90%	Language Arts Mathematics Social Studies Science	10%	English Language Development (ELD) through the content areas: Science, SS, Math
First	Spanish Speakers & English Speakers	90%	Language Arts Mathematics Social Studies Science	10%	English Language Development (ELD) through the content areas: Science, SS, Math
Second	Spanish Speakers & English Speakers	80%	Language Arts Mathematics Social Studies Science	20%	English Language Development (ELD) through the content areas: Math, Science, SS *(formal English reading instruction and informal writing begins)*
Third	Spanish Speakers & English Speakers	70%	Language Arts Mathematics Social Studies Science	30%	English Language Development (ELD) though the content areas: Math, Science, SS *(formal English reading instruction and informal writing continues)*
Fourth	Spanish Speakers & English Speakers	60%	Language Arts Mathematics Social Studies Science	40%	Math, Science, English Language Development (ELD) though the content areas, including informal writing *(formal English reading instruction continues and formal English writing instruction begins in the spring)*
Fifth	Spanish Speakers & English Speakers	50%	Language Arts Mathematics Social Studies Science	50%	Math, Science, English Language Development (ELD) though the content areas *(formal English reading and writing instruction continues)*
Sixth	Spanish Speakers & English Speakers	50%	Mathematics Pre-AP Science	50%	Pre-AP English Reading and Language Arts, Social Studies, Electives ESL/SIOP trained teachers
Seventh	Spanish Speakers & English Speakers	50%	Pre-AP Spanish Mathematics (Credit for Spanish 1 & 2 by assessment)	50%	Pre-AP English Language Arts, Science, Social Studies, Elective
Eighth	Spanish Speakers & English Speakers	50%	Mathematics Science AP Spanish (Spanish 4)	50%	Math, Social Studies, Technology Applications/Carrier Investigations, Elective

Half-day planning sessions every 9 weeks with all bilingual teachers have allowed the transition and expansion of the dual language program to be a positive experience. The teachers share lessons learned, challenges, effective strategies, and experiences implementing the program. Highland Elementary, as the pilot school initiating dual language classes in our district, has become the training site for the rest of the campuses. All other elementary teachers come to this school to observe their peers. Many other districts in south Texas and other states such as Florida, Washington, and New Mexico have visited our dual language schools.

Single School Contexts: Changes in Dual Language Program Designs

Now let us shift to school contexts where the dual language principal is the main instructional leader in charge of changes in the program. These examples illustrate the need to collaborate with staff in decision making and to pay attention to assessment data while making carefully informed decisions as program changes are considered.

AUTHOR: DR. MARJORIE MYERS, PRINCIPAL—KEY SCHOOL~ESCUELA KEY, ARLINGTON PUBLIC SCHOOLS, ARLINGTON, VIRGINIA

Equalizing the Spanish/English Minutes in a 50:50 Program

At Key School, math, science, and Spanish language arts are taught in Spanish, and English language arts and social studies are taught in English. Since becoming principal of Key, many teachers and sometimes parents have come to me to suggest changes in the program, including which subjects are taught in each language. When I arrived, the "specials"—art, music, and physical education—were taught in English because English-speaking teachers of these subjects had been assigned to my school. As our program continued to improve, our enrollment went up. By having more students, we were entitled to more staff, and I was thus able to hire Spanish-speaking art and music teachers. After we re-designed the schedule and counted the specials as instructional minutes, we realized that English time had previously been over 4 hours per day and Spanish only 2.5 hours. Now with the added specials in Spanish, there are 3 hours a day in English and 3 hours a day in Spanish. Lunch (20 minutes) and recess (30 minutes) are still mostly in English as it's the "language of the land." But the nice thing about schoolwide dual language is that the children are encouraged to speak both languages and many do just that.

AUTHOR: DR. EMILY BIVINS, FORMER PRINCIPAL—CARRBORO ELEMENTARY SCHOOL, AND CURRENT PRINCIPAL—COLEGIO FRANK PORTER GRAHAM BILINGÜE, CHAPEL HILL-CARRBORO CITY SCHOOL DISTRICT, CHAPEL HILL, NORTH CAROLINA

From 50:50 to 90:10 — Deciding to teach all students to read in Spanish first, then in English

When I served as principal of Carrboro Elementary in Chapel Hill, North Carolina, we paid close attention to the results of assessments in both English and Spanish each year as our dual language program continued to mature. Based on this data, we made another plan to shift from the 50:50 model to a variation of the 90:10 model. This plan focused on content allocation in each language and resources needed for struggling learners. The data clearly demonstrated the strengths in our program. Students demonstrated similar or higher levels of proficiency on English measures than non-dual language counterparts in each subgroup after Grade 2. Similar results were seen on the standardized Spanish assessments.

But several things jumped out at us—an achievement gap continued to exist between our Caucasian and Latino students in both languages, and all students needed additional support with oral language and grammar. We knew our Spanish speakers were not fully developing literacy at grade level in either language. We also had our Pre-K/Head Start program in English only. So our Spanish speakers were experiencing Spanish only from birth to age 3, English only for ages 4 and 5, and a bilingual setting in kindergarten. We combed through research and studied our implementation to see where things were not going well. We debated about what to do, and after many ideas, we made the decision to teach all students, regardless of home language, to read in Spanish first.

This made many parents nervous—would their child learn to read in English when formal instruction was not going to happen until Grade 3? We were apprehensive about this because research in 50:50 programs says teach biliteracy simultaneously. Our struggle was that we were teaching literacy in both languages in Grades K-2 and had not figured out how to contextualize content instruction with literacy. Thus, we made the switch to sequential development of biliteracy. Now the primary literacy instruction occurs in Spanish in Grades K-2, and the other subjects are taught primarily in English with contextualized literacy instruction. We provided a lot of parent education and were fortunate that parents had trust and confidence in our program and our decisions. At the same time, we converted two of our Pre-K/Head Start classes to dual language. We wanted our Pre-K to be all-in-Spanish classes, but politically that was not going to happen, so we regrouped with 50:50 and made it work.

Now 3 years later, our data supports our decision to change. The lag in student achievement in Grades K-2 is still there as students acquire both languages, but the lag is gone by Grades 3-5. English speakers are fluent Spanish readers and are transferring reading skills from Spanish to English. Spanish speakers are becoming fluent Spanish readers, and with some additional bridging support between Grades 2-3, they are also able to transfer their reading skills from Spanish to English. It was the right decision for our program.

Thus, we strongly recommend dual language principals use data to make program changes and decisions which work for your community. Be brave and always think about the least successful student in your program and what changes will support him or her, rather than spending a lot of time focusing on the political fallout that sometimes happens when you make these kinds of program changes. You can respond to those who are concerned by describing the needs of all the students you serve and by citing the research that backs up your decisions.

We have also struggled with making additional resources available for students who are struggling or advanced. When dual language began, our reading teachers and special education teachers provided supports only in English. So for a native Spanish speaker struggling with Spanish literacy in Grade 1, we were placing him with a Reading Recovery teacher in English. That child learned to read in English—some—and learned to read in Spanish—some. With attrition, we have slowly hired bilingual support teachers in reading and special education. We still need more, but we are now able to better match the language of instruction, native language, and diagnostic assessment information to determine what intervention the child needs and in what language. One size does not fit all. For example, my daughter struggled with learning to read in Grades K-1. In kindergarten, we assumed it was language acquisition, and she needed more time in Spanish. In Grade 1, it was clear we needed more information. There were deficits in which she was not making the transfer between Spanish and English literacy. She received services in English literacy support and that supported her Spanish literacy development simultaneously.

The biggest challenge we have faced is when to provide the services to ensure the students receive a true 90:10 day (or 50:50 as the students move into the upper elementary grades) and how we place our human resources in the right places to make it happen. Since we are a school within a school (two to three classes of dual language and two classes of English-only instruction), we still need monolingual support personnel for our English-only classrooms. Our district is also small and does not have the practice of moving people from school to school if needed. Thus, if we need a bilingual gifted education teacher, we must wait until there is attrition and try to hire one. We have worked on some creative solutions, particularly for gifted education. Our gifted specialists and classroom teachers have solicited parent and community volunteers who speak Spanish; provided training on programs like Junior Great Books, Problem Solver or Inquiry; and have provided resources and support for the services to be provided in Spanish. This elevates the level of Spanish, providing access to some of our advanced Spanish speakers who need the challenge in Spanish but may not yet be eligible in English. This is an area where we will continue to grow because not all services have the option for Spanish support at this time (e.g., speech, language, and gifted).

AUTHOR: ERIN BOSTICK MASON, ADJUNCT PROFESSOR—CALIFORNIA STATE UNIVERSITY, SAN BERNARDINO, AND FORMER PROGRAM MANAGER, DUAL LANGUAGE/ENGLISH LEARNER SERVICES—SAN BERNARDINO COUNTY SUPERINTENDENT OF SCHOOLS, SAN BERNARDINO, CALIFORNIA

How can I maintain the long-term focus on dual language immersion when there are so many other curricular initiatives that come along?

As administrators, we need to help make connections between the dual language program implementation process and other initiatives that come along. We need to help others see the underlying connections or differences. We need to see beyond the buzzword or the catch phrase and look at the pedagogy. This can help us stay the course and help staff see how initiatives may support our effort or hinder it. Understanding these connections can also help reduce the type of burnout that staff experience as a result of too many superficial changes in too short a time.

For example, in recent years, as the Internet and global economics have made our interconnectedness even more apparent and undeniable, many communities and school districts have started dual language programs under the banner of global education, preparing students for the 21st century, and preparing our labor force for the inevitable need to speak more than one language in order to compete economically. Furthermore, the Common Core now spotlights our attention on college and career readiness. It is up to all of us to make the connection between these initiatives and our current dual language work. This can be a rallying cry for dual language/immersion education.

At the same time, Response to Intervention (RTI) and efforts to recognize and close the achievement gap have prompted many schools to re-evaluate how well they are meeting the needs of culturally and linguistically diverse student populations. Unfortunately, most only review data through an English lens. A more regimented, standardized curriculum focused almost entirely on language arts and math and an accountability system that only recognizes achievement in English have added to the pressure and to the difficulty of starting and maintaining high-quality, fully implemented dual language programs. Instead, we need to remember the roots of the dual language vision, goals, and research. Dual language immersion *is* an intervention. In the terms of RTI, it is high-quality, culturally- and linguistically-appropriate initial instruction! It is one of the most effective ways to provide quality Tier 1 instruction for our at-risk students, those who are low-income, are English learners, or are culturally and linguistically diverse. Dual language administrators need to see beyond the hype and look more deeply at the pedagogy to make informed decisions about which initiatives support dual language and which impede it. This can help save energy and maintain momentum in the long journey towards fully implementing a dual language program.

Instructional materials and curriculum in the partner language provide a third example. In many places, dual language educators battle for access to high-quality partner language materials. Often, parallel materials and pacing guides in English and the partner language are viewed as the ultimate sign of equity. However, we need to carefully analyze the quality and appropriateness of the materials and pacing. In recent years, many English language arts textbooks spend most of the kindergarten year teaching the alphabet. Parallel materials in Spanish, for example, spend the year teaching the alphabet in Spanish, even though it is a much more phonetic, rule-abiding language than English. Most students can master the Spanish alphabet in less than a year, and few bilingual reading specialists would need the whole year to successfully teach it. In this case, the English curriculum is dictating Spanish literacy instruction and essentially slowing the learning process. Dual language immersion is designed to accelerate learning for our students. Accelerated learning closes the achievement gap. Parallel does not necessarily mean equitable or appropriate. These are the conversations administrators and lead stakeholder teams need to facilitate.

Budgeting and Financial Support

Now let us turn to the practical reality of financial support for the program. The dual language program needs creative thinking among central administrative staff to ensure that all leaders in the school district embrace the program. From our educational history of the past four decades in the U.S., central administrators have tended to view programs that deal with languages other than English as a separate world of either the foreign language staff or the bilingual/ESL staff. Services for new immigrants have been funded mostly by separate federal and state initiatives, and most innovations for foreign language teaching have been started with stimulus funds from the federal government.

Dual language is very, very different because it is a mainstream program taught through two languages. Thus, the budget for dual language comes from the regular funds for all curricular areas. The teachers are funded by the same human resources category in the budget as all educators in the school district. While a special grant from federal, state, or foundation funds might be awarded to an enterprising leader of the dual language program, the grant is usually awarded for 1 to 3 years, and the school district must be prepared to fully fund the program in the long term. The following authors provide advice on a variety of categories of funding that should be considered in planning the budget for the dual language program, but the possibilities are not limited to these examples. We recommend being open to budgeting creativity and including all instructional leaders in the dialogue.

> AUTHOR: DORA TORRES-MORÓN, LANGUAGE AND LITERACY EXECUTIVE DIRECTOR—DALLAS INDEPENDENT SCHOOL DISTRICT, DALLAS, TEXAS

One significant area rarely discussed is the dual language program budget. The school board and the community, which includes the parents, will want to know the program's effectiveness. It is critical that the program have an adequate budget to accomplish its goals.

If extra teachers or curricular materials are needed to start the program, then additional funding will be needed at the beginning of the program implementation. But teacher positions for dual language programs are where true cost savings can occur, in contrast to programs for English learners that are remedial add-ons requiring many new teachers. Dual language programs are designed to have the same student-teacher ratio as mainstream classes in general. If the program has been well planned in advance and is implemented grade by grade, new bilingual staff may be hired as replacements for those who leave the school district, without adding significantly to budget costs.

Funding should always be allocated for assessment and accountability, allowing for an evaluation component. This includes purchasing testing materials in both English and the partner language. Depending on who completes the program evaluation, you may need to set aside funds for the program evaluator. Sometimes the evaluation is done in-house and is less formal. If you already have a program in your district and you want to know how effective it is, you may want to get an outside evaluator, which will then require a budget. Whether it's an internal or an external evaluator, it's essential to complete an annual evaluation in striving for continuous improvement.

When planning to hire an outside consultant or dual language expert to provide supplementary professional development, funds should be allocated to pay for consultants, travel expenses, and trade books, if applicable. This is an expense I highly recommend; campus and district staff benefit greatly from bringing in professional experts. Central office may help fulfill this expense through the professional development department; or, if you have a partnership with an institution of higher learning, they might be able to help. Sometimes the vendor from whom the district purchases books in volume will bring in a speaker at no cost. It's always good to ask! An additional way to cut the cost of this much-needed service is to work together with another district to share the cost. Teachers will also benefit because they get to compare notes with other staff teaching in different contexts.

Monies should also be allocated for additional books and materials, as well as a travel allotment for teachers to attend conferences and/or visit other districts that are also implementing a dual language program. This can be very helpful. Parents enjoy summer school enrichment activities for their children; this may require a transportation expense. Make sure to budget for parent involvement activities and snacks for parent and student gatherings and end-of-year achievements. Certificates, given at the end of the elementary and middle school program and for end-of-year achievements, are always nice and make for good public relations.

Budgeting for resources. Bilingual resources that include a variety of genres and an assortment of materials (e.g., visual, audiovisual, art, technology, textbooks, periodicals, computer applications, etc.) are required to meet the goals of bilingualism and biliteracy. Technology resources should be available in both languages. Remember, the technology department and the libraries are abundant resources! Working with the district library and media services is a must in order to expand your budget; consider it an auxiliary budget. Including both library media services and the technology departments in your task force committee will help obtain the supplemental materials

Chapter Four: Leadership—Program Design, Scheduling, Budgeting   85

and hardware you need for your program without straining the designated funds for dual language. The library/media services and technology departments can help you locate bilingual websites and computer applications you don't have time to search for and download. When planning problem-based learning activities, these departments are there with a multiplicity of ideas and services, especially in large school districts. For example, for our dual language program, the technology department purchased iPad® mobile digital devices and flip cameras to use in dual language classrooms. The librarian reviewed our curriculum and made sure to purchase the bilingual books we needed for the library at each school and in the classrooms. In the summer, she put together a summer reading program for our dual language students.

Also, when considering continuing a dual language program through secondary, realize that materials are hard to come by. It's important for the district to collaborate with other neighboring districts in order to get material recommendations. More and more vendors offer these resources in both English and the partner language, especially when the partner language is Spanish. Books and other resources for professional development and parent involvement activities make up another important materials acquisition category for dual language programs.

> AUTHORS: WILMA VALERO, DIRECTOR OF EDUCATIONAL SERVICES FOR ENGLISH LANGUAGE LEARNERS, AND PATRICIA MAKISHIMA, COORDINATOR OF DUAL LANGUAGE EDUCATION—SCHOOL DISTRICT U-46, ELGIN, ILLINOIS

Instructional resources. In collaboration with other district administrators, it is extremely important to identify English and partner language district resources for literacy, math, science, and social studies that are aligned with the language of instruction as determined in the Dual Language Curriculum Alignment Plan.

These resources in the partner language and in English should be the same across the district and meet the high expectations we have for our program, with the only difference being the language of instruction. Students and teachers should have immediate access to these resources, and professional development must be designed and in place for those teachers who are new to the district and not familiar with these resources. Adequate resources means having a broad variety of instructional resources in both languages that support literacy and content area learning across all subject areas and all grade levels, in which the cultural aspects of our global society are respected, recognized, and validated.

Building capacity. Just to make sure you have included the physical spaces needed for the dual language program, we must not leave building capacity out of the planning process. At the school level, in collaboration with the Plant Operations department, a feasibility study needs to be conducted in order to determine short- and long-term space availability. Based on your school population, space needs to be available for the projected growth of the program. This has to be a very strategic plan that ensures the sustainability of the program for the participating stakeholders of the school community.

Transportation. As an administrator, you should include transportation for all students to enrich their participation and meet the linguistic balance of the classrooms. Sometimes budget constraints do not allow districts to commit funds to this area. However, this is a very important component for parents, in order to commit to their child's participation in the program. By providing transportation, we support the goal of consistent attendance, which results in lower attrition rates. This component has increased the participation of both English-dominant students and English learners. In addition, the community views this as a statement of the district's commitment to the dual language program.

Leadership Responses to "Bilingual Concerns"

The last two sections of this chapter include, first, an example of dual language leadership concerns that sometimes can become "political," followed by a summary of vital skills required for dual language school administrators to sustain a quality dual language enrichment program in the long term. This example illustrates that school leaders must be clear and knowledgeable regarding the dual language program goals and be prepared to respond to concerns raised by educators and policy makers influencing the program outcomes.

The U.S. has a complicated history regarding bilingual schooling, which influences decisions regarding the name of the program and how the program is perceived. This can be seen in the story that follows. When bilingual schooling began to expand in North America in the 1960s, two-way integrated bilingual schools for both English learners (language minority) and English speakers (language majority) were developed in metropolitan areas with diverse neighborhoods, and these were called simply "bilingual schools." Whereas in the same time frame, the Canadian bilingual program model developed for English speakers (language majority) became known as "immersion." These two terms—"bilingual" and "immersion"—are sometimes confused and misused by the U.S. media and the general public because in the English-only movement "immersion" is used to mean "sink or swim" in English-only classes when referring to programs for English learners. Linguists call this "submersion." It gets still more confusing when dual language schools use the term "immersion" for their program; some dual language programs are called "dual immersion" and others "bilingual immersion." But the main point of all these names is that students are immersed in the school curriculum, taught by using two instructional languages, rather than one. (To understand this complex history, see Collier & Thomas, 2009, and Thomas & Collier, 2012.)

> AUTHOR: DR. MARJORIE MYERS, PRINCIPAL—KEY SCHOOL~ESCUELA KEY, ARLINGTON PUBLIC SCHOOLS, ARLINGTON, VIRGINIA

The "B" word. Not long after the beginning of my first year at Key School, the superintendent came over to my school, walked into my office, and said he was there to find out how I defined bilingual education. He had received complaints from the Key community and from my staff that I was using the word "bilingual" to refer to the program. I remember thinking that was a very strange request, especially since he had just hired me to run this program at Key. I proceeded to define bilingual education as the umbrella to all programs serving linguistically diverse students. I then went on to carefully explain two-way bilingual enrichment programs where both language-majority and language-minority students learn and thrive side by side in classrooms to the benefit of all. He asked me if I knew of the League of United Latin American Citizens (LULAC) and if I'd ever been to the National Association for Bilingual Education (NABE) conference. He was concerned that the politics connected with these two organizations was not something Arlington or he was interested in taking on. I mentioned to him that although my parents were monolingual speakers of English when my Air Force fighter pilot father was stationed at Torrejón Air Base in Spain from 1957-1961 and we had to live in Madrid, my parents enrolled me in a Spanish school, Liceo Anglo Español. By January of my first year, I was getting along in Spanish, and 4 years later was completely fluent and have been ever since. I have always been proud of being bilingual. He said, maybe so, but I was not to use the word "bilingual" when referring to the program at Key. Instead I was to use the word "immersion." Okay, so, no "B-word" when referring to two-way partial Spanish immersion in Virginia. A rose is a rose by any name.

As I network with principals across the country, we note that the offices that oversee dual language programs can vary and thus influence program goals. In the District of Columbia Public Schools, it fell under the Office of Language Minority

Affairs (also called the Bilingual Education office), and funds came from Title VII; while in Arlington, funds came from the Foreign Language Office (now known as the World Languages Office). In DCPS, it was a program to support English learners; in Arlington Public Schools, its funding and focus is more a program to teach Spanish to English speakers, although the classes are two-way and include Spanish speakers. Politically they are very different programs. In practice, they are the same.

Political challenges. One of the political challenges Key School faced turned into a positive outcome. In the early 2000s, I was notified that the Commonwealth of Virginia had proposed a Senate Bill to prohibit non-English speakers from studying any content area in their primary language. Senator Barry had introduced that bill, and it was moving along fairly well. I sent out a message to the PTA and asked that folks send messages to Senator Barry to ask him to pull or at least reconsider his bill. After receiving innumerable calls and petitions, apparently he said, "Who are those guys?" (à la Butch Cassidy and the Sundance Kid). He decided

to accept our invitation to visit Key School. In one fifth-grade Spanish class, the children were sitting on the carpet reviewing the periodic chart of chemical elements. A Latina student, who had been with us since kindergarten, responded to a question about the chart in Spanish. Later as we were walking the halls, we saw this same student, and Senator Barry stopped her. He asked her in English if it was hard to learn in two languages. She said it was all easy for her. She was getting good grades, and she loved school. But best of all, she was speaking to him in perfect English after he had just heard her in the Spanish class speaking in Spanish. When we returned to the library, Senator Barry asked me what he could do for us. I responded that he should not legislate our instructional program, that he should let us do what we knew was good for kids. Senator Barry returned to Richmond and killed the bill. It was a win for two-way Spanish immersion/dual language in Virginia, an English-only state.

A decade later, in March 2012, the House Joint Resolution No. 497 was passed, commending the Francis Scott Key Elementary School Dual Language (Two-Way Immersion) Program. With lots of "whereases," ending with "Whereas, most students in the Key School/Escuela Key immersion program are able to communicate effectively in two languages by the fifth grade, helping them grow up to become global citizens prepared to meet the challenges of the future; now,

Chapter Four: Leadership—Program Design, Scheduling, Budgeting

therefore, be it RESOLVED by the House of Delegates, the Senate concurring, That the General Assembly hereby commend the Francis Scott Key Elementary School Dual Language (Two-Way Immersion) Program on the occasion of its 25th anniversary, as an expression of the Virginia General Assembly's congratulations and admiration for the program's commitment to bilingual education." Oh my! The "B" word is written in an official document from this English-only state!

In School Year 2012, I also submitted Key School to the Colegio del Año competition of the Ministry of Education of Spain for the 25th anniversary of our bilingual/immersion program. We were selected by the International Spanish Academy as the number one elementary school out of 40 schools that applied. This is a great honor, and the recognition comes with about $5,000 worth of books from major Spanish publishing houses, as well as access to the Aula Virtual AVE, that our students and staff can use to supplement their learning and teaching in Spanish. What a wonderful year for our two-way dual language/bilingual immersion school!

AUTHORS: DR. ELENA IZQUIERDO, ASSOCIATE PROFESSOR—UNIVERSITY OF TEXAS AT EL PASO, AND DR. TRACY SPIES, ASSISTANT PROFESSOR—UNIVERSITY OF NEVADA, LAS VEGAS

Conclusion: Dual Language Leadership Skills and Dispositions

Leadership is vital in establishing and ensuring the sustainability of dual language programs. In addition to developing a vision and collaborative school culture, leadership is needed in establishing communications with school and district officials regarding the goals and guidelines for dual language education, with the expectation that it is an integral component of the district offerings and has the resources and curriculum supports needed for dual language program implementation and sustainability.

Hunt (2011) identifies four key leadership skills and dispositions of principals who sustain high-quality dual language programs: collective mission, collaborative and shared leadership, trust, and flexibility. While Hunt's research is limited to one principal's influence at the campus level, the principal voices and examples of leadership decisions in this book demonstrate these four leadership skills and dispositions while working with district-level administrators to help negotiate policies and practices that enhance and support dual language learners.

A clear and collective mission must be evident at each campus. Principals view each district-level mandate through the lens of that mission. As campus leaders, it is important for you to protect and maintain that vision in order to sustain a successful dual language program. In order for that to happen, principals have to work with district-level administrators to build a collective mission between the district and the campus. Understanding the collective ideas that embody the dual language program allows campus and district leaders to work in unison to address policies and challenges in working with English learners.

This book provides many examples of **shared and collaborative leadership**. At the campus level, dual language teacher leaders must be highly engaged in the implementation and leadership of your programs. These same skills and traits administrators use to build shared leadership on your campus must also be evident in your interactions with district-level administrators. Each entity shares responsibility for the education of all students, and decisions are made building on each other's perspectives (Hunt, 2011).

Principal leaders work diligently to build trust in the dual language program with district-level administrators. There is **a high level of trust in the dual language philosophy** at the campus level. Teachers believe in the power and strength of dual language programs. Principals utilize this strong belief system to help district-level administrators begin to trust the effectiveness of the model. While the research is presented to district-level administrators in staff development sessions, the true building of trust comes from seeing the program in action. Through a willingness to open their doors, campuses are able to demonstrate the power and effectiveness of a well-designed program.

Finally, campus-level administrators work diligently with district-level administrators to understand **the importance of flexibility in decision making** in regard to assessment, curriculum, and hiring practices. Many times, decisions are made at the district level to ensure equity across programs. However, the focus should be more on what each program needs in order for students to have access to the same levels of high-quality education. The mandates originally designed to make everything equal among student groups can actually hinder English learners within the dual language program from achieving at the highest levels.

A collective mission, collaborative and shared leadership, trust, and flexibility are skills and dispositions of successful leaders of dual language programs (Hunt, 2011). Dual language programs are not isolated programs, but must function within the district's educational program. Each decision at the district level has a direct impact on the success and sustainability of the dual language program. As successful campus leaders, it is critical that principals and teacher leaders employ Hunt's four leadership traits to educate and advocate for dual language at the district level.

Dual language programs are unique, and it is important that they are not segregated or viewed as separated from a district's overall systemic instructional program. Dual language programs should be viewed with the same consideration and regard as gifted and talented, special education, or International Baccalaureate programs. Typically, those who know the most about dual language are at the campus level. This leaves the responsibility for implementing and sustaining dual language programs on the shoulders of principals and teacher leaders. Campus leaders have a tremendous responsibility and obligation to ensure dual language programs are viewed as integral components within the district's overall instructional framework.

Related to the skills and dispositions previously presented by Hunt (2011), there are several responsibilities or action steps campus leaders should follow in order to ensure dual language programs are considered integral components of a districtwide educational plan. These action steps include: developing and communicating the ideals and beliefs of the dual language program; being knowledgeable and active in curriculum, instruction, and assessment; keeping current with recent research and best practice in dual language and sharing key studies with district leaders; and reaching out to the community to discuss issues and communicate success in the program (Marzano, Waters, McNulty, 2005).

Campus leaders must be well grounded in the ideals, beliefs, and research foundations of dual language education and assume responsibility for communicating those beliefs and research findings to district administration. This allows not only individual campuses to promote best practices, but it also keeps the district involved in cutting-edge research to promote high-quality programs. In order for district-level administration to see dual language as an integral component to the overall education of students, they must truly understand the benefits of the program. The same powerful leadership skills principals use to build belief in the program at the campus level must be utilized to build enthusiasm and passion for the program at the district level.

District leaders should be invited to the campus. Campus leadership should show administrators firsthand the power of learning in two languages. Student successes in both of their languages need to be shared. During campus visits, teachers should demonstrate how they plan lessons and analyze assessment data. They should also show how dual language teachers plan together to align instruction. Through these steps, campus leaders are helping develop a better understanding of the powerful benefits of dual language and the roles of curriculum, instruction, and assessment in dual language. In this way, principals encourage district leaders to reflect on the premises of dual language education for decisions throughout the planning and implementation process, ultimately ensuring sustainability of the dual language program within the overall educational program in the long term.

All administrative leaders at each campus are obligated to have knowledge in curriculum, instruction, and assessment and to be active in the decision-making process in regard to these three areas. Principals should develop hands-on knowledge of how curriculum and assessments are developed and sequenced. Specific attention should be given to the alignment of curricular standards and assessment decisions in both instructional languages that directly impact English learners and their education in the two languages. With proactive attention, principals can ensure that curriculum, instruction, and assessment mandates will not hinder the dual language program design or learner outcomes.

The final responsibility of the campus principal in educating and advocating for dual language programs is outreach. Principals must advocate at all stakeholder levels for dual language education. With district offices, this means encouraging district leaders to view all decisions through the lens of dual language program beliefs. It also means being the first to celebrate and communicate the successes of the program to the district and to the community.

It is time to move beyond politics and inconsistent practices because of differing ideologies and understandings in school districts. We need educators and administrators to keep informed regarding what existing research tells us about effective programs and quality education. Principals, central administrators, superintendents, and school boards must also pay attention to the sociocultural climate in an educational setting and its effect on second language acquisition. In addressing these areas, leadership is achieving the most important aspect of dual language programs in the district—ensuring their sustainability. Leadership matters!

CHAPTER FIVE:
ASSESSMENT—ACCOUNTABILITY AND DUAL LANGUAGE SOLUTIONS

In previous chapters, the authors have brought up many assessment issues because program decisions, budget planning, and teaching practices all intersect with data collection on student achievement and evaluation of the program. In this chapter, we focus on the guidance that our collaborative authors have provided on assessment practices and how the findings from data collection can inform our leadership decisions.

Mandatory Assessments

State curricular tests in English and other languages. First steps involve examining the mandatory testing required by your state and by your local school district. Because school policy has been heavily influenced by the federal legislation No Child Left Behind (NCLB), each state in the U.S. has chosen or developed a state test that measures student achievement in Grades 3 through 8, as well as in various subjects tested at high school level. The state test given in English is the high-stakes measure to which most superintendents pay the greatest attention.

Some states have developed their standards-based assessment measures in languages other than English, so English learners can be assessed on curricular measures in their native or dominant language while they are developing mastery in English. In New Mexico and New York, these state tests are available in Spanish for all grades and subjects tested. New York state has also developed tests in 21 languages other than English including Chinese, Haitian Creole, Korean, and Russian. Illinois and Texas have developed Spanish versions of their state assessment measures for the elementary school grades, and in 2014, Massachusetts initiated a Spanish-language edition of their state mathematics test. The state of Oregon now provides assessments in Spanish in mathematics and writing, and the state of Washington has test questions on CDs translated into Spanish, Russian, Korean, Chinese, Vietnamese, and Somali, for which the students must provide answers in English. California has developed standards-based state tests in Spanish, which can be used for both English learners and for native English speakers who are attending dual language Spanish-English immersion programs. Yet, these tests in other languages are less valued than the English measures in our society, at the present time. We believe this perspective is slowly changing, but it will take major shifts in current attitudes to truly respect and value multilingualism. But why do we want policy makers to change their perspective?

What should really matter to school leaders is the English learners' most accurate measure of their academic achievement at the time of testing. The problem occurs when states prematurely use testing in the students' second language (English) for high-stakes decision making before the students have fully acquired English. In this case, their scores are artificially lowered because they have not yet fully acquired the language of the test. The most valid and reliable measure of the true level of their achievement is the first language test.

If they are third graders, have they mastered the third-grade curriculum? Content knowledge is content knowledge, no matter what the language of testing. If high-stakes decisions need to be made, the most valid measures should be used. In addition, the longitudinal research on English learners clearly shows that while the students are acquiring the English language, the achievement test in their primary language is the most powerful predictor of their eventual attainment in English (Collier & Thomas, 2009; Thomas & Collier, 2012). For example, Spanish speakers not yet fluent in English who started the dual language program in kindergarten and score at grade level in Spanish in reading across the curriculum in the third grade can be on grade level in English across the curriculum in fifth grade—if you have provided a well-implemented dual language program. This is true for both a state test and a norm-referenced test.

English proficiency tests and biliteracy assessment. In addition to mandatory testing of students' achievement levels in reading and math, school districts are required to test English learners' proficiency levels in English each year and demonstrate students' growth in English. Most states have mandated formal assessment measures for English proficiency development, and states must keep track of the number of students classified as English learners in each school district, including the number of students reclassified as English-proficient, as federal support funds are allocated according to the results of these assessments. Another mandatory assessment for all students is literacy development in the early grades. For dual language programs, equal weight must be given to measurements of literacy development in the partner language as well as in English, even though it may not be a state requirement. The goal of a quality dual language program includes academic proficiency in the two instructional languages, and for very important, pragmatic reasons. We strongly recommend that every dual language program test in the two instructional languages (even if local funds are required) because equal emphasis on the two languages leads to higher cognitive development, greater student engagement with instruction, and other documented advantages of dual language education (Thomas & Collier, 2012).

In addition, there exists potential confusion between tests that measure literacy development and the "Reading" measure on state and standardized tests. The Reading subtest on each state test, as well as norm-referenced tests, combines knowledge of social studies, science, and language arts. In other words, it should be titled "Reading Across the Curriculum." It should not be thought of as a literacy test measuring discrete reading skills. Most school leaders in central administration pay close attention to the Reading and Mathematics subtests of the state test as the main measures to assess students' grade-level achievement.

Program Evaluation

To understand the role of the assessment data that your school district collects, it is important to reflect here on the larger task of program evaluation. Evaluation of your dual language program must be based on both qualitative and quantitative data. Data collection may include many types of measurement, including interviews with administrators, faculty, staff, parents, and students; visits to classrooms using classroom observation instruments; and testing students across all curricular areas in both program languages, as defined in the previous section. The program evaluation begins in the planning stages of the dual language program, with a well-defined program design and clear plans for measuring the program's instructional processes and strategies. This program design includes all levels of how the program is being implemented and the program's intended and actual outcomes for all the participants.

What do we mean when we say "well implemented" or "implemented with fidelity"? We're referring to fidelity to research-based program features. These features provide the underpinning of your program evaluation because without fidelity of implementation, your program's full potential effects may not be seen in your testing data. What is your written vision for your program—the elements that will make it successful for all students? We are defining the specifics of well-implemented dual language programs in this three-book series, so our definition is quite complex. However, here is an overview of our definition of "a well-implemented dual language program" that we use for conducting our research studies.

- **Administrators at both school and district levels fully support the dual language program** (superintendent, school board, central office staff, and principals) by providing full financial and administrative resources for hiring good teachers who are academically proficient in the languages of instruction and choosing high-quality classroom materials and equipment.

- **Fidelity is defined for the dual language model chosen**, and all staff fully understand the non-negotiable components of the model and the research rationale for the key program features.

- **Careful attention is given to instructional time in *each* of the two languages,** with deep proficiency development of both languages throughout the academic curriculum.

- **Regular dual language program planning meetings are scheduled,** at which staff can talk out what is working well and what might need to be changed through collaborative group decision making.

- **All bilingual and English-speaking teachers work together creatively and collaboratively.** Teachers who are assigned as team-teaching partners appreciate and value each other and together plan cross-cultural thematic lessons that meet students' needs in all curricular subjects.

- **Thoughtful choices of assessment instruments** for both languages across the curriculum are a crucial early step for continuous program evaluation.

- **High-quality, ongoing staff development** in research-based and effective practices is provided for all dual language teachers and administrators.

- **Dual language teaching includes:**
    - Minimal lecturing by the teacher—direct instruction is intentional and of short duration, and routines and procedures are modeled and consistent.
    - Cooperative learning is implemented effectively, with many varied work groupings—pairs, groups of four, learning centers, whole-class, etc.—and consideration of students' language proficiencies.
    - The following are evident in all classrooms: problem solving, creative projects, varied activities, high-level thinking, stimulating learning.
    - Teachers are sensitive to cross-cultural issues and provide emotional support for all.
    - Students are engaged and actively participating in meaningful learning.
    - Students actively participate, whatever the language of instruction (L1 or L2), with intentional and explicit non-verbal and verbal clues to meaning for both content and language provided by teachers and fellow students.

While this is a very general overview of teaching practices in dual language classrooms, it provides a framework for defining program evaluation issues when observing classrooms. Dual language program evaluation is a complex topic to be addressed in our future publications.

Testing in Both Languages

The remaining sections of this chapter focus on the decisions administrators need to make regarding testing student achievement on academic tests across the curriculum. To further illustrate the range of testing decisions administrators are faced with when reflecting on the needs of both the English learners and the native English speakers attending dual language classes, let's examine some of our collaborating authors' perspectives on assessment in their varied state and district contexts. The next two sections discuss testing decisions regarding the two languages of the dual language program and uses of the required testing to identify curricular and instructional improvements that need to be addressed.

> AUTHORS: WILMA VALERO, DIRECTOR OF EDUCATIONAL SERVICES FOR ENGLISH LANGUAGE LEARNERS, AND PATRICIA MAKISHIMA, COORDINATOR OF DUAL LANGUAGE EDUCATION—SCHOOL DISTRICT U-46, ELGIN, ILLINOIS

Districts implementing dual language programs must take into account the academic and the language components of assessment in both languages, as reflected in the dual language curriculum alignment plan (CAP). The assessment framework must reflect the language and academic growth of English learners and of their classmates learning in the partner language. The nature of the dual language program requires assessment in both languages, which creates the challenge of balancing the amount of assessment conducted throughout the year. The purpose of these ongoing assessments is to guide teaching effectiveness by addressing the differentiation needed in instructional practices to reach all students. Teachers must be trained in the administration of these assessment tools to ensure consistent administration, confidentiality, and inter-rater reliability. They also need to learn how to use the data to guide classroom instruction. Data collection is one of the most important supports for sustaining and promoting the program within the community.

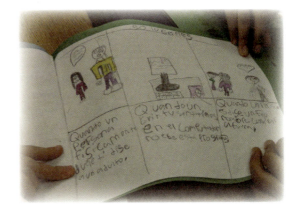

AUTHORS: IRIS GONZÁLEZ ORNELAS, BILINGUAL/ESL/DUAL LANGUAGE PROGRAM COORDINATOR, AND MANUEL ENRIQUE ORNELAS, FORMER MIDDLE SCHOOL PRINCIPAL—EAST CENTRAL INDEPENDENT SCHOOL DISTRICT, SAN ANTONIO, TEXAS

Student Academic Achievement

State tests. Students' scores on state assessments measure our academic achievement and program success. All our elementary campuses are Title I campuses, which means that at least 60% of our students at each campus participate in the free and reduced lunch program. Our population is primarily composed of middle, low-middle, and low-income families. Despite the fact that our dual language students are not the most affluent, their scores on state assessments are the same as native English speakers in our district and in many cases higher. In some instances, where a small number of students are achieving at a lower level in a particular subject, it has been the result of ineffective classroom instruction. For example, our dual language students were not scoring where they needed to be on the science test, but neither were the English-only classrooms. Replacing teachers, providing professional development, and supporting curriculum alignment resolved the problems. Following those changes, dual language students in fifth and seventh grade have scored higher in science than the rest of the English-only classrooms. In middle school, the dual language students are now scoring higher on the mathematics state assessment than the English-only classes.

Other important indicators of success. Students in our dual language program not only achieve academically, they are also leaders. When interacting with them, one soon notices the confidence they have in themselves. They are articulate, confident, and mature. They take on leadership roles within their schools and in the community.

For the past 5 years, we have offered the Dual Language After-School Fine Arts Program. Dual language teachers and community members volunteer their time to teach the students drama, folkloric dance, choir, drawing, and photography. At the end of the school year, a fine arts production consisting of more than 100 students is presented to the parents and community. In our experience, this is a great opportunity for students to learn about other cultures and practice their language skills in a different social context.

Challenges. As administrators, we do not have full flexibility to test students in the language in which they are learning or to test them based on second language acquisition research. We are pressured for students to test in English as soon as possible. In our program, even though we have more flexibility than other states, it is still a challenge. Table 5.1 describes the assessment guidelines for our district.

Table 5.1
Assessment Guidelines for Dual Language Students at East Central ISD

ASSSESSMENT TOOL	NOTE:

Language Proficiency Tests:
Woodcock-Muñoz
    Spanish & English:
        Oral (PK-6)
        Reading & Writing (K-6)
	All PreK and kindergarten dual language students are tested at the beginning of the school year. All students/all grade levels are tested in the spring at the end of the year if they have not reached proficiency level in one of the languages. (Students scoring a four will no longer be tested in that language.)

Tejas LEE & TPRI—through 2nd grade (Texas state Early Reading Assessments in Spanish & English)	Beginning of year (BOY) (either Spanish or English—all students) Middle of year (MOY) (Tejas Lee Spanish) End of year (EOY) (both languages)
TELPAS (Texas English Language Proficiency Assessment System)	For English learners only, K-12 (once a year)
EDL (Spanish Reading Inventory)	3rd Grade BOY/MOY/EOY
STAAR (State of Texas Assessments of Academic Readiness)	
STAAR: 3rd grade	Spanish: Reading & Math (unless determined otherwise by Language Proficiency Assessment Committee [LPAC])
STAAR: 4th grade	Spanish: Reading & Writing (unless determined otherwise by LPAC) English: Math
STAAR: 5th grade	Spanish: Reading (unless determined otherwise by LPAC) English: Math & Science
STAAR: 6th grade	English: all subjects unless Newcomer student with LPAC recommendation

The goal of our program is for third-grade students to take the state assessment in Spanish (reading and mathematics), and for fourth-grade students to take reading and writing assessments in Spanish and mathematics in English. In fifth grade, students take reading in Spanish and mathematics and science in English. Then from sixth grade on, even though some of the content areas are taught entirely in Spanish, the state assessments are in English.

Since we know that students learn at different rates, and newly arriving immigrants in all grades are just starting the process of English proficiency development, we meet in the spring to decide, for each individual student, the language he/she will be tested in according to their second language proficiency level. This practice has worked well for our district. Now with the new Texas state assessment, the STAAR, we are facing a large challenge. Students taking state assessments in Spanish will not have the right to some accommodations. The state rationale is that the students do not need accommodations (e.g., bilingual dictionary) because Spanish is their native language. They have not realized that some students taking the state assessment in Spanish are second language learners of Spanish. And the challenge is also there for the second language learners of English. These students are emerging bilinguals who have limited academic language in the beginning stages of second language acquisition. Furthermore, some bilingual students are not yet biliterate. State assessment guidelines sometimes force administrators and programs to rush students into testing in English, at the same time compromising the fidelity of the program. An academic assessment in English can give us an indicator of the start-point in English development for each English learner, but it is not appropriate to use this score as a measure of a student's academic knowledge until the student reaches a high enough proficiency level in English to "show off" what he/she truly knows. The same is true for an academic assessment in Spanish when the students taking the test are not yet far enough along in acquisition of the Spanish language.

Understanding the "How Long" Research Findings

We have found in our longitudinal research (Collier & Thomas, 2009; Thomas & Collier, 1997, 2002, 2012) that it takes groups of students, who by first grade are on grade level in primary language, an average of 6 years to reach grade-level achievement in their second language, when they have received high-quality schooling with instructional work in both their primary language and the second language. This is true regardless of students' socioeconomic status. An average of 6 years means that some individual students may get there sooner, and others will take longer, but the group mean is 6 years. Students who do not develop literacy in their primary language and receive no cognitive or academic support in first language take still longer than 6 years to reach grade level in second language, sometimes never reaching grade-level achievement. (See Collier & Thomas, 2009, for more information on these concepts and the theoretical and research foundations for these findings.)

Lindholm-Leary (2001) and Escamilla (reviewed in Escamilla, Hopewell, & Butvilofsky, 2013) have also conducted longitudinal research examining the pattern of development of both first and second languages in school, illustrating that emergent bilinguals are on two language trajectories that are interrelated. As cognitive and academic development occurs in a student's primary language, the knowledge and skills transfer to the second language, which can be demonstrated on a test as the student develops the vocabulary and fluency in the second language to express what he/she already knows in the first language.

When students attend a high-quality, well-implemented dual language program for all the elementary school years in Grades K-5 (and some attend PreK-5), you should expect the majority of dual language students to reach grade-level achievement in their second language by the end of fifth grade, if not sooner. In the meantime, the majority should be on or above grade level in their first language by first grade. In fact, many students in dual language classes score above grade level in first language as they progress through school. In our research findings, we typically find that, for example, sixth-grade dual language students are scoring at seventh-grade level in academic tests across the curriculum in first and second languages.

There is one exception to this pattern of an average of 6 years. Because of their student demographics, some schools have one-way, rather than two-way, dual language contexts, in which most of the participating students are of the same language background. This could be, for example, a group of Spanish-speaking students who are all acquiring English as a second language. If very few native English speakers are enrolled in classes with the English learners, the English learners do not have same-age peers to assist them with natural acquisition of English. Interacting with same-age peers can be a key support in second language acquisition.

But the solution is not more English. Instead, in a dual language program, year after year we keep students on grade level in their native language while they're working on acquiring English through meaningful academic work for a portion of the instructional time. In this one-way context, we find that on average students reach grade level in second language by seventh or eighth grade. This is an important rationale for continuing the dual language program through Grades K-12 (including preschool, if you have it). And in the future, when native English speakers enroll in your school district, they should be invited to participate in the dual language program.

In your assessment practices, it is very important to understand student progress in second language acquisition and celebrate the appropriate gains students are making. Each year, you should see gains, with your students getting closer and closer to grade level in their second language. But it is absurd to base high-stakes decisions on unrealistic expectations for second language learners. That's why the tests in students' primary language are so important. They are giving you the best indicator that your students are on grade level, and that's what truly counts.

Another challenging question, even for experienced dual language educators, is whether or not the language of assessment and the language of instruction must always be the same in a dual language program. For example, let's say you are offering the calculus course in Mandarin Chinese in your dual language high school. Dual language students can be tested in English at the end of the year and do well on the test, even though their course was taught in the partner language—as long as there has been adequate, focused support for exploring similarities and differences between the two academic languages, including the opportunity to connect content area learning in one language to the other on a regular basis throughout the course. Once the students have reached a comfort zone with oral and written second language, and they have acquired the vocabulary in the subject area in which they're being tested (which is a good reason to alternate the language for each subject from year to year—if math is being taught in Mandarin Chinese this year, next year offer the next math course in English), then testing in either language can be a valid measure. The policy makers are looking for those scores on the English test, especially at secondary level. If your dual language students have been taught a rigorous, on-grade-level course in the partner language, they can do equally well on the test in English. With planned and consistent bridging/transfer support across the two languages, our research has found that dual language students are able to demonstrate what they know in their second language in courses taught through their first language—or vice versa (Thomas & Collier, 2002, 2009, 2010, 2014).

Let's listen to some other assessment concerns from two of our authors who are principals in school districts where only a few schools are implementing two-way dual language.

AUTHOR: DR. EMILY BIVINS, FORMER PRINCIPAL—CARRBORO ELEMENTARY SCHOOL, AND CURRENT PRINCIPAL—COLEGIO FRANK PORTER GRAHAM BILINGÜE, CHAPEL HILL-CARRBORO CITY SCHOOL DISTRICT, CHAPEL HILL, NORTH CAROLINA

Aligning Assessments in English and Spanish

Assessment was the toughest beast we encountered in our initial 6 years of the dual language program. Our state and locally required assessments are English-only, and no one seemed interested that we thought it necessary to measure the students' progress in Spanish. In literacy, we tried several commercial resources, but found they were direct translations and did not work in the early reading levels. We contracted with a retired bilingual educator and curriculum specialist, and she created an assessment in Spanish that mirrored what we used in English (Fountas & Pinnell). This project went on for several years, but we were committed to having an instructional and assessment program in Spanish that mirrored our approaches in English. Many other dual language programs we talked with used balanced literacy in English and a basal reader in Spanish, but we were committed to having balanced literacy in both languages. While not perfect, our assessments were a step in the right direction.

We also began assessing our students on their Spanish proficiency using the IPT (Idea Proficiency Test). We measured each grade level for 2 years and had a real sense of where the strengths and weaknesses of our program were. This helped us with the decision to switch from Spanish and English simultaneous biliteracy development (a 50:50 model) to sequential biliteracy development, with Spanish reading taught first to all students (English speakers and Spanish speakers) and formal English reading introduced in Grade 3. As a result of this program change, all students have developed strong Spanish proficiency so that they can do grade-level work in Spanish in the upper elementary grades. And all students became more competent readers in both languages.

AUTHOR: DR. MARJORIE MYERS, PRINCIPAL—KEY SCHOOL~ESCUELA KEY, ARLINGTON PUBLIC SCHOOLS, ARLINGTON, VIRGINIA

Passing the State Tests

With the advent of adequate yearly progress (AYP) and NCLB, we began what is now life in public schools. The first year we gave the tests, two elementary schools in our district of 35 schools passed the state Standards of Learning (SOL) tests. The second year of the SOL tests, I received a phone call from the communications office stating that they wanted me to be present at a press conference. I started whining that I didn't want to represent the failing schools. It was then that the Schools and Communication representative said, "No, your school passed; that's why we need you at the press conference." Honestly, I had not even looked at the results, so passing was not on my radar. I went to the press conference, talked about my school's passing, and yet I knew it wasn't a real pass. At that time, only children who were mainstream students were considered in the pass rates. That was prior to the subgroups of today. So, as I took credit for this pass, I knew in my heart that my strugglers were not part of the final successful results.

I must admit that seeing Key School as the only new school to pass the tests the second year of testing was heady. It had an amazing effect on the way the community viewed us. We were no longer the strange school that taught Spanish, but rather a successful school in the neighborhood that was attractive to the community. Long before NCLB, I would test all my students and publish the results. I wanted the administrative offices to know that we have English learners and special education students who were struggling and yet making gains. Nevertheless, the publicity from this "win" turned around how people viewed our school and the program. After that year, we had so many English and Spanish speakers of middle class and higher socioeconomic status apply to the school that we had to hold a lottery for admission to the school. Many children had to be turned away. When I first became the principal of Key School, someone commented to me that the folks in the fancy neighborhood behind us felt Key was an eyesore to them. After this change in how we were perceived, Key School became the reason housing prices went up and more educated parents wanted to live in the neighborhood to ensure their children could attend Key and become bilingual.

Communication Across Administrative Levels in Large School Districts

The next authors provide examples of assessment policies and practices that have occurred in large school districts in which central administrative staff created policies that conflicted with the goals of the dual language program. These examples illustrate the importance of continuing communication and collaboration between administrators at all levels in order to identify problems and to propose solutions that serve all students' needs.

> AUTHORS: DR. ELENA IZQUIERDO, ASSOCIATE PROFESSOR—UNIVERSITY OF TEXAS AT EL PASO, AND DR. TRACY SPIES, ASSISTANT PROFESSOR—UNIVERSITY OF NEVADA, LAS VEGAS

The interdependent use of two languages for schooling relies on the informed and intentional design of delivery of instruction, assessment, curriculum, and staffing for dual language education. Dual language programs must utilize multiple measures in assessing linguistic and academic progress in both languages. Let's look at some examples of inequitable practices that frequently occur in districts across the nation, where districts mandate policies and practices that do not take into account the goals of the dual language program. In these cases, campus leadership is responsible and obligated to educate and advocate for the dual language program, within the overall instructional programs of the district.

Language of Assessment

In this first example, the district curriculum office, in conjunction with the program for English learners, mandated that English learners districtwide would take specific assessments at certain grade levels in English. One mandate was that all fifth-grade English learners would take the state science test in English. Curriculum and bilingual district specialists made this decision based on the linguistic complexity of this science assessment in Spanish, making the argument that the vocabulary and sentence complexity of the English test was easier for English learners than the test in Spanish. These specialists were concerned that the English learners in the district did not have the sophisticated, academic Spanish required for the state science exam. On the surface, this decision appeared to be grounded in the concern for attaining accountability standards. The district administration wanted to ensure English learners reach the academic goals set before them. Further reflection, however, indicated a larger programmatic issue that needed to be addressed districtwide by the curriculum office and the English learner program. *Why didn't English learners have the sophisticated, academic Spanish used in the state science exam?* This question was harder for district administrators to answer and would require long-term, comprehensive change. Mandating all English learners to take the state science exam in English was easier to do than addressing the programmatic issue of why English learners were not developing the Spanish academic language in science. This mandate contradicted the beliefs and outcomes of dual language education. Dual language emphasizes learning and consequently assessing in two languages. Instruction in these programs focuses on developing strong academic and literacy outcomes in both instructional languages.

How did leadership address this issue? Dual language leaders at the campus level, both teachers and administrators, began questioning the district curriculum and bilingual specialists about the reasoning behind the decision to mandate all-English science testing. They continued to probe and question the assumption that English learners did not have the sophisticated, academic Spanish required for the science state exam. One campus principal invited the district leaders to spend time in both the Spanish and English dual language classes during science instruction. She believed the leaders needed to see qualitatively the success students were having in science during Spanish time. They visited frequently to watch students' transition from learning in Spanish one day and continue that learning the next day in English. To the district-level administrators, it became clear that English learners in the dual language program did have the level of academic Spanish required in the science state exam. They also realized some of the English learners within the dual language program would perform better in Spanish than in English. District leaders realized that while most English learners districtwide were struggling with science in Spanish, English learners in the dual language program were not. As a result, the mandate for English science testing was lifted for the dual language program.

Had this mandate remained, it would have had a significant impact on the programming and perception within the dual language program. First, students would have received a mixed message about the equal importance of both languages. Testing only in English would send a message that it is more important to test in the English language. Second, although the program had clearly designed instructional minutes for science instruction in English and in Spanish, it would have been a natural tendency for teachers to spend more time in English during science instruction in order to prepare them for upcoming assessments, since this is often a teacher belief that is hard to overcome. The research cited previously has shown that the language of the test does not have to be the instructional language, but teachers are difficult to convince on this issue. Finally, had this mandate remained, the dual language program would not have achieved what it promises to do—which is to prepare students for a global society. Limiting students to science only in English weakens their preparation for work in the sciences internationally.

Benchmark Assessments

In another school district, district curriculum and bilingual specialists mandated that students in Grades 3-5 would take all state assessments and district benchmark tests in English. District administrators were concerned with achievement data for English learners in middle school. Middle school principals complained that elementary schools were not preparing students for the rigor of all-English classes in sixth grade. District leaders believed mandating English-only assessments would encourage teachers to use less Spanish with students and better prepare them for the rigor of middle school.

The fundamental premise of this mandate was that elementary students should be spending more time in English to better prepare them for middle school. The underlying message from district leadership created doubts that bilingual programs could effectively prepare students for all-English instruction. More specifically, it was unclear to the district's decision makers how continuous native language development supported English learning. District leaders perceived that the time students spent in their first language detracted from students acquiring English. These decisions were based on aggregate English learner data rather than by individual language program. Consequently, the examination of aggregate English learner data did not take into consideration the English learners in the dual language program who were reclassified as fluent English proficient upon leaving elementary school. The majority of English learners in the dual language program attained sufficient levels of English proficiency to be reclassified. In reality, district administrators and middle school principals only examined the data for students who were still in need of services. Transitional bilingual or ESL programs served the greater part of these English learners.

This mandate countered the basic premise behind the philosophy of dual language education. Beyond the cultural competence component, dual language is built on the foundation of long-term language, literacy, and academic learning equally in both languages. Mandating that assessments be conducted in English in an effort to require more instructional time in English would not yield the higher cognitive outcomes district leaders were anticipating.

How did leadership address this issue? In order to sustain the dual language program, it was critical for the principal and teacher leaders to educate district administration on the long-term outcomes of well-implemented dual language programs. With the bilingual director, the campus principal met with the top district administrators to explain the research. Each of them was aware of what the research indicated but was uncertain about the implementation and day-to-day oversight of the program. Questions arose such as "How do you know teachers maintain the language?" and "How can kids switch from one language one day to another the next? I couldn't do it." More notable was the question, "Aren't students losing valuable time to develop English when they are spending half their instructional time in Spanish?" Clearly, the district-level administrators did not have an understanding of second language acquisition or the role of first language in the process of English acquisition.

As in the previous example, the campus principal invited key district administrators to see the program in action. The principal, district administrators, and dual language teacher leaders walked sequentially through K-5 classrooms. Together they looked at the language distribution in the program and how the program increased in rigor in both languages as students progressed through each grade. Teachers sat with district administrators and explained instructional techniques (e.g., preview/view/review, consistent graphic organizers) selected to specifically support students transitioning between languages. District administrators spent time with students enrolled in the program. They asked them what it was like to learn in two languages. The series of visits culminated in a debriefing meeting with district administrators, the campus principal, and dual language teacher leaders. In this final meeting, campus leaders utilized classroom examples seen during the visit to demonstrate the academic losses students would suffer if forced into all-English instruction. Campus leaders focused on the cognitive advancement of students in their native language, the problem-solving skills developed when learning in two languages, and the students' preparation for a global society. As a result, the district administrators lifted the mandate for English-only assessment for dual language programs. They also wanted to further explore implementing the model districtwide and expanding it to middle school level and beyond.

Had this mandate remained, the dual language program would have come to an end. The program would have been moved to what seemed to be an early-exit transitional bilingual program with no clear language distribution. Students would not have had the benefits of developing cognitively in their native language while acquiring English. Nor would students have left school with the academic and linguistic skills to compete in an international job market.

As seen in the previous example, district leaders can make districtwide decisions based on English learners as a single unit without regard to second language acquisition and how to best support students learning in two languages. It is not uncommon for districts to mandate the use of particular curricular materials and consistent sequences of instruction to support the high mobility of students within districts. For dual language programs, it is important that the curricular materials and sequences selected are supportive of students learning in both languages.

Districtwide Strategic Planning Initiatives

Our next contributor to this chapter on assessment served for several years as bilingual superintendent of a K-12 districtwide bilingual program in Woodburn, Oregon. The two main heritage languages of this school district are Russian and Spanish, with 78% of the students Spanish dominant, 11% Caucasian English dominant, and 11% of Russian heritage. The Russian immigrant community arrived in Woodburn in the 1960s and started a Russian-English bilingual program soon after their arrival. The Spanish-English program in Woodburn schools was strengthened in each decade that followed, until the two programs now encompass all schools in the district. This is a Title I district, with 80% of the students participating in free and reduced lunch, 60% entering as English learners, and one of every five students coming from a migrant background. In Chapter 7, we will present more information on the design of this innovative program.

> AUTHOR: DAVID BAUTISTA, ASSISTANT SUPERINTENDENT—OREGON DEPARTMENT OF EDUCATION, AND FORMER SUPERINTENDENT—WOODBURN SCHOOL DISTRICT, WOODBURN, OREGON

The paragraphs that follow describe the Woodburn School District's revised 2012 strategic plan, illustrating how assessment and evaluation are an integral part of each step taken to transform a whole school district that is working to graduate all of its students bilingual/biliterate. Critical initiatives for enriching the bilingual educational system across all grades in Woodburn schools call for bold and innovative strategies. Each year the community members, students, teachers, and administrators update the revised plan. The superintendent remains an observer in order not to influence the process towards one particular point of view.

Initiative 1. Teachers at all levels will develop aligned and articulated instructional frameworks for best practices in the content areas at each level (K-3, 4-6, 7-8, 9-12). We envision a clearly articulated K-12 system with banded instructional loops that identify key proficiencies necessary for success at each step in a student's educational journey. Targeted, individualized intervention systems will be in place for students not meeting proficiencies, while a proficiency-based system will also allow students who reach proficiency more quickly to engage with challenging curriculum and instruction within the system. Because the state reading assessment, the Oregon Assessment of Knowledge and Skills, is offered only in English, reading scores do not accurately reflect the development of reading skills for students in our bilingual programs. The district uses the Aprenda, a nationally-normed, academic exam in Spanish, along with the state reading exam to determine reading proficiency and development for students in Spanish-English dual language programs. The district is working to develop a comparable academic exam in Russian for use at each grade level. To successfully target interventions, the district will use the Oregon state exam, Aprenda, and the locally-developed Russian exam to correctly differentiate between struggling readers and predicted English reading delays for students in bilingual enrichment language programs.

Initiative 2. At the elementary level, our students' performance data indicates the need to focus on the improvement of mathematics teaching and learning. Woodburn School District plans to provide support implementing intensive professional development that impacts all elementary school teachers in one of two distinct program offerings. For teachers who lack mathematical skills and confidence, the district will provide math instruction, offered by more advanced math teachers within our district. Elementary teachers with strong math skills will earn an Oregon Teacher Standards and Practices Commission-approved graduate level Math Specialization certificate offered at the district by a university partner focused on high impact teaching strategies aligned with the Common Core State Standards and Smarter Balanced Consortium frameworks. Five of these specialists will in turn serve as math coaches in their schools, offering math instruction for elementary teachers who lack skills and confidence to teach math.

Initiative 3. At the middle school level, Woodburn School District will complete the bridging of our proficiency-based teaching and assessment programs already in existence at the elementary and high school levels. This will be accompanied by the launching of a new International Baccalaureate (IB) Middle Years Program, raising

expectations for students to participate and succeed in college preparatory programs, and increasing student academic self-efficacy (Eccles, Vida, & Barber, 2004). True college readiness should include college awareness activities and college eligibility preparation no later than middle school (Wimberly & Noeth, 2005). The IB high schools will also implement the Middle Years programs for Grades 9 and 10. Middle and high school teachers will work toward alignment and articulation, with the IB framework at the core, to help support this work in the key years when we know our students are transferring deep cognitive thinking between their first and second languages.

Initiative 4. At the high school level, the program will support a college-attending culture by expanding the number of classes available for dual high school/college credit, knowing that students who garner college credits while in high school are more likely to graduate on time and earn higher GPAs in college. To achieve this vision, Woodburn School District will increase the number of middle and high school teachers who complete 28 credit hours of discipline-specific classes needed to qualify as a *College Credit Now* instructor. The district will also expand Career and Technical Education programs to allow students to explore different career options and to earn dual high school/college credit in fields that may not require 4-year college degrees. Both of these programs allow students to deeply explore areas of academic interest in a rigorous context but with the supports to be successful.

Initiative 5. Woodburn School District will extend education beyond school walls, traditional calendars, and K-12 aged students. Each high school student enrolled in Woodburn and each K-8 family in the district will receive a mobile learning device that extends learning beyond the classroom. Woodburn's summer program, previously limited to only migrant students, will be open to all K-12 students. Our evening Family University, offering English and technology classes for migrant parents, academic supports for school-age children, and pre-school classes, will be expanded to support more families who wish to participate while literacy- and math-based family offerings in schools will be increased and promoted. The district will also use funds to expand our limited summer school program. In addition to literacy interventions, a pre-kindergarten program will be available for all incoming kindergartners. Providing an early transition for our students, the majority of whom have not attended pre-school, the program will also give an opportunity to collect data and get to know students' strengths and needs.

The current 2014 website of Woodburn School District includes these visionary statements: "Our mission: Our promise is to engage, inspire, and prepare all students to learn and lead in a global society." "Our Vision: Woodburn School District is an outstanding multilingual school district, which motivates and empowers all students to succeed." "We value accountability, civic responsibility, diversity, equality, family, integrity, learning, multilingualism, parent-community partnerships, safety, and the individual." "Our goals: All students will graduate college-and-career ready. All students will meet or exceed growth targets in writing, reading, and math. All students will have the opportunity to achieve high academic competence in two or more languages. All students will have the opportunity to complete post-secondary level coursework prior to graduation."

Assessment and Evaluation for the Future of Dual Language Education

The examples in this chapter of visions for the future, as well as struggles with policies that do not support the dual language program, are all part of the process of assessment and evaluation. An evaluation of your entire dual language program must include stepping back and examining elements that work well, as well as things that need to be changed. But assessment and evaluation involves much, much more than simply examining student achievement on the annual tests. Ongoing staff dialogue needs to occur at the classroom level, among the team-teaching partners, within the dual language strand and the schoolwide programs, and extending to the contexts of the whole school district, the state, and national policies that impact the program.

> AUTHOR: ERIN BOSTICK MASON, ADJUNCT PROFESSOR—CALIFORNIA STATE UNIVERSITY, SAN BERNARDINO, AND FORMER PROGRAM MANAGER, DUAL LANGUAGE/ENGLISH LEARNER SERVICES—SAN BERNARDINO COUNTY SUPERINTENDENT OF SCHOOLS, SAN BERNARDINO, CALIFORNIA

Support Systems for Dual Language Education for the Long Term

How can I make compromises in the short term and still maintain progress toward fully implementing dual language/immersion in the long term? How do I balance district, state, or regional directives that I know are not supporting our program?

Systemic reform takes long-term effort by many stakeholders. It is a continuous cycle of unearthing the parts of the system that are counter-productive and re-designing those components so they support the ultimate objective of creating multilingual, multicultural graduates. Since dual language/immersion programs grow with the students from kindergarten to twelfth grade, this truly is a long-term process. In an era when many consider 3 to 5 years to be long term, systems find it a challenge to stay focused on a single vision and program implementation process for the required number of years. We have seen this pattern in the PROMISE Initiative Pilot Study in southern California (2006-09), Title VII grants, Foreign Language Assistance Program (FLAP) grants, Title III grants, and in our regional network.

Roughly speaking, a program is still breaking new ground until it has graduated the first few cohorts. Once the first groups have graduated, a program can finally analyze summative data and look for patterns and trends from Grades K-6, K-8 or K-12 in order to refine the program's implementation. In some districts, the average stay for a principal or superintendent is 3 to 5 years. Therefore, initial implementation often spans more than one administrator's tenure. Teachers and support staff also move or get reassigned. Administrators need to nurture a broad team of leaders including teachers, support staff, district and school office staff, parents, community members, and even students who are poised to serve as branches of a tree, reaching out to facilitate change within the system and create success with dual language/immersion education. This team is vulnerable to burnout and high turnover. Therefore, we must include a wide range of stakeholders representing all parts of the system and continually reinvest in their capacity to lead this implementation process for dual immersion education. As members move or leave, we need to include new members and give them access to the same information and networks that others enjoyed.

In the end, none of us live or work in a utopia. Our systems are always a work in progress. Furthermore, there are tremendous formal and informal pressures upon us to conform to the current system, even if the majority of us are consciously embracing the change process. In addition, there are times when short-term actions may conflict with the optimal path towards dual language/immersion implementation. We all have to accept compromises sometimes, perhaps only for the short term, until we can leverage support for the more optimal path. The key is to illuminate for ourselves and others the most effective, research-based path in the long term. Why are we compromising? And, how we can work to eventually create a path to the more optimal route? For example, having all classrooms provide English Language Development at a uniform time school-wide is a common management strategy that enables an administrator to hold staff accountable for delivery. Some may believe this is necessary if there are compliance issues at a site and resistance to providing English Language Development. However, we need to keep in mind the impact on dual language/immersion. Does it mean target language instruction is interrupted or cut short? How can we minimize the negative impact and work towards a more optimal path in the long term?

In other cases, schools may have issues around a lottery system for kindergarten enrollment due to a limited number of bilingual staff. All energy can become consumed by finding a solution to the lottery debate. However, at the same time, we need to question why there are not enough bilingual teachers to meet the demand and create a path toward resolving that deeper issue. We have to make the best compromises we can in the short term, while never losing sight of the research-based ideal. We all have to make concessions and prioritize which steps to take first toward long-term redesign. It is essential to understand what relevant research states, what is ideal or most beneficial, where we are in relation to that optimal choice, and then clearly communicate why we are making that choice. Too often, research gets confused with local compromise. Understand why you are doing what you are doing. Keep the optimal in mind, and make the best strides you can toward that vision. Help others understand what the optimal would be, work toward that shared vision in the long term, and make the best compromises you can in the short term.

Eventually, change will be required at almost all levels of the system, but not all at once. Creating a dual language/immersion program is like a river's current shaping the stone. Some changes will come or be required in a flash flood. Others will take years of persistence to erode an obstacle and replace it with a smooth path of support. That is why we need to connect with others, even if we may have to look far and wide. Luckily, social networks and digital communication make this easier. We need to link our islands and network as much as possible. Invite all parts of the system to learn and work together. Empower ourselves. These school systems are social constructs. Although powerful, they were made by humans and can be changed by humans just like us—moving one step at a time, choosing our priorities, and keeping our vision high for all to share.

Accountability and Dual Language Solutions

Many voices in this chapter have expressed the paradoxes in which dual language programs live within the broader policy context in the U.S. On the one hand, the extra testing and accountability that has come with NCLB federal funding and states' subsequent systems of measuring student progress has led to a focus on the achievement of English learners (emergent bilinguals) for the first time. These emergent bilinguals are now classified as a subgroup that must be counted and their progress measured. (They are still called "limited-English-proficient [LEP] students" by the federal government, even though many students and their parents find this term offensive.) While policy arguments go back and forth between federal and state officials as to how soon the beginning ESL students who are English learners must be tested on the state achievement tests in English, our bilingual/ESL field is at least no longer ignored or hidden from view, given the new accountability requirements. And yet teachers, schools, and school districts feel penalized for working hard to serve these students well, with unreasonable expectations for how soon these students should be tested on English curricular measures.

Our Thomas and Collier research findings (1997, 2002, 2009, 2010, 2012, 2014) illustrate how astoundingly successful English learners can be on the accountability tests when given the opportunity to be schooled in high-quality, well-implemented dual language programs. And this is also true for all subgroups attending well-implemented dual language classes. We can celebrate this validation of the possibilities and potential of this powerful program that are far outside the limited box that NCLB and the present educational reforms are pushing us into.

But at the same time we must not accept unrealistic expectations for short-term gains in English by the policy makers who think it only takes 1 or 2 years to learn English as a second language. It is essential that we continue to explain to policy makers the complex developmental processes that must occur in students' first and second languages during the school years—linguistic, academic, cognitive, emotional, social, and physical—for all our students to do well in school (see the Prism Model in Collier & Thomas, 2009, Chapter 4). English learners and other at-risk groups not participating in dual language education are still being over-identified as having special educational needs in a variety of exceptionality categories. This practice could be lessened significantly with attention to students' cognitive and academic development through both their first and second languages. In a high-quality dual language program, as English learners reach grade-level achievement in their primary language and gradually develop comparable skills in their second language, students will reach grade-level achievement in English in an average of 6 years.

All dual language leaders must tackle the challenge of educating those policy makers with shortsighted vision. The longitudinal research findings are quite clear and generalizable throughout all regions of the U.S. Dual language programs have the potential to change the lives of many students of all diverse backgrounds. As dual language leaders, we can transform our schools into contexts that prepare our students for a very new and different multilingual, multicultural, interconnected world.

Chapter Six:
Parents, Partnerships, and Advocacy

Parents are the lifeline of your dual language program. They are your most important allies. Often, parents are the ones who keep the vision alive because this is a lifetime commitment for dual language families. They want their children to become proficiently bilingual. Parents appreciate the rich multilingual and multicultural communities we live in, and they want to expand the role school plays in bringing diverse children together. They want their children to be at ease in multicultural/global contexts, to be able to navigate the professional worlds and life experiences, and to be able to cross national boundaries that await them as adults. In dual language classes, parents envision all their children participating in classrooms where students of diverse socio-economic and cultural backgrounds value and respect each other and work collaboratively.

Parents become crucial advocates and valuable partners with dual language educators when decisions are made at critical junctures in the program's development. For example, families whose children are attending dual language classes in elementary school sometimes contact their middle school's administrators to make sure the middle school staff understands and embraces the program and will be a part of the dialogue and planning as the program moves up grade by grade. If a new school board member or newly hired administrator is initially not supportive of the dual language program, parents often step in to explain the research, rationale, and commitment of the community to dual language education.

In this chapter, our collaborating authors share their experiences with community and family partnerships across a range of school contexts. The most important message all of these stories impart is to keep the communication flowing with all parent groups and to be creative and flexible in responding to the needs of each diverse parent community. Parents serve the important role of growing and sustaining the program as they become knowledgeable about this type of enrichment bilingual schooling. They become your partners in recruiting new families to the program and explaining the rationale to newly arrived immigrant parents who are often initially skeptical about their children being schooled through both their home language and English. The following author describes five different parent groups with varying functions that have become crucial advocates and allies for the dual language program at her former school, as well as her own experiences as a dual language parent.

AUTHOR: DR. EMILY BIVINS, FORMER PRINCIPAL—CARRBORO ELEMENTARY SCHOOL, AND CURRENT PRINCIPAL—COLEGIO FRANK PORTER GRAHAM BILINGÜE, CHAPEL HILL-CARRBORO CITY SCHOOL DISTRICT, CHAPEL HILL, NORTH CAROLINA

Parent Groups in One School

I strongly believe that parents are partners in education, their child's first and most important teacher, and vital to the success of any school. Parents are a huge support in a dual language school, but their needs vary based on their background and experience with dual language. We provide a great deal of parent education and advocacy work with families at Carrboro Elementary School, where we house a Spanish-English dual language strand that occupies approximately two thirds of the school's classes. There are several parent groups that are critical and necessary.

First, every school in our state has a School Improvement Team that writes and monitors the School Improvement Plan. The parents and staff on this team must understand dual language, the research on dual language, and why it is a vital program in our school. Each year, I provide resources and materials (articles, presentations, etc.) to this group to explain why, for example, the school leadership team recommends teaching language through academic content using the Sheltered Instruction Observation Protocol (SIOP) model (Echevarría, Short, & Powers, 2006; Echevarría, Vogt, & Short, 2008), or why teachers need release time for unit planning, or why we analyze data.

Second, our school PTA is critical to our work with dual language. They focus on community building, advocacy, and fundraising for the entire school. One significant area of community building is bridging the disconnect between dual language and English-only classrooms and families. The school PTA plans events, programs, and celebrations that highlight the entire school population, and they have made a conscious effort not to have dual language/non-dual language events or programs. They also advocate for things like redistricting and policy changes at the Board of Education level because those decisions impact our ability to develop and maintain a supportive multilingual, multicultural community. In my tenure here, our school has gone through one big redistricting and is preparing to go through another. With dual language, neighborhoods can't be picked up and moved, because the children may not have access to dual language programming at another elementary school. Parents and school staff have also invested a lot of time in building relationships and establishing a school community where parents are powerful advocates for all children in our school, whether they are in dual language or not.

When dual language is a strand in a school, it is important to share information about dual language with all stakeholders in the school, whether they are directly involved or not. Don't make it seem like dual language is the only show in the school because if it is portrayed this way, those not involved begin to feel resentment toward dual language. Every program is worth acknowledging, every student is worthy of praise, and every family is worthy of celebration.

Our school has two other parent groups that are specific to dual language. One is Padres Unidos, the dual language parent group, organized and run by parents to provide updates on dual language planning, to participate in decision making as needed, to share resources available for dual language families, to provide advice for new parents, and to serve as advocates for the program. This group met monthly when the program was first established. Now they meet quarterly for formal meetings. The first meeting of the year is Dual Language 101. I make a presentation on dual language research, school data, our rationale for having dual language, etc. Teachers provide model lessons for parents to experience what their children are experiencing at school. We finish with experienced parents sharing with new parents what has worked for them—how to help with homework when you don't speak the language, managing children's stress, etc. If the year does not begin with this meeting, the parents overwhelm the teachers with individual conferences where the teachers get to say this 48 times to individual parents. This initial meeting helps to lower new parents' anxiety, to communicate the rigor and high standards of the program, and clarify the kind of support required from home.

The parents decide what the Padres Unidos programming will look like for the remainder of the year. We have done things like role playing how to set up play dates with families who don't speak your language, how to access community resources available in Spanish, how to use web resources in Spanish and English, and how to navigate middle school transition. The program also addresses program changes, literacy development in English and Spanish, and math instructional differences in Central and South America compared to the U.S. Sometimes parents plan their own program, and at other times, they ask for school help. I meet with the parent leaders for the year as they organize topics for their meetings. With topics determined, they work from a checklist of things to do for each meeting, such as getting meetings on the school calendar/website, distributing fliers, and arranging for translators, listening devices, and handouts. Good planning for these parent meetings includes being aware of the needs of both language groups and being inclusive in the decision making.

The other dual language parent group is the Hispanic parent group. Our Hispanic parents come primarily from Central America, and many live in poverty in our community. They have specific needs as newly arrived immigrants that warrant a separate parent group. They have also felt more empowered as a parent group when they are working together rather than within the PTA. They meet every other month (they want to meet more often!), have dinner, and discuss a parent-selected topic of education.

These are very important meetings that bond the newly arrived Hispanic families to the school and the dual language program and demonstrate the role the school serves as strong support for the whole family and community. Sometimes the topics are related to school—reading at home, homework help, what school accountability means, discipline, and math support. They also organize important sessions that involve community resources, such as budget/finance, fair and quality housing, legal issues, or after-school/summer activities. Sometimes they want adult-learning opportunities such as English classes (taught by university volunteers two nights a week at school) or computer classes (taught by one of our teachers each week). The school tries to be responsive to the needs of the parents. It is a two-way street because the parents are always asking what they can do to help the school. We talk about when/where they can volunteer, fundraising opportunities, cultural events, and special programs. Hispanic parent nights draw about 90% of our Spanish-speaking population. Funds for the minimal expenses for these meetings come from Title I and "at-risk" funding, as well as from funds the parents raise.

This may seem like a lot of parent groups, but we highly recommend that you ask parents what they want or need and then give it! We have found that too much information is a good thing, even when the information shows a problem with the program. Parents are more supportive of the changes if you have been detailed in explaining the problem as well as the potential solutions.

Parent Cross-Cultural Communication and Advocacy

Advocacy is a huge part of parent education—and advocate is what parents can and need to do. With our Spanish-speaking parents, we talk a lot about U.S. schools and the role of parents in U.S. schools—rights, responsibilities, etc. Parents talk about how different this is for them culturally. We are not seeking to assimilate parents into U.S. schooling, but we do want parents to understand what they can do, and we want teachers to be mindful of parents' cultural expectations, as well.

For example, I have a teacher from Central America, and an English-speaking dad began demanding different classroom experiences for his daughter at the beginning of the year. We had to work through the cultural incongruence for both of them. In another situation, a Latina mom felt her son was not being challenged enough but thought it a sign of disrespect to talk to the teacher about it. We helped that mom and teacher figure out what to do next so both parties felt comfortable, and the interests of the child were met.

Both Spanish- and English-speaking parents play a huge role in advocacy for dual language instruction. They have written letters, talked with Board of Education members, and hosted prospective parents and schools interested in starting dual language. They talk about their experiences, both good and bad, and what they think teachers and the school need. They always offer to help new programs get started or help the central office/Board of Education with problem solving to make our program better. One of the current topics is expansion of our program to be a schoolwide model. Parents have been essential in voicing their advocacy and desires to decision makers.

We strongly recommend that you encourage your parents to speak out as advocates for the dual language program. They are the best public relations tools we have. Our community and school board listen to them, sometimes more than to the school staff.

Principal as Parent

Six years ago, I became a dual language parent. Prior to that, I reassured parents that their children were going to be fine in dual language, and I had no idea what I was saying. I have three children, now in Grades K, 3, and 5. If only I knew then what I know now. When my oldest child entered kindergarten dual language, after Pre-K only in English, I began to notice changes. She became withdrawn, whined more, and began developing nervous habits, but the teachers all told me she was fine and delightful in school. I assumed something was wrong with my child. I then recalled all my previous meetings with concerned parents who shared similar experiences about their kindergartner. My child was under stress. It was the first time in her life when, for half the day, she did not have a clue what was going on around her—and she had never been in the middle of this much socioeconomic, linguistic, or racial diversity.

I found it difficult to reassure myself, so I talked to other people—colleagues whose children were students in their dual language schools, friends who had older dual language students. I knew removing her from dual language was not an option for me on so many levels. I realized I needed to do some things differently outside of school so my child could handle the challenge school provided. We cut out new extracurricular activities and focused on what she was good at, so she built confidence. We altered the amount of sleep and down time she got at home. All of these things helped, and she eventually got used to the set up and began to learn Spanish. Now when I talk about dual language with parents, I talk a lot about how children can be impacted by the stress of the day, the pace, the two languages, etc. It's important that, as a principal, you remember that you may know a lot more than parents about dual language, but parents know a lot more about their child, so be sensitive to parents' concerns.

When my second child entered kindergarten, we started a strand of 90:10 dual language to jump start the English-speaking students' experience in Spanish because we did not have enough Spanish speakers for this class. I placed my second daughter in this class and have now seen the pros and cons of the different program models play out in my own children. I am not sure which model I will select for my son next year, but knowing there are two models really helps me to dispel fears that 90:10 would not work in our community or that 50:50 is the only way to go. It will also give me data to demonstrate the high level of Spanish and English proficiency students in 90:10 are capable of achieving, since this has continued to be a political concern for our Board of Education and parents.

My second and third children have had the opportunity to have dual language experiences in Pre-K/Head Start in the school. Since they were younger when they began, they don't seem as aware that school is different from other experiences they have had. They will ask questions when we have a new babysitter or are going to someone's house they don't know, such as "Do they speak English or Spanish or both?" They are working through contextualizing what to do when they meet someone new. It is amazing to watch. When this happens to me as a monolingual, who is trying to learn Spanish, I feel instant fear that I will not be able to communicate and things will be terrible. I never see those behaviors in my kids. What a life skill to have!

Having children in dual language has made me a better leader and parent. I feel that as a parent I am able to provide for my children something I never had—a bigger worldview and the ability to navigate it with confidence, both linguistically and culturally. As a leader, I am able to lead with 21st century skills in mind—collaboration, cross-cultural competence, proficiency in multiple languages, critical and creative thinking. Pedagogy that supports these skills, relevant instructional resources and materials, and a focus on learning that goes well beyond reading and mathematics have all supported our school in being more effective with a worldview of the entire child and what he/she will face in the future.

In summary, principals of dual language schools must be prepared to support all parents, and in turn, all your families will reward you with essential support for your school. Parents are your most loyal partners, once you truly understand and respect their concerns. The idea of having four different parent groups in one small school at first seems at odds with the idea of collaboration, but Dr. Bivins finds that each parent group serves a unique and important function, and at the same time, they support each other and are all proud of their school. In fact, in this school, a fifth parent group has recently organized around a truly basic need—providing food for their families. A Burmese/Karen refugee group resettled in Chapel Hill. They became parents at Carrboro Elementary and requested permission to grow a community organic garden, which became an important source of food for their families. The Karen families work the land lovingly, mentoring all of the children who attend the school. Each class at the school has also planted greens, herbs, and flowers just outside their classroom door, so that the children across all grades incorporate science lessons on life cycles, including chickens that lay eggs on the school grounds (and sometimes even in children's hands!).

Parental response, even in the first years of a new dual language program, can be quite rewarding. In a Southern community that had no previous experience with bilingual schooling, the principal reports that Harrisonburg parents have responded with excitement and amazement.

AUTHOR: GARY PAINTER, PRINCIPAL—SMITHLAND ELEMENTARY SCHOOL, HARRISONBURG CITY PUBLIC SCHOOLS, HARRISONBURG, VIRGINIA

Parental interest in our two-way dual language program at Smithland grows each year. As of the second year of implementation, 45 students of Spanish- and English-speaking background are participating in the kindergarten classes, while 40 students are enrolled in the first-grade classes. Students from our neighborhood are automatically enrolled, with a small number of slots held for students living outside the Smithland school boundaries. The popularity of this program has already resulted in numerous applications and waiting lists each year.

The parents meet with me during the first and second semesters to have their questions answered and to learn details about the program and plans for grade expansion. The parent group has organized play dates and picnics and created a

parent video to show at informational meetings. In addition, they provide support for teachers during parent conference days by ensuring classes are covered while all 85 families meet with the teachers. The partnership with parents has been powerful!

Results from a family survey were outstanding, with 100% of the parents reporting overall satisfaction with Smithland's dual language program. Some of the comments included:

- "Mom, learning Spanish has changed my life." (My all-time favorite quote from a first grader!)
- "We can now retain and embrace our Latino roots and culture."
- "The program is well structured, and the results have been amazing!"
- "It is a great opportunity, and we hope to get as many people involved as possible to ensure the program continues."
- "We feel strongly that to be educated in two languages at this age is a wonderful gift to give to a child."
- "My daughter had an eye appointment and the doctor's assistant was bilingual. Once she became aware that my daughter is in the dual language program, she started speaking Spanish only, and they did the entire exam in Spanish. I was so proud! Thank you for everything you do to keep this program going!"

Parent Challenges

Sometimes, though, not everything goes so smoothly. Throughout this book, you have seen, through the voices of the principals and school district leaders, that dual language implementation has its challenges, along with its rewards. As an example of a very big challenge, the next story examines some of the difficulties that can occur when the school community has not participated in the planning for implementation of a new dual language school, and thus the community support is not there.

> AUTHOR: DR. MARJORIE MYERS, PRINCIPAL—KEY SCHOOL~ESCUELA KEY, ARLINGTON PUBLIC SCHOOLS, ARLINGTON, VIRGINIA

From 1983 to 1995, I worked in the District of Columbia Public Schools (DCPS) as secondary ESL-math teacher, bilingual counselor, central office ESL coordinator, assistant principal at Cardozo High School, and finally principal of H.D. Cooke Elementary School. The Office of Minority Language Affairs had been awarded a federal grant to make H.D. Cooke a two-way bilingual enrichment school, and I was hired to run it. The position was my first job as a principal and the first time in years to be back in an elementary school. From the beginning, it was clear that the groundwork had not been laid sufficiently to involve the community in the process of converting a neighborhood school into a two-way Spanish-English bilingual school in a section of town where the population was split between Hispanic and African American families. Although they lived side by side, these neighbors did not always see eye to eye. The buy-in for bilingual schooling was not there for either group, and with no community input or education, this community was mobilized to resist implementation of the program.

In a short time, the rumors had gotten out of control in the neighborhood. One rumor was that with this grant, African American children would be denied their own language (English), and teaching them in Spanish would cause them to be held back in their education. Parents were already fighting at the school board level to have language services provided in Standard English for African American children, equal to those services provided to English learners through Title VII funding. Having their children learn Spanish was not part of the original plan.

With this community unrest, I decided to hold a PTA/community meeting to explain the two-way Spanish/English program to the parents and community. The afternoon of the planned meeting, a school board member representing the neighborhood recommended I cancel the meeting. She was accompanied by a Spanish-speaking policewoman from the community who told me that if I wanted to have the meeting, she had my back.

Being naïve and new at this principal thing, I assured her that I would say nothing controversial, and I doubted many people would attend. Unbeknownst to me, the media had gotten wind of the meeting, and it was being announced on the radio. That night, much to my surprise, the multipurpose room of the tiny school had a standing-room-only crowd. People were out on the street unable to get in. All of the major TV stations were there, and a central office representative from the communications division was sent to help. I gave my presentation about how two-way bilingual enrichment would work and how research showed that children would benefit from—rather than be harmed by—studying in a second language as well as their first language.

Once I finished my presentation, one of the community parents stood up and started to rally the audience with the idea that the plans for using this grant to implement bilingual schooling would destroy the education of African American children in the community. He also went on—and I agreed with him—about the fact that the 100-year-old school needed new wiring, new floors, and new windows in order to be a safe environment for the students. He felt the $1 million grant should be used to rebuild the school, not create a detrimental program. At that point, others started weighing in, and things were getting a bit loud; nevertheless, I was willing to continue fielding questions. The communications representative stepped up, took the microphone from me, and very professionally thanked everyone for their interest and for coming to the meeting. He then declared the presentation over. I said, "Good night," and walked upstairs to my office to get my purse and then went out the back and down the fire escape stairs to my car as I did every night. The policewoman followed me upstairs and out to my car. Neither of us felt threatened, and she kept telling me how interesting the plan was and how she would love for her children to have such an opportunity. That night I was quite surprised to see myself on the eleven o'clock news with the comment that I had needed a police escort to get out of the building.

That evening gave me quite a reputation. A few days later, I requested a meeting with the superintendent. After hearing my appeal that I needed more time to bond with the community, he called in one of his assistant superintendents to find out the status of the grant. They informed me the grant had been moved to John Adams Elementary School, a few blocks away, and would no longer be at H.D. Cooke Elementary School.

As sad as I was to lose the grant, it was a blessing. Things calmed down at the school, teachers could concentrate on their students, and learning began to take place.

By 1995, I had worked in DCPS for 13 years. I loved being in the city and working for the children and families I so loved, but I wanted to run a two-way bilingual enrichment program and that wasn't going to happen any time soon at H.D. Cooke Elementary School. The only school in DCPS at that time with two-way bilingual schooling was Oyster Elementary, and Oyster already had a dedicated principal. Much to my amazement, I saw an ad in *Education Week* for a principal for Francis Scott Key

Elementary in Arlington, Virginia, only 4 miles from my home in Washington, D.C. I applied for the position, and after extensive interviews with Arlington parents, staff, and central office personnel, I was offered the position as principal of this schoolwide two-way Spanish-English school and have been there since.

At Key School-Escuela Key, our parents are phenomenal partners with us in every aspect of school decision making and participation. They serve as outspoken advocates for the dual immersion program that makes us all so proud. Community support is absolutely crucial to a dual language school's success.

Parent involvement can be another type of challenge in large urban school districts where a large percentage of the students, including many English learners, are being served in the dual language program. In these contexts, you may experience political challenges from those who advocate for monolingual English instruction for immigrants. Convincing parents to enroll their children in the dual language program can be difficult in regions of the U.S. (such as the southwest U.S., as well as the borderlands along the French-Canadian and Mexican-U.S. borders) where languages other than English have been de-valued and where parents may have experienced physical punishment for using their home language at school when they were growing up. These sociolinguistic patterns remain hard to overcome, but parents are the key. Once a parent advocacy group is solidly behind your program, they are your best allies. The next author presents her experience and passion on these issues.

AUTHOR: DORA TORRES-MORÓN, LANGUAGE AND LITERACY EXECUTIVE DIRECTOR—DALLAS INDEPENDENT SCHOOL DISTRICT, DALLAS, TEXAS

Parent Involvement

Parents play an integral part in developing and growing your dual language program, as they are critical for the success of any educational program. Informed parents are involved parents. It is the parents who are the first to fight for your program whether in the board room or in the community, so it is wise to keep parents informed and included in the planning and decision-making process. Inviting parents to the school to see how the program is implemented is the best way to keep them informed and to create a positive feeling about the program. If parents are new to the program, invite them to see how students are learning in the upper grades, so they can keep the end goals in mind—proficient bilingualism and biliteracy as professional adults.

Advising parents. It's also important to discuss with parents any issues that might come up—before they come up! The school should always be accessible to address parents' concerns. For example, talk to parents about their child's first weeks of school or what to expect when their child first enrolls. Parents may panic when their child begins to cry or is stressed when he does not understand what the teacher is saying. Preparing parents about what to expect beforehand and providing tools on how to address concerns will help avoid surprises and generate more support for both the student and the school. Talk to parents about how they can prepare their child for a new way of learning. Providing information on how a child acquires and develops a second language is critical for all stakeholders and is necessary to create a smooth transition.

When reaching the stage of continuing the dual language program into the secondary level, it is important to talk to parents about the expectations for the program and the goals they have set for their child. Expectations must be spelled out and articulated ahead of time. Parents need to be prepared to make decisions regarding electives and extracurricular activities as part of their secondary plan. Depending on the activities their child may want to participate in, students may need to be prepared to take some classes during the summer in order to continue their dual language classes in the fall while adding extracurricular activities, such as band or sports. This can be a planning nightmare for parents, students, and the school, if not considered carefully as they grow the dual language program. This will also help in deciding which courses you will offer in Spanish at the secondary level. And, if a middle school course will be counted as high school credit, the staffing has to be considered, since the teacher certification requirements differ.

Parental service to the program. Another useful way to involve parents is asking them to help the school evaluate materials you plan to use in the program. This is extremely helpful, especially if you don't speak the partner language. Make sure to include the different cultures represented on your campus during parent meetings. This is an opportunity to talk about how the education system works in the United States (useful for immigrant parents) and how it works in other countries. Parents are happy to share multicultural linguistic differences, too; for example, Spanish is spoken in over 20 countries, so the vocabulary and customs can vary, including variations by socioeconomic class.

Parents want to remain involved and want to know what their role is, so continuous communication is very important. They also want to know where their child is within the different phases of language development and what to expect at each phase. Parents who don't speak English know that their heritage language is valued in the academic environment when they are included in the curricular decision making.

Remember, parents are the best advocates, so enlist them to welcome parents new to the school and to invite other parents to visit the program. This will create added interest in the dual language program. Be sure these parents are able to articulate the goals and benefits of the program and have been informed regarding the language acquisition process and the research behind the program.

Student and parent advisory committees. It is extremely important that both the parents and the students play an integral part in the decision making during the development and implementation of the dual language program. In order to have continuous communication with students, it is a good idea to organize a student advisory committee and a parent advisory committee. It's remarkable what students will share and the significant input they can provide to improve program services. It will help grow the program, and families will become the ultimate advocates! Both parents and students are eager to request as many opportunities as possible for students to practice language, such as volunteering to translate at after-school events or community organization meetings. As part of the committees, they can also help organize university-sponsored events, such as out-of-the-country excursions.

Students also benefit greatly from participating in leadership and character development opportunities, leading to self-efficacy. Creating opportunities for students to feel proud that they are working on mastering two languages and being knowledgeable about world events is a great advantage to families. As students mature, they need opportunities for developing their sociocultural identity and demonstrating their ability to present their multilingualism and multiculturalism as an asset.

Developing Partnerships

Higher education partnerships. The dual language plan should always include major stakeholders of the community (i.e., school board members, school administrators and all education staff, business leaders), along with partnerships that include institutions of higher learning and community service organizations. One of the best suggestions I can provide is including an institution of higher learning as a major partner. A university can provide a wide variety of assistance, including being an active partner

Chapter Six: Parents, Partnerships, and Advocacy

in developing your program, providing the teachers needed for your dual language program, and generating ideas on best practice, professional development, and program evaluation. The newly certified teachers can come better prepared if you communicate your expectations to the university ahead of time. The bilingual professors and their bilingual students can provide invaluable assistance in helping you develop and decide on the type of model to be implemented in your district. In addition, university partners will increase the credibility of your program and will actively communicate the importance of implementing a dual language program to your community.

In Dallas ISD, our partnerships with Southern Methodist University, University of North Texas, and the University of Texas at Arlington provide professional development, stipends for teachers to obtain their ESL/bilingual certification, and unique summer programs, such as visiting Central American countries. This provides teachers a new experience in learning about different educational systems, as well as strengthening the teachers' academic knowledge and proficiency in the partner language. Community and business partners can cultivate increased services such as providing internships, mentorships, volunteer opportunities, service-learning projects, and leadership opportunities for the secondary students.

Community organizations and summer enrichment. The summer months are the perfect time to add to the very demanding curriculum and an optimal time to build upon what has been learned. It is a time to provide summer enrichment activities that specifically address the second language and increase opportunities to use the language. A summer program is especially important for the early grades, PK-2, when students are learning early literacy skills. The summer program should include conversation and reading to build skills for early reading success. Engaging in active discourse and reading for enjoyment builds skills for early reading success in both languages. Word study in both English and the partner language should also be a part of the summer program, in a playful and hands-on context.

For secondary students, it's even more important to practice their partner language. I can still remember talking to middle school dual language students as part of a student focus group. I asked them what we could have done better in elementary to enhance or enrich their dual language experiences; almost in unison, they responded with two suggestions. They wanted more opportunities to use their second language, whether it was making oral presentations or practicing with others who knew the language well, and they had really enjoyed learning about other cultures and wished they could learn more about different cultures around the world! I was left breathless.

We decided to involve the students in more after-school or summer activities within the community. They could volunteer to translate at a local community event or business and provide presentations in their second language. Students could also tutor younger students using their second language and volunteer hours could be recorded as part of their graduation requirements. Our summer and after-school events took on a whole new meaning.

When students begin taking a more active role in extracurricular activities, summer is also the time to get ahead with high school credits, in order to allow more time for taking additional partner language classes or begin acquiring a third language. Once students learn a second language, they are suddenly anxious to learn a third!

Partnerships with sister schools. Summer is also a time to explore possibilities for travel to other countries. Exchanges and group trips to new cultural contexts are a wonderful way to expand horizons for both teachers and students. This can lead to student exchanges with sister schools in other countries. Through email and Internet connections, students and faculty in the sister schools can develop joint units of study and exchange knowledge and information (Brown, 1997; Cummins & Sayers, 1995).

School partnerships with dual language communities and families can stimulate wide-ranging creativity in learning contexts when you listen to the voices within your school community and respond with collaborative planning and resources. Using your school community's "funds of knowledge" (González, Moll, & Amanti, 2005), with dual language parents as partners in schooling, is one of many possibilities for strengthening the bonds between families and schools and valuing the knowledge that parents of all socioeconomic and cultural backgrounds bring to the dual language classroom.

Another important opportunity is created through family's connections with relatives in their countries of origin. New technologies each year lessen the distance between communities around the Earth, and this instant connecting allows for many creative lessons to emerge when sharing across languages and cultures. For example, teachers can Skype a student's grandma twirling traditional large tortillas in a tiny village in northern Mexico; create joint music-making across diverse contexts (*http://www.playingforchange.com*); develop a technology unit on urban living that is exchanged between Mandarin Chinese-English dual language high schools in San Francisco and Beijing; videotape biliteracy development among families, and share the videotapes across generations (Brown, 1997). All of these examples, and many more, have taken place in dual language classes.

For the last contribution to this chapter, we finish with a resounding cheer for advocacy for dual language programs. Many ways of examining advocacy for dual language programs have been discussed in this chapter, and Marcia Vargas provides an overview of advocacy strategies at all levels that help to sustain our dual language programs.

> AUTHOR: MARCIA VARGAS, FORMER EXECUTIVE DIRECTOR—TWO-WAY CABE (CALIFORNIA ASSOCIATION FOR BILINGUAL EDUCATION)

Advocacy

In 2006, *Time* magazine's cover story titled "How to Bring Our Schools Out of the 20th Century" described skills students will need, in addition to the traditional academic disciplines, to be successful in today's 21st century economy. Those skills include: (1) knowing more about the world—sensitivity to foreign cultures; (2) being conversant in different languages; (3) thinking outside the box—creativity and innovative skills; (4) seeing patterns where other people see only chaos; (5) becoming smarter about new sources of information—having the ability to rapidly process information and distinguish between what's reliable and what isn't; and (6) developing good people skills—having strong communication skills and the ability to work in teams and with people from different cultures.

When I read this article, it occurred to me that all of those skills are incorporated within high-quality, well-implemented dual language programs. High-quality dual language programs are those described by Cloud, Genesee and Hamayan (2000) as enriched education models. These models pursue the goals of bilingualism and biliteracy, academic achievement in two languages, and multicultural competency, with positive cross-cultural attitudes and high levels of self-esteem. To accomplish these goals, dual language students are instructed in a minimum of two languages. Academic achievement research on these programs (Collier & Thomas, 2009; Lindholm-Leary, 2001; Thomas & Collier, 2012) has been very positive, demonstrating that dual language students achieve as well as, or better than, their peers in monolingual English programs. In addition, research affirms the benefits of bilingualism and biliteracy, including increased job opportunities, expanded travel experiences, appreciation of other cultures and languages, lower high school dropout rates, higher interest in attending colleges and universities, enhanced academic and linguistic competence, development of skills in collaboration and cooperation, and cognitive advantages.

One of the challenges for dual language programs is ensuring the long-term permanence of the program despite administrative, staff, and student population changes. We can promote our dual language programs by telling our stories—the stories that test data do not tell. In order to make sure these programs continue through ongoing educational changes, I offer some possibilities and recommendations for promoting and advocating for our dual language programs at several levels: school, district, community, state, national, and international. These activities are not new, but this is a beginning list of possibilities that school leaders, teachers, and parents can use to promote and advocate for their programs.

At the school level. It is the responsibility of everyone involved in dual language programs—students, parents, teachers, administrators, and other staff—to be advocates for their program. It is imperative to have administrative support and leadership for the program. Whether the dual language program is a strand within a school or a schoolwide program, there must be a schoolwide focus on bilingualism and biliteracy. This bilingual focus can be accomplished by ensuring that environmental print throughout the common areas of the school reflects the languages of the students and of the program. Opening announcements and school assemblies should be provided bilingually, not necessarily through concurrent translation, but through the use of headphones for one linguistic group or using an alternate day/event schedule. Awards can be given to school staff, parents, and students to recognize them for the use of their bilingual skills.

In addition, dual language students must be assessed in both the partner language and English in order to have data to share the students' progress in both languages with the community. Administering surveys and interviews to all dual language participants—students, parents, and staff—can provide additional data for the program. The data obtained from test scores, surveys, and interviews can then be disaggregated, analyzed, and the results shared with site staff, district staff, and the outside community.

Professional development opportunities must be provided for dual language teachers to become knowledgeable in all defining characteristics and guiding principles of the model. By providing this professional development in the partner language of the program, teachers can increase their own levels of proficiency in that language in addition to acquiring the content of the activity. This professional development must also include a social justice focus. Dual language teachers must teach students to think critically, to challenge mainstream knowledge and conventional wisdom. They must have high expectations for all their students and then create the environment for their students to reach those expectations. By affirming and building on the knowledge their students bring, dual language teachers and administrators create both a safe and risk-taking environment. By creating opportunities for students to know more about themselves and others as they work in heterogeneous cooperative teams with others different from themselves, they acquire the cultural competence that today's global society demands.

When the dual language program is a strand within the school, efforts must be made to include all students and staff in the quest for bilingualism and biliteracy. The dual language classes can make yearly presentations to the whole school to showcase their bilingual and academic skills. Student activities can be offered in the partner language of the program to involve students who are not in the dual language strand. These activities might include an after-school club, with physical education games taught in the partner language, and cross-cultural music and dance activities. Students should be knowledgeable about the dual language program and taught to be ambassadors for the program with their peers, as well as with outside visitors.

Successful dual language programs offer regular parent meetings to address concerns and offer educational opportunities to learn more about dual language education. Parent involvement and education should assist parents in becoming ambassadors for the program. Parents will become confident and can then use their skills by escorting visitors and explaining the dual language program. English classes for parents not yet proficient in English and classes in the partner language for those parents who do not speak the partner language can also be offered. Effective programs can showcase accomplishments by assisting parents with the organization of celebrations/potluck dinners to honor their participation in the dual language program. Through these celebrations, dual language students and their families are affirmed for their participation in programs that prepare them to be successful in today's global society.

At the district and community level. The first level of advocacy at the school district level is for the district to be fully prepared to provide adequate resources for the dual language program, with all facilities, bilingual staff, curricular materials, and extracurricular support systems in place. The dual language program is the ongoing, mainstream curriculum, taught in two languages instead of one. All district administrators are required to understand and fully support dual language inside and out and to be prepared to sustain the program for all the decades of your service to your school system.

District and community information dissemination is also a critical component of effective dual language programs. Marketing brochures that explain the dual language program should be created and distributed throughout the community. It is critical to revise these marketing pieces periodically so they reflect the current status of the dual language program. Dual language students and parents themselves are very effective in communicating the success of the program as they present and share their experiences with district administrators, community, and civic groups. Another way of promoting the focus of the program is to create special awards, such as an "Award for Promoting Bilingualism," to recognize local district, community, and civic groups or individuals for their efforts.

The local media provide an additional way of disseminating information to the local community. Administrators can contact the local media to invite them to cover special dual language events, including presentations and celebrations. Dual language staff, students, and parents should be encouraged to write letters to the editor sharing positive aspects or research on bilingualism and on dual language student accomplishments.

Another way of publicly recognizing the efforts of the dual language program is to encourage dual language students to participate in and apply for special recognitions including writing/poetry contests and leadership opportunities. Dual language parents, teachers, and administrators should also be encouraged to apply for district and community Parent/Teacher/Administrator of the Year recognitions. These are all opportunities to highlight the program and create a reputation of success. Many districts and several states (California, Illinois, New Mexico, New York, Oregon, Texas, and Washington) have instituted a seal of bilingualism/biliteracy to recognize high school graduates who demonstrate academic excellence in attaining proficiency in one or more languages other than English. This seal is attached to diplomas and transcripts of graduates who excel in listening, speaking, reading, and writing in multiple languages, according to criteria established by each state.

At the state and national level. As the dual language program is communicating success at the local community level, it is time to reach further. Dual language staff, students, and parents should be encouraged to present their successes at state and national educational and leadership conferences. Administrators can invite elected officials to visit their dual language program. They can also write letters and visit elected officials to share the success of their program, as well as working to support pro-language legislation and candidates.

At the international level. Bilingual or multilingual education is commonplace in many countries outside of the U.S. Dual language program staff, students, and parents can connect with foreign consulates and embassies to acquire instructional materials and special recognition, including bilingual certification for dual language staff and students from countries that speak the partner language, as well as recognition and awards for dual language schools. Teacher and student exchange programs can be initiated with the partner language countries to enhance the language and cultural aspects of the program. Real-life, meaningful opportunities allow students to use their language and cultural skills acquired through the dual language program.

All of these suggestions should be considered as a beginning to create a reputation of success for the dual language program. When a program has the reputation of success, it is difficult to dismantle or change it. The more we publicize the successes of our programs, the more knowledgeable everyone becomes and the less likely that a program will be changed. Dual language programs really are the programs that will equip our students with the skills to be successful in the 21st century!

In summary, parents and the whole school community, including school administrators and school board members, are crucial partners in the whole process of designing, implementing, and sustaining the dual language program. Without this close partnership among all diverse families of the community, the impact of dual language schooling may be lessened. With a sustained community effort, the dual language program will increase the academic success of all student groups and lead to higher student self-esteem and confidence, greatly improved student motivation, better school attendance, and increased cognitive stimulation for both students and teachers from the use of two languages

and from experience with multiple cultural perspectives (Thomas & Collier, 2012, p. 113). In the long term, we are graduating dual language students with high academic proficiency in two languages, ready for the global, interconnecting world of the 21st century. And, we are also preparing families to continue to connect to their linguistic and cultural roots across generations. As children mature, the love that comes from keeping these roots and connections is unbounded.

Chapter Seven: Secondary Dual Language Education— Moving into Middle and High School

Creating Secondary Dual Language Programs

As dual language programs spread to many regions of the United States, more and more school leaders are choosing to expand their programs, ensuring a complete dual language education experience, Grades K-12. As the program is grown grade by grade, the secondary educators preparing for this innovation have time to plan carefully. But many express astonishment at how fast this occurs! We strongly recommend that the middle and high school administrators who represent the feeder schools for the dual language program be included from the very beginning of the planning process, when the program is just getting started at preschool and/or kindergarten level.

Dual language implementation at the secondary level presents different challenges than those for elementary school. The number of dual language students arriving from the feeder schools influences the number of courses that should be offered in the partner language, and the availability of subject-certified bilingual staff who are academically proficient in the partner language often presents an obstacle to staffing. Scheduling is always complex at both middle and high school levels. But the elementary dual language program expectation that 50% of the instruction be provided in each language influences the choices for balance of coursework in the partner language and in English in the secondary years.

An average of two core classes in the partner language each year is considered the minimum, and with proper master schedule development and student choice, the number can be as high as four classes in the partner language (Sizemore, 2011; Sandy-Sánchez, 2008).

Several of our collaborating authors have written about their school districts' dual language programs at secondary level. The following section provides some of the steps taken by the principal at Collinswood Language Academy when the Charlotte-Mecklenburg School District decided to expand the Collinswood dual language program from a K-5 to a K-8 campus, including central office funding for the building of additional classrooms to house the middle school program.

AUTHOR: NICOLETTE GRANT, PRINCIPAL—COLLINSWOOD LANGUAGE ACADEMY, CHARLOTTE-MECKLENBURG SCHOOLS, CHARLOTTE, NORTH CAROLINA

The Middle School Expansion of Collinswood Language Academy

How do you reflect on the establishment of the first two-way dual language program in the state of North Carolina (begun in 1997) and the successes achieved by its founding principal—and then expand it to grow a successful K-8 dual language program? That was the challenge I faced when I took the helm of Collinswood Language Academy.

Having 4 years of experience as the assistant principal under the leadership of María Petrea and her intentional succession planning truly prepared me for this challenge. I am completely committed to the students and a firm believer in the benefits of dual language instruction. I have grown professionally while working at Collinswood and attended numerous professional development sessions regarding second language acquisition, brain research, effective classroom strategies such as the Sheltered Instruction Observation Protocol (SIOP), Thinking Maps, cooperative learning, and research on dual language education.

So how did I begin the expansion planning? Collinswood Language Academy was a firmly established and nationally recognized K-5 program. When the Charlotte-Mecklenburg School District decided in 2008 to expand this successful K-5 program to a K-8 program, I rolled up my sleeves and got to work.

My first step was to create a middle school planning committee and to study the characteristics and structures of effective middle school dual language programs. I involved fourth- and fifth-grade students, staff members, and parents in a series of meetings to determine the elements of the current program that must remain and the suggested revisions needed to further the language and cultural proficiency of middle-school-aged students. This committee collected and analyzed information about existing middle schools, both those with dual language programs to align language curricula, and non-dual language schools within the district to ensure equivalent course offerings. I also spent a great deal of time studying the North Carolina Standard Course of Study for Grades 6-8 to make sure that any instructional decisions made about curricular materials, staffing, and course offerings aligned to state objectives.

The next stage included site visits to model language schools in the southeastern region of the U.S. I visited Blythe Academy of Language in Greenville County, South Carolina, to examine other teaching strategies for language development. I visited the Ron Clark Academy in Atlanta, Georgia, and I was blown away by the effective teaching strategies employed to engage and challenge middle school students. I also visited two-way dual language schools in Houston, Texas (Burbank MS), and West Palm Beach, Florida (Okeeheelee MS). From these school visits and networking with International Spanish Academy middle school principals, I had a clearer picture of how I wanted to develop the middle school at Collinswood.

Finally, I met with central office personnel in Charlotte-Mecklenburg regarding the fine details involved in school expansion needs and resources. I met with district representatives from project management and building management on the construction of our middle school wing, as well as representatives from the curriculum and textbook department to determine elective class offerings and instructional materials. This resource investment from the district central offices was crucial to the middle school expansion at our campus. I also attended the Magnet Schools of America conference and the North Carolina Department of Public Instruction's World Language Essential Standards Committee to strengthen my knowledge of the expectations we needed to set for our middle school students to ensure they would be thoroughly prepared for high school.

Throughout this process, I kept parents, staff, and students aware of our development through frequent communications. I held monthly meetings to share our progress, and I conducted several surveys to gather input from all stakeholders. I included progress updates at staff meetings and in the principal's newsletter to parents. I also had regular meetings with María Petrea, the former principal and former executive director in the school district, to share information and to solicit her input on the expansion plans. In March, I vigorously began the hunt for the best teachers to join our staff. Since several of the new teachers came from various Latin American countries, I also assigned an experienced teacher as a mentor to each new staff member to help them in the process of adjusting to living in Charlotte or in the U.S. for the first time. These dual language mentor teachers knew the school district very well and were experienced in dual language teaching.

In 2010, my first year as principal—after 4 years of serving as the assistant principal and 2 years of planning the middle school expansion and constructing the new wing—we opened the doors of our middle school program. Upon entering middle school, students were sorted into four houses, in which they would remain for their 3 years in the middle school grades. The "house" idea was borrowed from the Ron Clark Academy and from the Hogwarts Houses in the Harry Potter series (Rowling, 1999). Our houses are Earth/*Tierra*, Air/*Aire*, Fire/*Fuego*, and Water/*Agua*. The inaugural sixth-grade students in these houses selected their house colors, house mascots, and house chants. The houses will serve as their team-building support group, and the older members of each house will welcome in and care for the next group of sixth graders that enter their family.

During the first year of our middle school, we also created a student leadership class. This student group is integral in serving as a voice for the students, and the group continues to be involved in determining procedures and activities to meet the needs of our middle school students. In that first year, the student leaders decided on house banners, house lanyards, house field trips, middle school parties, and they even published our first student-created yearbook, which documented the first year of our program expansion.

I am proud to report that the first year of our program was a great success! Ninety-eight percent of our sixth graders passed the state End-of-Grade (EOG) Test and 100% of our students passed the math EOG. Collinswood was named a State of North Carolina Honor School of Excellence for the 2011 School Year. We were also named a National School of Excellence by the Magnet Schools of America (one of the top five in the U.S. in School Year 2014), we received the International Spanish Academy's School of the Year Award in School Year 2012, and we are accredited by Spain's Ministry of Education.

In School Year 2012, we successfully added our seventh-grade classes and the eighth-grade classes in School Year 2013. We are working with the district to provide more classroom space, as the popularity of our K-8 program continues to grow. We booked our first international trip for the school's first eighth-grade class, funded by community and grant fundraising, and in March 2013, a group of 45 students and staff traveled to Spain and spent 10 days visiting Seville, Córdoba, Madrid, Toledo, and Barcelona. This was truly a fitting and well-deserved educational experience for our International Spanish Academy students who had spent 9 years studying the language and culture of Spain, as well as Latin America.

It has been my sincere honor and privilege to be the principal charged with growing the middle school program at Collinswood and upholding the legacy established by my mentor, María Petrea. Each year, the feeder high school continues to expand the number of content classes offered in Spanish by bilingual teachers certified in their subject specialty, as well as high-level AP Spanish courses with credit for university study, for the dual language graduates of Collinswood and other dual language middle schools in the Charlotte-Mecklenburg School District.

The next example of expansion of a dual language program to secondary level comes from the experiences of two authors from East Central Independent School District in the metropolitan area of San Antonio, Texas. In Chapter Four, we were introduced to this dual language program's expansion into multiple elementary schools, and the instructional schedule for dual language classes for Grades PK-8 is provided on page 78. The description below of the dual language expansion, first to intermediate schools for Grades 4-5, and then into the middle school level for Grades 6-8, illustrates some aspects of the complex decision making needed for secondary programs. This school district's dual language program is now in place districtwide for all Grades PK-12.

> AUTHORS: IRIS GONZÁLEZ ORNELAS, BILINGUAL/ESL/DUAL LANGUAGE PROGRAM COORDINATOR, AND MANUEL ENRIQUE ORNELAS, FORMER MIDDLE SCHOOL PRINCIPAL—EAST CENTRAL INDEPENDENT SCHOOL DISTRICT, SAN ANTONIO, TEXAS

Expansion to Intermediate (Grades 4-5) and Middle School (Grades 6-8)

The transition of the first cohort of students to the intermediate school (Grades 4-5) was not as seamless as the expansion among the elementary campuses. The principal at the receiving intermediate school was aware of the program, attended professional development sessions, and participated in the book study on dual language, yet chose to remain "low key" with the program and the program demands. By this time, the dual language parents had seen the amazing gains their students had made in the elementary grades. They knew what needed to happen to prepare for the dual language program to continue. The principal at Highland Elementary and I, as curriculum coordinator, could not dictate to the intermediate principal what to do, though recommendations were strongly suggested. The parents organized themselves, designated a spokesperson and requested a meeting with the intermediate principal. The principal then called us to assist with the process.

The following year, a new principal was assigned to the intermediate school. She knew the instruction, staff, and parental demands of a dual language program. Therefore, she did everything possible in a short time to learn about the program at the intermediate school. She met with the dual language parents every month for coffee and doughnuts. At these meetings, she listened to the parents and offered the assurances of support they needed.

The dual language students have done very well academically at the intermediate campuses. Fourth grade at one of the intermediate campuses is self-contained. Fifth grade is departmentalized, and there are four teachers. Social studies and reading/language arts are taught in Spanish, while math and science are taught in English. All teachers are bilingual/ESL certified.

The phase-in to middle school (Grades 6-8) was definitely a new frontier to conquer! Luckily, Manuel had become the new principal at the middle school. Since he had initiated the dual language program at the pilot elementary school, we chose to take a similar approach. At a faculty meeting, we informed the staff that the dual language students were going to enter sixth grade the following year. We presented the idea of having students take two courses in Spanish and explained the rationale for the decision. First, we looked at our existing staff and their certification. Then we posted a crucial question, "Are any of you interested and able to teach your content area in Spanish?" Soon a science teacher who is also bilingual/ESL-certified volunteered. Then a math teacher followed.

The biggest challenge of implementing a dual language program at the secondary level is finding teachers for the courses in Spanish who are both certified in the content areas and deeply, academically proficient in Spanish—and able, at least initially, to teach the courses with limited resources and materials. The teacher will need to create and present the subject matter concepts and information in Spanish at professional, adult levels of language use for challenging middle school courses. The Internet is an important resource for this process. During the planning year, these teachers participated in a book study; chose instructional materials; attended local, state, and national bilingual education conferences; visited other middle schools in Ysleta ISD and Canutillo ISD, Texas; and attended other professional development sessions.

In Texas, fifth grade is the last year bilingual students can take a state assessment in Spanish, and our dual language students continue to take Spanish language arts in fifth grade. In sixth grade, we have chosen to have students take Pre-AP English Language Arts. Therefore, the English teachers attend the same professional development sessions as the dual Spanish teachers, with one topic being explicit teaching of non-transferable skills between the two languages.

In sixth grade, dual language students are required to take Pre-AP science in Spanish, math in Spanish, and Pre-AP English Language Arts. In seventh grade, students take math in Spanish, Pre-AP English Language Arts, and Pre-AP Spanish (Spanish III). Students receive high school credit for testing out of Spanish I and II. In eighth grade, students take math in Spanish, Pre-AP English Language Arts, and AP Spanish (Spanish IV).

Many of our middle school dual language students have already been identified as gifted and talented and enjoy the rigor of these classes. As explained in Collier and Thomas (2009) and Thomas and Collier (2012), the process of becoming an additive bilingual, developing academically and cognitively through one's two languages, often leads to giftedness, or higher cognitive development than that of monolinguals (Baker, 2011; Bialystok, 2011). Many are requesting to take Pre-AP math in seventh grade so they can take algebra in eighth grade. They should be given that opportunity. We must consistently monitor and adjust the courses offered at the middle school to ensure student participation in the program and simultaneously offer rigorous courses that will prepare them for high school and college.

A challenge for the dual language program is that students at middle school level have more choices for the classes they want to take. At this age, they want to be with friends, and they have other interests and passions they want to explore through electives. Therefore, we must keep the students focused and informed of the program benefits. They need to be included in the parent information sessions and in the decision making. We motivate them to become school and community leaders by having them attend youth leadership institutes, present at dual language conferences, and participate in the campus/district fine arts program. Parents and students once again sign a commitment letter to participate in the dual language program at the secondary level.

These two perspectives on middle school development from North Carolina and Texas have illustrated some of the initial program design decisions that can be quite different for secondary when compared to elementary school dual language programs. The next two authors, a mother-daughter dual language partnership, describe steps in building the master schedule for dual language courses at the secondary level and the important role student leadership can provide in assisting with the course planning.

AUTHOR: CINDY SIZEMORE, FORMER DISTRICT DUAL LANGUAGE COORDINATOR, AND CURRENT ASSISTANT PRINCIPAL—EASTWOOD KNOLLS INTERNATIONAL SCHOOL, YSLETA INDEPENDENT SCHOOL DISTRICT, EL PASO, TEXAS

Developing the Secondary Dual Language Program

Developing a secondary dual language program is a daunting task, yet a very rewarding one. To accomplish this, it is necessary to develop a team headed by a strong leader who understands and believes in dual language education as integral to the personal development and academic success of each student. The team leader is not necessarily the person with the highest title on the campus, but the person with the passion, the knowledge, and the position—whether it be teacher, instructional specialist, or counselor—to successfully build and guide the dual language program. This requires understanding and carefully navigating the many programs, people, and needs that must be woven together.

Elementary and secondary program differences. The dual language team must also understand how the elementary dual language program is structured, students' elementary exit levels in each language, and most importantly, the curricular and regulatory requirements of secondary schools. An elementary program, no matter how successful, cannot be imposed on a secondary school. The structures of elementary and secondary are incompatible, particularly the freedom that an elementary teacher has to combine subjects, set his/her time schedule, and maintain the same group of students throughout much of the day. Developing a program based on percentage of the school day does not work in secondary school, which is divided into class periods with different teachers. The current definition of a secondary dual language program is a minimum of two core content classes in the partner language per year, to include language arts courses in both English and the partner language. When possible, electives should also be offered in the partner language.

Course planning. Developing middle and high school dual language programs begins with understanding the district's requirements for all secondary students. What core and elective courses are required? When can high school credits be earned? Is it a block schedule, a traditional schedule, or a blended schedule? What electives are offered and how many electives do students typically take? Do certain students lose an elective in order to be placed in an intervention class? Remember, dual language students have all the core classes of monolingual students, plus the core, non-negotiable, partner language arts class that might include an advanced language course from the district's world languages program. Many schools use Pre-AP and AP classes to both meet the language development needs of the students and provide an opportunity to earn both high school and, possibly, university course credits.

Academic abilities in both languages. Most importantly, what needs to happen to ensure dual language students leave eighth grade with near equal academic abilities in both languages? This is critical. If the gap between academic English and academic ability in the partner language is not closed in middle school, the high school cannot offer core content classes in the partner language. The students' frustration level with the language, combined with challenging academic content, will lead them to leave the program.

Two student groups in particular tend to fall out of the program between middle school and high school. There are the students who are already working hard to master the increasingly complex academic content, let alone the increasing complexity of academic vocabulary, grammar, and syntax in a second language. Then there are the academically high-achieving students who are acutely aware of their differing abilities in the two languages and the increasing gap between them. These students are working to develop a profile that positions them for competitive secondary opportunities. They will not jeopardize academic success by taking courses not offered at the advanced level or courses taught in their weaker language that may result in lower grades and academic ranking. In order to be successful, a program must have a robust student population that represents all levels of student achievement along with the appropriate coursework and supports.

Electives. Loss of electives can also lead students to drop out of dual language programs. One of the great opportunities of middle and high school is the chance to choose some classes based on personal interest. This is significant, as adolescence is all about increasing independence and making personal decisions based on individual goals, needs, and wants.

Band? Orchestra? Art? Sports? Technology? Journalism? Hmmm... what shall I choose? Wait, what's that you say? I can't have an elective because I have to take Spanish language arts and write essays, read novels, and do grammar worksheets? Hold on—this is in addition to all the essays, novels, and grammar I already have to do in English? Are you crazy?!?! No way! I'm out!

Can you blame them? Who wants an extra language arts class instead of a chosen class with others who share the same interest? This is a difficult obstacle to overcome and requires extremely creative scheduling. Dual language students must develop high levels of academic literacy in both languages, and they must have the access and opportunities afforded to all students. Both are non-negotiable if a school truly wants a solid dual language program that extends from kindergarten through twelfth grade and graduates students who attain near equal academic abilities and literacy in both languages.

Curriculum development. The secondary dual language planning team must align courses, recruit certified bilingual faculty, and choose high-quality materials. After the elementary grades, quality curricular materials and textbooks aligned to state and national standards become increasingly scarce. Will the secondary schools develop their own dual language curriculum? Is there a team prepared to do so? Is there time to make that a reality? An extremely important caution must be given here. It is not sufficient to have students read material in English and then discuss it or even write about it in Spanish, for example, as the partner language. Well-written Spanish materials are critical for the development of high levels of literacy in Spanish. So much knowledge about language is acquired consciously and subconsciously through reading—syntax, vocabulary, voice, and nuances of language that are impossible to gather without this constant exposure. We become better writers by becoming better readers and being exposed to well-written literature, stories, texts, and articles. The written word, whether it is a scientific article, historical fiction, or a canonical piece of literature, models for us how to write.

Bilingual language development across all subjects. Students must be exposed to authentic language in all subjects over time. Looking back at the elementary program, what content was taught in which language? In the middle school, it is important that students take content areas in Spanish in which they may not have had the opportunity to develop confidence and subject-specific language during their elementary school years. For example, if students had many years of math taught in Spanish in elementary, it is important that they take some of their required math in English in middle school. Students understand math, but many do not believe they can do math in English simply because they have not yet done so. This is true whether students began the program English dominant or Spanish dominant. They must be given the opportunity to develop cognitively with depth and complexity of subject-specific language and confidence in the content in both languages over time. If science has long been taught in English, then in middle school, it is important that it be taught in Spanish. The literacy requirements and writing styles in science are very different from the literacy taught in language arts classes. Students learn how to write a lab report or develop a hypothesis and defend it by reading lab reports and scientific articles in Spanish and then modeling their own after what they have read. In high school, it is important that students continue to develop academic abilities in both languages across all content areas by taking at least 1 year, preferably 2, in each core content area in the partner language. The development and refinement of language never stops in either language.

Bilingual personnel. Just as quality curricula in the partner language become more elusive in secondary schools, so do personnel. As a country, we struggle to find well-qualified, effective teachers, especially in the shortage areas of math and science. Now add the fact that we are hunting for a teacher who is not only highly qualified, but also knows the content inside and out and can relate to teenagers. This teacher must also understand language acquisition and be able to teach in the partner language for both native and non-native speakers of the language. Given the scarcity of highly-qualified, effective dual language secondary teachers, it does not make sense to staff each grade level in each content area with these teachers and then ask them to teach part of the course in English and part in the partner language. Human resources, while an important consideration in program design, are not the only consideration. The goal of developing deep cognitive abilities in each language necessitates students having the opportunity and requirement to wrestle with language through complex learning situations. This requires time—long stretches of time—preferably the year's length of the course, when expectations and supports are present for reading, writing, understanding, and communicating in the academic language of the discipline in a single language.

Adolescence. It is important to remember that secondary students are entering adolescence and beginning to look to peers more closely for belonging, for guidance, and for advice. They are developmentally pulling away from adults and beginning to develop a need for autonomy and independence. They are also forming likes and dislikes for academics, athletics, music, and social groups. Some students are excelling, and some are struggling; many express a desire to quit the dual language program. This is natural. They do not want to continue what they did in elementary school; they don't want to be different than their peers; and sometimes, they don't want to put in the extra effort to refine and enhance their abilities in their non-dominant language.

This is also a time when parents may pull away from their commitment to the program, saying their children know enough of the target language and are fine continuing in an all-English education. Parents may also experience the normal parent-tween/teen conflict and decide—thinking that perhaps dual language is not the battle to pick with their adolescent—that they will let their child make the decision. The dual language program must motivate students to choose to remain in the program. There must be elective choices that appeal to students and rewards that entice them to commit to a program that requires extra work, but provides great payoffs both in the immediacy of the adolescent world and long term in college preparation and competitiveness, as well as in the real-world economy.

> AUTHOR: SHEA SIZEMORE, DUAL LANGUAGE STUDENT LEADER AND GRADUATE—YSLETA INDEPENDENT SCHOOL DISTRICT K-12 DUAL LANGUAGE PROGRAM, EL PASO, TEXAS

Student leadership. In middle and high school, the dual language program transforms into a completely different creature than its elementary counterpart. This happens because the educational expectations shift. Students (and their parents) go into high gear thinking about university acceptance looming on the horizon, and they start to realize that what worked in elementary school can no longer work in the "serious" years of middle and high school. This is where the ideas of program ownership and student leadership come into play. In middle school, if the parents still believe in dual language education, there is a chance they can convince their reluctant student to continue. But that's not how a program will survive past its infancy in elementary school. To create a thriving K-12 dual language program, it is important to foster a sense of ownership among students early in their dual language years. Providing opportunities for student leadership not only helps ensure continued participation, but also allows students to give input into the dual language program's content and rigor and helps to ensure inclusiveness.

It is essential for a student advisory board to be created for high school. The advisory board allows students access to the teachers and administrators who run their program so that students can assist in related decisions. The students will be able to suggest changes to improve the program's function and viability because the students are living in the process of learning. Through the advisory board and participation in the ongoing self-evaluation process, students can advocate for additions to their program. For example, there could be courses in medical Spanish for students on the path of health professions, theatre in Spanish for upcoming actors, and engineering in Spanish for the more mathematically inclined.

Assisting in class creation and program adjustments are not the only responsibilities of student leadership. Through the student leadership structure, students interact with peers and participate in decision making, which allows the dual language secondary program to grow in strength and value. Students need to know they are the ones who own and mold the dual language program for their own futures.

One particular aspect of the Ysleta ISD high school dual language program that Cindy Sizemore created when she was the district's dual language coordinator is important for other school districts to consider seriously. The high school dual language students are asked to provide community service for a specified number of hours in a context in which their bilingualism is required. Through that experience, the students are able to understand and appreciate the deep level of adult proficiency in listening, speaking, reading, and writing required in both of their languages to serve the community effectively. If a student has chosen, for example, to be a medical interpreter in the emergency room of the hospital (a responsibility that Shea Sizemore chose), both coursework and certification are required because that is a life-and-death support position. The high level of adult bilingualism/biliteracy required for community service highlights the reality of the necessary abilities in the two languages and the crucial role that students will serve in their communities as bilingual adults.

The next author narrates the story of the evolution of the K-12 bilingual program in the public schools of Woodburn, Oregon. The town consists largely of Russian and Latino immigrants, with a significant percentage of the Spanish-speaking community coming from an Indigenous heritage from southern Mexico and Guatemala. These Indigenous students receive schooling through their second and third languages (Spanish and English). In the schools and throughout the community, the multicultural heritages of the residents continue to be expressed through food, religion, music, dress, and language. The innovative K-12 Russian-English and Spanish-English dual language programs created in all the Woodburn schools for both the Russian-speaking and Latin American-heritage students ensure academic success and prepare students for a multilingual, multicultural world.

> AUTHOR: DAVID BAUTISTA, ASSISTANT SUPERINTENDENT—OREGON DEPARTMENT OF EDUCATION, AND FORMER SUPERINTENDENT—WOODBURN SCHOOL DISTRICT, WOODBURN, OREGON

Planning and Sustaining the Dual Language K-12 Program

It has taken the work of the last four superintendents to plan and sustain the bilingual program that now exists in Woodburn schools. Despite the political and ideological nature of the topic of bilingualism, the program has prevailed and gets better every year.

The program began with Title VII funding in the late 1960s and early 1970s, providing some bilingual/ESL schooling for students in Grades K-5. After the state granted more funding to support English learners in 1992, study groups made up of administrators and teachers in Woodburn

examined research and best practices. The group concluded they wanted to create a stronger bilingual program, starting with Grades K-1 and adding a grade each school year. After several years of planning, this educational effort started in 1997. As of School Year 2013, out of 20 kindergarten classes, Woodburn has only three English-plus classes (designed for the parents who opt out of bilingual schooling), with two Russian-English and 15 Spanish-English kindergarten classrooms making up the remainder. (See Table 7.1.) The English-plus classes spend the majority of the instructional day in English with at least 30 minutes of instruction in either Spanish or Russian. But the large majority of Woodburn parents prefer bilingual schooling for their children, at all grade levels, because they see how well it works. The district graduates around 96% of their students who started school with no proficiency in English. These bilingual classes included 13% Caucasian American native English speakers, with approximately 56% of the Spanish-speaking students classified as English learners in School Year 2012. In that same year, 86% of the total school population participated in the free and reduced lunch program.

Small high schools. In 2006 (at that time, this author was the bilingual director), with grant funding, Woodburn School District converted its failing comprehensive high school into a thriving small school model. Within the first 2 years as small

schools, the district's high school dropout rate fell from greater than 10% to less than 3%. This in turn made the district's achievement gains even more compelling, given that most at-risk students were now staying in school and being assessed. Participation in the district's International Baccalaureate program more than doubled. With the majority of students from traditionally underserved subgroups, the district's greater-than-90% completion rate demonstrates that all students can achieve high goals and aspirations.

Beginning in 2009, Woodburn School District used a district vision for powerful teaching and learning to begin a professional development process for district leaders in partnership with the Center for Educational Leadership from the University of Washington. These consultants engaged teacher leaders, principals, and district leadership in data-based self-evaluation of instructional practices. Out of this effort, these district leaders developed a rigorous teacher evaluation system and K-12 walkthroughs that involved collaboration between administration and teachers, with weekly professional development time

Table 7.1

Woodburn School District Bilingual Schools and Educational Structures, SY 2013

Heritage ES	914 students—K-5 Russian/English strand, Spanish/English strand, English-Plus strand 75:25 Language Model
Lincoln ES	734 students—K-5 Spanish/English strand, English-Plus strand 50:50 Language Model
Nellie Muir ES	521 students—K-5 Spanish/English strand, English-Plus strand 75:25 Language Model
Washington ES	577 students—K-5 Spanish/English whole school 50:50 Language Model

The main K-5 objective is to achieve 5th grade bilingual proficiency based on reading, writing and math measures.

French Prairie MS	580 students—Spanish/English 50:50 Core Content Classes
Valor MS	612 students—Russian/English strand, Spanish/English strand 50:50 Core Content Classes

The middle school bilingual program is structured to provide at least 3 core-content classes in native language (Spanish or Russian) in sixth grade. Students take at least 2 core-content classes in native language in seventh and eighth grade. In eighth grade, students are expected to take Advanced Placement (AP) in Spanish. Aspects of the program such as scheduling, teacher licensure, and teacher language and content skills continue to be addressed yearly.

Academy of International Studies (AIS)	268 students
Wellness, Business & Sports School (WeBSS)	315 students
Woodburn Academy of Art, Science & Technology (WAAST)	358 students
Woodburn Arts & Communications Academy (WACA)	333 students
Woodburn Success Alternative High School (WSHS)	170 students

At the high school level, the bilingual program objective is to provide at least one core-content class in native language, in addition to native language arts, from ninth to twelfth grades. High school seniors can receive a bilingual-intercultural certificate based on their results from the International Baccalaureate (IB) language diploma or achievement in Advanced Placement language classes. Students' accomplishments in Russian and Spanish in the International Baccalaureate and Advanced Placement language classes are evidence of success. However, the number of participating students needs to increase. The Academy of International Studies provides bilingual/ESL coursework and support for recent arrivals at high school level, many from Spanish-speaking countries.

committed to the transformation of teaching and learning. Supporting teachers in effectively addressing the needs of second language learners was a common thread in each of these initiatives. Through this work, all teachers are focused on teaching and learning with K-12 alignment in a proficiency-based system, with school-based and cross-school Professional Learning Communities developing common formative assessments aligned with the Common Core State Standards.

Current challenges include telling the Woodburn story so the general public can recognize the huge benefits that a well-focused bilingual/intercultural K-12 education provides for all students. Another challenge is to continue to hire well-prepared bilingual teachers who have a deep understanding of the political and social issues that work against many disenfranchised students. Administrators lead these challenges with the will to act courageously to transform the lives of many students through bilingual/intercultural pedagogy and understanding social justice issues. Conversations continue about equity, race, and ideological issues that need to be confronted in the Professional Learning Communities at the school and district level in order to keep the program moving forward.

These conversations provide the opportunity to continue to analyze system issues that need to be addressed, such as inequitable outcomes in terms of college and career readiness, improving mathematics instruction, lack of appropriate first language reading assessment instruments for Russian-speaking students, lack of opportunities for undocumented resident students to access financial aid needed for post-secondary education, and the ongoing reality of high poverty rates in the community. But as long as the strong presence of Woodburn's strategic plan, Diverse in Culture, Unified in Mission (*http://www.woodburnsd.org*), guides continuing development of these language and cultural enrichment programs, the future looks solid for Woodburn students.

The next author introduces another successful high school dual language program developed in the public schools of Omaha, Nebraska, to respond to the needs of native Spanish-speaking students. This unusual and creative high school program started small and has grown year by year as more and more dual language students enter the program from the five elementary and three middle schools that feed the high school. The uniqueness of the program includes a dual language contract that all participating families and students and dual language educators must sign; a significant number of core content courses offered in Spanish; the support systems in place to ensure that every dual language student graduates from high school, is admitted to university study, and is supported financially; and the development of the Omaha South High

Education Academy, which gives students the opportunity to explore a career in education while still attending high school and provides the connections with teacher preparation courses at the local university (thus "growing their own" future bilingual teachers).

> AUTHOR: DR. RONY ORTEGA, PRINCIPAL, ALICE BUFFETT MAGNET MIDDLE SCHOOL, AND FORMER ASSISTANT PRINCIPAL, OMAHA SOUTH HIGH MAGNET SCHOOL—OMAHA PUBLIC SCHOOLS, OMAHA, NEBRASKA

Omaha Public Schools High School Dual Language Program

The American classroom landscape has changed dramatically over the past decade, and the number of students who arrive in school with a language other than English is rising rapidly. For example, Omaha Public Schools (OPS), the largest school district in Nebraska with 51,070 students in School Year 2014 and over 7,000 employees, saw an increase of 157% in English learners from 1999 to 2009 (National Clearinghouse for English Language Acquisition, 2011a). Today, OPS serves over 7,000 English learners and 8,739 former English learners (reclassified as proficient in English) in Grades PK-12. While 79% of these students speak Spanish, there are over 109 different languages spoken within the group.

How school districts respond to this demographic shift toward a more linguistically, culturally, and academically diverse group of students will impact educational outcomes. Fourteen years ago, OPS had both the vision and the native Spanish-speaking students to lead the state in starting a two-way 50:50 dual language program. While providing a means to improve the English proficiency and educational outcomes of English learners, the initiative has most importantly offered both native Spanish and native English speakers the enrichment opportunity to become bilingual, biliterate, and bicultural. Today, the OPS K-12 dual language program serves about 2,500 students at six elementary schools, three middle schools, and one high school, Omaha South High Magnet School (OSHMS).

OSHMS is an urban magnet school for Information Technology, Visual Arts, Performing Arts, and Dual Language. While OSHMS draws students from throughout the city, the school largely reflects its surrounding community with about 1,602 Hispanic students out of 2,272 total. At OSHMS, students have the opportunity to "major" in any one of the four magnet areas, including Dual Language. The option to major gives students a focused path of study and also prepares them for the process of selecting and completing a major at a college or university.

Our high school dual language program is set up as a college preparatory program, with the expectation that bilingual students will attend college after high school. We currently have 330 dual language students in Grades 9-12, but dual language enrollment at the high school is projected to increase to 860 students within 5 years because of the increase in our feeder programs. In 2012, OSHMS graduated the first group of 21 dual language students who began in kindergarten and remained in dual language through their senior year, with 18 of them enrolling in various colleges and universities. The classes of 2013 and 2014 produced 60 more dual language graduates, with each class earning over $2.1 million in scholarships to continue in university studies. The program has a 100% high school graduation rate, and the goal remains to have 100% of dual language graduates attend a college or university.

Dual language team. We have been fortunate to have financial support and backing from our district, building principal, and K-12 dual language district supervisor. This has allowed us to assemble a great dual language team at the high school, including several teachers, a coordinator, counselor, bilingual liaison, and administrator—all of whom are bilingual. Our dual language teachers are content-area endorsed, and some also hold or are working on a district-paid bilingual education and/or ESL endorsement at the University of Nebraska at Omaha. The dual language teachers share a common planning period that we use weekly to discuss student concerns, develop curriculum, and participate in the Student Assistance Team meetings. This common planning period, coupled with various other means to monitor students, allows us to maintain great relationships with our students while also providing a way to quickly address any concerns.

Rigorous curriculum. At OSHMS we have a traditional nine-period schedule, and dual language students take their core content classes in dual language—about half of their daily schedule. Dual language courses are taught exclusively in Spanish or 50:50 Spanish/English. We offer 31 core content dual language courses, including honors, AP, and college dual enrollment options. The most recently developed dual language courses include Physical Science, and upper-level math courses in probability and statistics. In addition to the required dual language core content courses, students are expected to take Spanish as a subject each year of high school. These Spanish courses are geared for native Spanish speakers and are capped by AP Spanish Literature and AP Spanish Language. For English class, freshman and sophomore dual language students are scheduled with the same teacher. In fact, due to the limited number of bilingual teachers, several of our dual language teachers loop with students and have them in class multiple years. This is actually a benefit to both students and teachers. Students enjoy a lasting relationship with the teacher during their 4 years of high school, while teachers know the students well and can support them readily and effectively from day one.

Beyond ensuring that we offer a rigorous high school curriculum within a team structure, our dual language coordinator and counselor work side by side to ensure dual language students are in the right classes and on track to meet college admission requirements. One-on-one formal appointments are made yearly with students to discuss progress, needs, post-secondary goals, and remaining high school courses. Though last year's dual language juniors exceeded the school, district, and state average on our state's reading test, students' ACT scores are not where we expect them to be. For the 2014 School Year, we implemented an ACT test preparation course, which is open to any interested junior or senior. Within the dual language program, we ensure all students take the ACT test during their junior year.

Another way we have built a community that accepts and encourages academic excellence is by placing dual language sophomores, juniors, and seniors in a grade-level-specific dual language advisement class with dual language teachers as mentors. This weekly advisement class provides us with additional time to disseminate grade-level or college information, assist students with state test preparation, and check on the overall progress and engagement of our students. We consistently monitor this academic progress and engagement, not only through advisement, but also through dual language teacher team meetings and by academic reports that are checked biweekly by the dual language coordinator or bilingual liaison. All dual language students who fall behind academically are required to attend school-provided tutoring during their lunch time until their grades and school work are satisfactory. This expectation is laid out in our student, parent, and school dual language contract. Dual language students who repeatedly fall behind are placed on the Student Assistance Team, and a meeting of this team is scheduled with the student, parent, and dual language school staff.

Parent, student, and school dual language contract. All incoming ninth-grade dual language students and parents are required to meet with our dual language coordinator, counselor, or administrator, and after they have agreed to our dual language contract, they are officially part of the high school program. The contract outlines expectations for the student, the parent, and the dual language school personnel. For example, it is an expectation that the dual language students agree to additional support when they are struggling academically and that they not be involved with any gang, drug, or other criminal behaviors. It is also an expectation that the parents be involved in the student's education, have a working telephone where they can be reached, and attend parent-teacher conferences twice a school year, at a minimum. Parents and students who are repeatedly unable to meet their end of the contract can be exited from the dual language program through our Student Assistance Team process, but this is a very rare occurrence. One of many expectations parents and students hold for the dual language school personnel is the facilitation of at least three college/university applications and three scholarship

applications for all dual language students before graduation. These applications are typically supported through our dual language senior-level Wednesday advisement class and our College & Scholarship Saturday program.

College & scholarship Saturday program. The dual language coordinator and counselor run our dual language College & Scholarship Saturday program where dual language students report on Saturday mornings. Community volunteers, many from local colleges and universities, offer one-on-one support to students in completing their college essays and applications, as well as scholarship applications. Since the inception of our Saturday program, our dual language student scholarship dollars have dramatically increased:

Class of 2010 (13 dual language students) = $182,700*

Class of 2011 (21 dual language students) = $1,579,814

Class of 2012 (37 dual language students) = $2,456,111

*The dual language college and scholarship program began in 2011. The class of 2010 did not participate in this program.

As our scholarship dollars have increased, so too have our college and university student matriculations, supporting our goal of having former dual language graduates return to teach in our K-12 dual language program. To help meet the challenge of finding bilingually certified teachers, we hope to grow our own by intentionally and energetically recruiting dual language students who express an interest in education into our Education Academy.

Education academy. The Omaha South High Education Academy was created to help meet the demand for highly qualified teachers in Omaha Public Schools. The Education Academy at OSHMS is unique because of its focus on recruiting and developing bilingual teachers for our rapidly growing dual language program. This academy has three goals:

1. Provide students the opportunity to explore a career in education.

2. Allow students to explore the challenges facing public education in the 21st century.

3. Prepare students to decide if they want to pursue a career in education.

Students enter the Education Academy during their junior year of high school and have the opportunity to take two courses. If students want to continue with a career in education, they can take the internship course their senior year. These courses are offered for dual enrollment with our local community college, Metropolitan Community College.

- Junior Year: Honors Introduction to Education (3 college credits)
- Senior Year: Education and Training Internship (2 college credits)

In addition to these education courses, dual language students are encouraged to accrue as many college credits as possible through dual enrollment courses at the community college and through our AP partnership with the University of Nebraska at Omaha. The goal is to connect high school studies with college plans, help students save money for college expenses, and accelerate students' entry into the workforce.

Conclusion. It is to no one's surprise that our student demographics are changing and our English learner population is increasing. However, these students, on average, achieve at rates below their native English-speaking peers, particularly in the secondary years (Fry, 2007, 2008). This means schools must better prepare themselves to address the particular linguistic, cultural, and learning needs of these students. Research shows that dual language programs are an effective way to meet the needs of Hispanic English learners and close the achievement gap (Lindholm-Leary, 2001; Thomas & Collier, 2002, 2012). Our Omaha Public Schools K-12 Dual Language Program has created an opportunity for English learners to retain and build upon their native language and culture, which are seen as resources, not deficits. Our high school dual language program has permitted students to reach high levels of both English and Spanish proficiency and academic achievement. What's more, this program has helped to increase our graduation rate, scholarship dollars, and college enrollments. With a commitment to high academic achievement and clear, shared goals, the overall success of our dual language program rests in the fact that students and parents are empowered in a program that plays to their strengths and that validates and affirms their native language and culture. We look forward to continuing the growth and effectiveness of our two-way 50:50 K-12 dual language program!

Bilingualism/Biliteracy Seal Legislation

Another major development occurring in recent years that has powerful implications for secondary graduates of dual language programs was first begun in the state of California. A statewide bilingualism/biliteracy seal placed on a student's diploma recognizes and honors those students who have reached deep academic proficiency in English and in another language. State legislation for the seal has been passed in the following states since 2011: California, Illinois, New Mexico, New York, Oregon, Texas, and Washington. As of March 2014, there is pending legislation for the biliteracy seal in Massachusetts, and Department of Education initiatives in Delaware, Indiana, Maryland, Minnesota, New Jersey, North Carolina, Ohio, Rhode Island, and Utah (American Council on the Teaching of Foreign Languages, 2014). Bilingualism/biliteracy seal legislation is a growing movement whose time has come, even in states that previously experienced English-only policy initiatives!

Each state is working on defining the credentials for this award, and the qualifications can vary from state to state. For example, New Mexico's Bilingualism/Biliteracy Seal emphasizes bilingualism first as a means of recognizing each tribe's sovereignty in the use of their languages in public school settings and their individual preference of oral tradition over a written language. But while the specifics may vary, the initiative to create this potentially prestigious award continues in regions throughout the U.S. For student graduates of dual language programs, this recognition becomes an important credential for admission to continuing studies in post-secondary education and a powerful skill to add to their resume when applying for professional jobs that require bilingualism. The following authors describe the development of this seal of bilingualism/biliteracy in Albuquerque Public Schools, several years before the New Mexico state legislation was passed and signed by the governor in 2014.

> AUTHORS: LISA HARMON-MARTÍNEZ, AP ENGLISH 12/LITERATURE AND COMPOSITION TEACHER, LANGUAGE ARTS DEPARTMENT CHAIR, BILINGUAL DEPARTMENT CO-COORDINATOR, AND MISHELLE L. JURADO, SPANISH LANGUAGE ARTS TEACHER, BILINGUAL DEPARTMENT CO-COORDINATOR—ALBUQUERQUE HIGH SCHOOL, ALBUQUERQUE PUBLIC SCHOOLS, ALBUQUERQUE, NEW MEXICO

As the oldest high school in Albuquerque, New Mexico, Albuquerque High School (AHS) has a legacy of academic excellence. In 2014, our school graduated 45 students of diverse cultural and linguistic backgrounds with the Albuquerque Public Schools Bilingual Seal. This seal signifies the recognition of dual language students' bilingual and biliterate development through content and language arts classes in both English and Spanish. The bilingual seal is an honor awarded to students who have taken course requirements set by their schools and/or school districts. The state of New Mexico is now developing requirements which will guide districts and schools in creating this path to the state Seal of Bilingualism/Biliteracy. In order to complete their seal requirements, students at AHS must also pass a portfolio presentation their senior year in which they demonstrate their language development over the course of their education. In this way, the seal encourages students to work toward a high level of proficiency in both languages, including the completion of AP-level content classes now offered in Spanish.

In 2011, our program graduated 22 Bilingual Seal recipients with an average GPA of 2.1, while in 2014, 45 students received their Seal with an average GPA of 3.6. Each year the number of applicants, as well as the number of those who have achieved the seal, has increased. As student success has grown, so have supports provided for them by the AHS Bilingual Education Department, centrally located in the school. Given the rigorous course requirements students must take each year, and in order to identify possible program participants early in their high school career, we revisit bilingual seal requirements in Spanish Language Arts classes yearly—a core class requirement for the seal. At the start of each school year, dual language students' schedules are reviewed to monitor language acquisition and development in both English and Spanish; student grades are also reviewed each semester to ensure students' progress in completing course requirements for the seal. The AHS Bilingual Education office is the academic hub for the program, where students find the academic, linguistic, and social support they require to be successful in school and after graduation.

While the Bilingual Seal is meaningful as an academic recognition, it is also clear that the seal means even more to the students, as their language and culture are central to their identity, careers, and future in our global society. Cerrie Ali Jurado (Class of 2016, Albuquerque High School) affirms the seal means a great deal to her, but even more importantly she notes, "Working towards the seal helps

 me keep in mind that I need both languages to live my life to the fullest with my family. I do not want to have superficial conversations with them; I want to discuss, debate and argue in the language being used … whether I am in the U.S. or in Mexico." Clearly the two languages mean more to this student than just academics—they are lifelines to her family in both countries.

Another important aspect for many students is the link to careers with the Bilingual Seal. Brandon González (Class of 2009, Río Grande High School) said, "I believe that receiving my bilingual seal has opened up many opportunities in professional fields, such as the U.S. Army, by being able to communicate effectively with my soldiers who are Spanish speakers and then translating for my chain of command, which is necessary for effective communication, especially in the Army. … and it landed me a job with one of the most renowned police departments in the country …." Students convey the importance of having the seal to demonstrate to employers and higher education institutions their linguistic proficiency, beyond social language.

Many of our students view themselves as integral citizens in our global society. Alondra Tarín (Class of 2014, Albuquerque High School) explains it best: "The bilingual seal represents change and evolution of who we are as people. It is no longer enough to live in only one language because that would mean exclusion of many aspects of the world, including cultural and even important international affairs. The seal proves that I committed to this global change, but it's also a reminder that there are hundreds of other languages to be learned. Yes, the seal is important in representing my cultures, but it is also only the beginning of great change."

Conclusion

The continuation of dual language schooling into the secondary years is an ever-expanding frontier for bilingual educators in the U.S. It represents another strong sign that schools in all regions of this country are in a major process of transformation. The world is changing rapidly as we begin to value the interconnections that continuously developing new technologies have brought us. And along with the need for communicating effectively across national boundaries and cultures has come a recognition that our youth in the U.S. have been growing up in insular contexts that limit their awareness. Now with global immigration, refugee resettlement, and daily opportunities for connecting with people of diverse languages, cultures, and social classes within our own neighborhoods, U.S. schools have become one of the best opportunities for assisting all of our youth to be prepared for a very different intercultural future.

The examples provided in this chapter are just the beginnings of experimentation. As competent secondary dual language educators, we will be called upon to be creative as well as collaborative. We must start with the structures that exist now at the middle and high school levels and develop a wide range of services and new educational opportunities that meet the needs of all of our diverse students. In many of these new secondary dual language programs, the world languages coordinator and the bilingual/ESL coordinator work together to create a secondary program that serves the needs of both the English learners/emergent bilinguals and the native English speakers who have been schooled together in the dual language program during their elementary school years. Joining these two very different perspectives leads to creativity and new awareness. This transforms bilingualism into an additive context for all students, minority and majority, working together.

We are innovatively and lovingly preparing our youth linguistically, cognitively, and socioculturally for their adult roles in our world.

Our next book in this series will focus on middle and high school innovations in dual language education with many collaborating authors sharing their experiences and the new educational opportunities they have created for—and with—secondary dual language students. We hope you will join us!

Epilogue

Are you inspired now, or perhaps relieved that your challenges and decision-making processes are similar to other administrators implementing dual language programs? Throughout this book, our collaborative authors have demonstrated that dual language education can work. In fact, it works really well! It's hard work, but worth it. Our research has shown that the results can be astounding, as measured by school tests, attendance, and engagement with learning.

What do we see in the future—our vision for the next 10 to 20 years? In the U.S., dual language education will increasingly become the default, the mainstream curriculum. The typical U.S. school will be a dual language school. There are compelling reasons for this vision to come about, all of which are in the national interest ... gap closure and equal protection under the law for all students, plus raising student achievement across the board and serving our currently underserved students well in school programs that have dramatic impact on student motivation for learning.

Attitudes in the U.S. are changing positively towards bilingualism, with more and more parents demanding bilingual schooling for their children. Reports in the mainstream media have been highlighting recent neurological research on the bilingual brain, demonstrating many cognitive advantages that bilinguals and multilinguals have over monolingual humans. Proficient bilinguals outperform monolinguals in creativity, problem solving, divergent thinking, mental flexibility, executive function issues (such as attention to detail, ability to ignore distractions, task switching, working memory, conflict management), efficient cognitive/sensory processing, metalinguistic awareness, visual-spatial skills, AND for those of us "aging gracefully," bilinguals are more resistant to the onset of dementia and Alzheimer's (Baker, 2011; Bialystok, 2011; Grosjean, 2010; Lyons, 2014; Perry, 2013; Willis, 2012). Massive amounts of research favoring bilingual education in general and dual language education in particular have been reported in over five major meta-analyses as well as syntheses of major research studies in recent years (see Thomas & Collier, 2012). Yes, our time has come!

We see a future where policy makers actually pay attention to research findings when they make educational policy. We see a future where the federal and state governments put substantial funding into education programs that have large research-based effect sizes and that demonstrably raise student achievement, rather than promoting programs that don't make much difference. Dual language education has a huge positive impact on the lives of students, families, teachers, and administrators! We see a future where U.S. schools serve well the demographic reality of the next 25 years—this September of 2014, the majority of our students in U.S. schools are now multiethnic/multilingual/multicultural (Krogstad & Fry, 2014). We are not a monolithic country. Our schools must be designed to serve the greater diversity that is ours to affirm and celebrate.

We see states that are now taking responsibility for raising test scores of underserved groups of students—English learners, African Americans, Latinos, American Indians, Whites in poverty, students in rural settings and inner cities. The changes are coming whether education responds to them or not. To be a world citizen, these times call for learning at least two of the top three most-spoken world languages—Chinese, English, and Spanish. And for all students to experience additive bilingualism, they must develop literacy in their home language (if it is a written language), and continue developing cognitively in both home language and one or more additional languages. Dual language education fully provides that opportunity.

Dual language education is unifying. Dual language leaders can make all of this happen. You have seen in this book how these dual language administrators have taken research-based concepts and made them their own in their effective dual language programs. They took abstract theoretical foundations and data-based research findings and applied them to their local circumstances. They developed dual language schools greatly superior to what existed before. They did this in ways that are sensitive to local conditions that characterize their schools and school districts. Why did this work? Because they started with highly generalizable research knowledge and fundamentally sound theory. We now have the research knowledge base and the practical experience of dedicated dual language administrators and teachers throughout the U.S. to guide the way as we expand these opportunities for all our students.

Dual language education is for everyone. We can make this happen. We are powerful leaders with visions of the future. We know what our students need. We can create the schools of the 21st century for our deeply interconnected and transforming world.

WE ARE INFINITE
by Francisca Sánchez

there are songs in my head i could sing you[1] she said
songs that could set you free to soar beyond the horizon you see
in your dreams and imagine is the edge of earthly possibility
songs as mysterious as the hum that lulled you to sleep
once upon a time deep in the womb when you were fed
with the wax and wane of strumming blood
when all that you knew was contained in the span
of two hands spread wide and the steady beat
of a mother's heart

there are songs in my head she cried that could give voice
to the silence you hide like a piercing thorn worn deep
in the secret heart of the young girl you were before the curl
of time slowly unfurled to reveal the woman today
songs powerful enough to shatter the shame you've borne
from believing english only english first english the best
when you are not english and so not first, not the best
when you know in your head that none of it's true
and still inside there like a poisonous shard it rests

nonetheless, there are songs in my head still alive
after all this time so sublime they spill out now
from lips fragrant with unspoken rhymes
just waiting for our words to be heard yours and mine
for our language to pour its wild justice like a baptism of rain
with divine running through it so we can climb once more
to the shelter of stars that await our return healed, whole, holy

so our phoenix songs that carry within them
the tongues of the universe can sing back the shattered skies
why does it surprise you that there are words in my head
that can climb like brilliant kites to dizzying heights
that can illuminate our consciousness with the lights
of exploding stars and capture the first language we ever heard
even before we ever were even before we were taught to regret
that part of us that carries as benjamín[2] said
our mother's mother's mother in us why when we are infinite
beyond measure beyond imagination
why when there are songs in our heads we can sing

References:
[1] From Lorna Dee Cervantes, "There are songs in my head"
[2] Benjamín Alire Sáenz, "My Culture"

REFERENCES

American Council on the Teaching of Foreign Languages. (2014). *Seal of biliteracy: Update on state implementation.* http://www.actfl.org/sites/default/files/pdfs/SealofBiliteracy-StateUpdate-March2014.pdf

Baker, C. (2011). *Foundations of bilingual education and bilingualism* (5th ed.). Bristol, UK: Multilingual Matters.

Baker, C., & Hornberger, N.H. (Eds.). (2001). *An introductory reader to the writings of Jim Cummins.* Bristol, UK: Multilingual Matters.

Bialystok, E. (2001). *Bilingualism in development: Language, literacy & cognition.* New York: Cambridge University Press.

Bialystok, E. (2011). Reshaping the mind: The benefits of bilingualism. *Canadian Journal of Experimental Psychology,* 65(4), 229-235.

Blankstein, A. M. (2012). *Failure is not an option: Six principles that advance student success in highly effective schools*(3rd ed.). Thousand Oaks, CA: Corwin.

Brown, K. (1997). Balancing the tools of technology with our own humanity: The use of technology in building partnerships and communities. In J.V.Tinajero & A.F. Ada (Eds.), *The power of two languages: Literacy and biliteracy for Spanish-speaking students* (2nd ed.). New York: Macmillan/McGraw-Hill.

Center for Applied Linguistics (2014). *Two-way bilingual immersion directory.* Washington, DC: Center for Applied Linguistics. http://www.cal.org/twi/directory/index.html

Cervantes. L.D. (1982). Visions of Mexico while at a writing symposium in Port Townsend, Washington. In *Emplumada*. Pittsburgh, PA: University of Pittsburgh Press.

Clark, E.R., Flores, B.B., Riojas-Cortez, M., & Smith, H.R. (2002). You can't have a rainbow without a *tormenta*: A description of an IHE's response to a community need for a dual language school. *Bilingual Research Journal,* 26(1), 123-148.

Cloud, N., Genesee, F., & Hamayan, E. (2000). *Dual language instruction: A handbook for enriched education.* Boston: Heinle.

Collier, V.P. (1995). *Promoting academic success for ESL students: Understanding second language acquisition for school.* Elizabeth, NJ: New Jersey Teachers of English to Speakers of Other Languages-Bilingual Educators & Bastos Books. http://www.bastosbooks.com

Collier, V.P., & Thomas, W.P. (2004). The astounding effectiveness of dual language education for all. *NABE Journal of Research and Practice, 2*(1), 1-20. http://www.thomasandcollier.com

Collier, V.P., & Thomas, W.P. (2009). *Educating English learners for a transformed world.* Albuquerque, NM: Dual Language Education of New Mexico-Fuente Press. http://www.dlenm.org

Collier, V.P., & Thomas, W.P. (2013). *La educación de los estudiantes de inglés para un mundo en constante transformación.* Albuquerque, NM: Dual Language Education of New Mexico-Fuente Press. http://www.dlenm.org

Cummins, J. (2000). *Language, power and pedagogy: Bilingual children in the crossfire.* Bristol, UK: Multilingual Matters.

Cummins, J., & Sayers, D. (1995). *Brave new schools: Challenging cultural illiteracy through global learning networks.* Toronto: Ontario Institute for Studies in Education.

de Jong, E.J. (2011). *Foundations for multilingualism in education: From principles to practice.* Philadelphia: Caslon.

DuFour, R. (2004). What is a professional learning community? *Educational Leadership, 61*(8), 6-11.

Eccles, J.S., Vida, M.N., & Barber, B. (2004). The relation of early adolescents' college plans and both academic ability and task-value beliefs to subsequent college enrollment. *Journal of Early Adolescence, 24*(1), 63-77.

Echevarría, J., Short, D., & Powers, K. (2006). School reform and standards-based education: An instructional model for English language learners. *Journal of Educational Research, 99*(4), 195-210.

Echevarría, J., Vogt, M.E., & Short, D. (2008). *Making content comprehensible for English language leaners: The SIOP model* (3rd ed.). Boston: Allyn & Bacon.

Escamilla, K., Hopewell, S., & Butvilofsky, S. (2013). *Biliteracy from the start: Literacy squared in action.* Philadelphia: Caslon.

Fortune, T., & Tedick, D. (Eds.). (2008). *Pathways to bilingualism: Evolving perspectives on immersion education*. Bristol, UK: Multilingual Matters.

Freeman, Y.S., & Freeman, D.E. (2006). *Teaching reading and writing in Spanish and English in bilingual and dual language classrooms* (2nd ed.). Portsmouth, NH: Heinemann.

Freeman, Y.S., Freeman, D.E., & Mercuri, S.P. (2005). *Dual language essentials for teachers and administrators*. Portsmouth, NH: Heinemann.

Freeman, Y., & Freeman, D. (2007). *La enseñanza de la lectura y la escritura en español e inglés en salones de clases bilingües y de doble inmersión* (2nd ed.). Portsmouth, NH: Heinemann.

Freire, P. (1970). *Pedagogy of the oppressed*. New York: Seabury Press.

Fry, R. (2007). *How far behind in math and reading are English language learners?* Washington, DC: Pew Hispanic Center. http://www.pewhispanic.org/topics/?TopicID=4

Fry, R. (2008). *The role of schools in the English language learner achievement gap*. Washington, DC: Pew Hispanic Center. http://www.pewhispanic.org/topics/?TopicID=4

García, O., & Kleifgen, J.A. (2010). *Educating emergent bilinguals: Policies, programs, and practices for English language learners*. New York: Teachers College Press.

García, O., Kleifgen, J.A., & Falchi, L. (2008). From English language learners to emergent bilinguals. In *Equity Matters: Research Review No. 1*. New York: A Research Initiative of the Campaign for Educational Equity.

Genesee, F. (1987). *Learning through two languages: Studies of immersion and bilingual education*. New York: Newbury House.

Genesee, F., Lindholm-Leary, K., Saunders, W., & Christian, D. (2006). *Educating English language learners: A synthesis of research evidence*. New York: Cambridge University Press.

Genesee, F., Paradis, J., & Crago, M.B. (2004). *Dual language development and disorders: A handbook on bilingualism and second language learning*. Baltimore: Paul H. Brookes Publishing.

González, N., Moll, L.C., & Amanti, C. (2005). *Funds of knowledge: Theorizing practices in households, communities and classrooms.* Mahwah, NJ: Lawrence Erlbaum.

Grosjean, F. (2010). *Bilingual: Life and reality.* Cambridge, MA: Harvard University Press.

Herrera, S., Pérez, D., & Escamilla, K. (2010). *Teaching reading to English language learners.* New York: Pearson.

Howard, E.R. (2003). *Biliteracy development in two-way immersion education programs: A multilevel analysis of the effects of native language and home language use on the development of narrative writing ability in English and Spanish.* Ph.D. dissertation, Harvard University. http://www.worldcat.org

Howard, E.R., & Sugarman, J. (2007). *Realizing the vision of two-way immersion: Fostering effective programs and classrooms.* Washington, DC: Delta Systems and ERIC Clearinghouse on Languages and Linguistics.

Howard, E.R., Sugarman, J., Christian, D., Lindholm-Leary, K., & Rogers, D. (2007). *Guiding principles for dual language education* (2nd ed.). Washington, DC: Center for Applied Linguistics. http://www.cal.org/twi/guidingprinciples.htm

Hunt, V. (2011). Learning from success stories: Leadership structures that support dual language programs over time in New York City. *International Journal of Bilingual Education and Bilingualism, 14*(2), 187-206.

Izquierdo, E. (2011). Two-way dual language education. In R.R. Valencia (Ed.), *Chicano school failure and success: Past, present, and future* (3rd ed.). New York: Routledge.

Izquierdo, E. (2012). Leadership matters for learning English and learning in English. In M. Calderón (Ed.), *Breaking through: Effective instruction and assessment for reaching English learners.* Bloomington, IN: Solution Tree Press.

Krogstad, J.M., & Fry, R. (2014, August 18). Department of Education projects public schools will be 'majority-minority' this fall. Pew Research Center. http://www.pewresearch.org

Lambert, W.E. (1975). Culture and language as factors in learning and education. In A. Wolfgang (Ed.), *Education of immigrant students.* Toronto: Ontario Institute for Studies in Education.

Lazarín, M. (2006). *Improving assessment and accountability for English language learners in the No Child Left Behind Act* (Issue Brief, No. 6). Washington, DC: National Council of La Raza.

Lindholm-Leary, K.J. (2001). *Dual language education*. Bristol, UK: Multilingual Matters.

Lindholm-Leary, K.J. (2005). The rich promise of two-way immersion. *Educational Leadership, 62,* 56-59.

Lindholm-Leary, K.J. (2007). *Effective features of dual language education programs: A review of research and best practices* (2nd ed.). Washington, DC: Center for Applied Linguistics.

Lindholm-Leary, K.J., & Borsato, G. (2006). Academic achievement. In F. Genesee, K.J. Lindholm-Leary, W. Saunders, & D. Christian (Eds.), *Educating English language learners* (pp. 176-222). New York: Cambridge University Press.

Lindholm-Leary, K.J., & Howard, E.R. (2008). Language and academic achievement in two-way immersion programs. In T. Fortune & D. Tedick (Eds.), *Pathways to bilingualism: Evolving perspectives on immersion education*. Bristol, UK: Multilingual Matters.

Lyons, J. (2014). *Benefits of bilingualism*. Albuquerque, NM: Dual Language Education of New Mexico. http://www.dlenm.org

Marzano, R., Waters, T., & McNulty, B. (2005). *School leadership that works*. Alexandria, VA: Association for Supervision and Curriculum Development.

McConachie, S., Hall, M., Resnick, L., Ravi, A.K., Bill, V.L., Bintz, J., & Taylor, J.A. (2006). Task, text, and talk: Literacy for all subjects. *Educational Leadership, 64*(2), 8-14.

National Center for Education Statistics. (2011). *National Assessment of Educational Progress*. Washington, DC: Institute of Education Sciences, U.S. Department of Education. http://nces.ed.gov/nationsreportcard/studies/gaps/hwfaq.asp#big_picture

National Center for Education Statistics. (2013). *The nation's report card: Mega states: An analysis of student performance in the five most heavily populated states in the nation* (NCES 2013 450). Washington, DC: Institute of Education Sciences, U.S. Department of Education.

National Clearinghouse for English Language Acquisition. (2011a). *Omaha Public Schools. District Focus: Nebraska, School Year 2009-10.* Washington, DC: Author. http://www.ncela.gwu.edu/files/uploads/T3SIS_LEA/ne_omaha.pdf

National Clearinghouse for English Language Acquisition. (2011b). *What languages do English learners speak? NCELA Fact Sheet.* Washington, DC: Author. http://www.ncela.gwu.edu/files/uploads/NCELAFactsheets/ELLanguages2011.pdf

Olsen, L., & Jaramillo, A. (1999). *Turning the tide of exclusion: A guide for educators and advocates for immigrant students.* Oakland, CA: California Tomorrow.

Olsen, L., Bhattacharya, J., Chow, M., Jaramillo, A., Tobiassen, D., & Solorio, J. (2001). *And still we speak: Stories of communities sustaining and reclaiming language and culture.* Oakland, CA: California Tomorrow.

Perry, S. (2013, January). The bilingual brain. *Society for Neuroscience.* http://www.brainfacts.org

Rivera, C., Collum, E., Shafer Willner, L., & Sia Jr., J.K. (2006). An analysis of state assessment policies addressing the accommodation of English language learners. In C. Rivera & E. Collum (Eds.), *A national review of state assessment policy and practice for English language learners* (pp. 1-173). Mahwah, NJ: Lawrence Erlbaum.

Rowling, J.K. (1999). *Harry Potter and the Sorcerer's Stone.* New York: Scholastic.

Sáenz, B.A. (2004). My culture. In O. Santa Ana (Ed.), *Tongue-tied: The lives of multilingual children in public education.* Lanham, MD: Rowman & Littlefield.

Sandy-Sánchez, D. (2008). Secondary dual language guiding principles: A review of the process. *Soleado—Promising Practices from the Field, 1*(1), 8. http://www.dlenm.org

Singleton, G.E., & Linton, C. (2006). *Courageous conversations about race: A field guide for achieving equity in schools.* Thousand Oaks, CA: Corwin.

Sizemore, C. (2011). Planning for secondary dual language—Asking the critical questions. *Soleado—Promising Practices from the Field, 3*(3), 2-3. http://www.dlenm.org

Thomas, W.P., & Collier, V.P. (1997). *School effectiveness for language minority students*. Washington, DC: National Clearinghouse for English Language Acquisition. http://www.thomasandcollier.com

Thomas, W.P., & Collier, V.P. (2002). *A national study of school effectiveness for language minority students' long-term academic achievement*. Santa Cruz, CA: Center for Research on Education, Diversity and Excellence, University of California-Santa Cruz. http://www.thomasandcollier.com

Thomas, W.P., & Collier, V.P. (2009). *English learners in North Carolina, 2009*. Fairfax, VA: George Mason University. A research report provided to the North Carolina Department of Public Instruction. http://www.esl/ncwiseowl.org/resources/dual_language/ *and* http://wlnces.ncdpi.wikispaces.net/Dual+Language+%26+Immersion+Program

Thomas, W.P., & Collier, V.P. (2012). *Dual language education for a transformed world*. Albuquerque, NM: Dual Language Education of New Mexico-Fuente Press. http://www.dlenm.org

Thomas, W.P., & Collier, V.P. (2014). *English learners in North Carolina dual language programs: Year 3 of this study: School Year 2009-2010*. Fairfax, VA: George Mason University. A research report provided to the North Carolina Department of Public Instruction. http://www.esl/ncwiseowl.org/resources/dual_language/ *and* http://wlnces.ncdpi.wikispaces.net/Dual+Language+%26+Immersion+Program

Thomas, W.P., Collier, V.P., & Collier, K. (2010). *English learners in North Carolina, 2010*. Fairfax, VA: George Mason University. A research report provided to the North Carolina Department of Public Instruction. http://www.esl/ncwiseowl.org/resources/dual_language/ *and* http://wlnces.ncdpi.wikispaces.net/Dual+Language+%26+Immersion+Program

Wallis, C., & Steptoe, S. (2006). How to bring our schools out of the 20th century. *Time, 168*(25), 50-56.

Willis, J. (2012). Bilingual brains—smarter and faster. *Psychology Today*. http://www.psychologytoday.com

Wimberly, G.L., & Noeth, R.J. (2005). College readiness begins in middle school. *ACT Policy Report*. http://www.act.org

INDEX

A

Achievement gap/gap closure 11, 35–41, 58, 66–69, 80–82
Advocacy xix, 11, 92–93, 120–123, 131, 134–138
Albuquerque High School 161–162
Assessment/testing
    Biliteracy 96–97
    Comprehensive xviii, 42–43
    English proficiency 19–20, 96–97
    Language of 96–97, 99–102, 104–105, 107–112, 135, 144
    Spanish proficiency 105
    State curricular 95–96, 100, 106, 107–111

B

Bautista, David 111–114, 151–154, 178
Bilingual/bilingualism/bilingual schooling 14, 27, 30–31, 40–41, 87–90. *See also* Emerging/emergent bilinguals
Biliteracy 43, 80–82, 96–97, 105
Bivins, Emily 10–12, 15, 24–26, 50, 57–59, 80–82, 105, 120–125, 178
Book study list 60–61

C

Carrboro Elementary School 10–12, 24–26, 50, 57–59, 80–82, 105, 120–125
Colegio Frank Porter Graham Bilingüe 12
Collinswood Language Academy 51, 140–142
Communication Plan 30–31, 136–137
Cultural/Bicultural identity 1–4, 32, 38–43, 67, 159
Curriculum alignment plan 76–78, 86, 99

D

Dallas Independent School District 28–31, 54–56, 74-75, 84–86, 129–133
Demographics 11, 39, 103, 155
Dual language
    Budget 84–86
    Expanding the program 10–12, 22, 77–79, 140–145
    Features xiv–xix, 97–98
    Outcomes/goals xiv–xv, 1, 14, 28, 68, 82–83, 111–114, 114–116, 134–135, 155–159
    Program evaluation 74–75, 85, 97–99, 111–116
    Program model 73–77, 75–77, 80–82
        50:50 model 10–12, 79, 80–82
        90:10 model 10–12
        One-way 14, 28
        Two-way 5–6, 10–12, 14, 28, 40–41
    Research. *See* Longitudinal research
    Schoolwide 10–13, 50
    Strand 21, 82, 120–124, 136
    Student role 142, 145, 150–151
    Teachers. *See* Teachers/staff
    Transition to 27–38

E

East Central Independent School District 7–9, 32–34, 77–79, 100–102, 143–145
Emerging/emergent bilinguals 43, 102–103, 116–117
English as a second language (ESL)/English to speakers of other languages (ESOL) 5–7, 18–19
English learners/English language learners (ELLs) 5–7, 9, 14, 18–20, 35–38, 39–41, 76, 96, 116–117, 155

F

Families/parents xix, 7–9, 29, 68, 113, 119–131, 134, 149, 157

G

Grant, Nicolette Marie 51, 140–142, 178

H

Hamilton, Wanda 18–22
Harmon-Martínez, Lisa 161–162, 179
Harrisonburg City Public Schools 18–22
Heritage language 9, 111

I

Inclusion 3–9, 53
Instruction
    Decisions 32, 57–59, 76–77, 82–83, 111–113

Practices/strategies xvi–xviii, 24–26
Time/support in each language 77–82, 108–110
Irving Independent School District 28, 74–75
Izquierdo, Elena 39–43, 48–49, 90–93, 107–111, 179

J

Jurado, Mishelle 161–162, 179

K

Key School/Escuela Key 5–6, 13, 52–53, 59, 79, 88–90, 106, 127–129

L

Language acquisition/development xiv
Leadership 41–43, 65–69, 82–83, 90–93, 114–116, 150
Longitudinal research 3–4, 6, 102–104, 117
Lottery for native English speakers 7–8, 115–116

M

Makishima, Patricia 14, 35–38, 46–47, 56–57, 75–77, 86–87, 99, 180
Mason, Erin Bostick 1–4, 70–72, 82–83, 114–116, 180
Mobility 14
Myers, Marjorie 5–6, 13, 52–53, 59, 79, 88–90, 106, 127–129, 180

N

Native English speakers 1–3, 7–12
Networking/Networks 70–72, 75
No Child Left Behind 66, 95–96, 106

O

Omaha South High Magnet School 155–159
Ornelas, Iris González 7–9, 32–34, 77–79, 100–102, 143–145, 181
Ornelas, Manuel Enrique 7–9, 32–34, 77–79, 100–102, 143–145, 181
Ortega, Rony 155–159, 181

P

Painter, Gary 23, 61, 125–126, 182
Parents/families. *See* Families/parents

Partner language 75–77, 86, 139
Professional development xviii–xix, 25–26, 33–34, 54–57, 59, 61–63, 79, 112, 135–136, 152–154
Professional learning communities 57–59, 75
Program retreat 61–62

S

Sánchez, Francisca xiv–xx, 167, 182
School District U-46 14, 35–38, 46–47, 56–57, 75–77, 86–87, 99
Sizemore, Cindy 146–149, 183
Sizemore, Shea 150
Smithland Elementary School 22–23, 61, 125–126
Sociocultural xv–xvi, 1–4, 32, 38–39, 42–43, 65–69, 129
Socioeconomic status/Title I free and reduced lunch 3–4, 65-66, 100
Special education/Exceptionalities/Special needs 3–9, 117
Spies, Tracy 39–43, 48–49, 90–93, 107–111, 183

T

Tabet-Cubero, Edward 65–69, 183
Teachers/staff
    Bilingual 20, 50, 52–53, 149, 156
    Certification 46, 52–53, 61–62, 144
    International 51–53
    Staffing practices 47–49, 156
Torres-Morón, Dora 28–31, 44, 54–56, 74–75, 84–86, 129–133, 184
Transitional bilingual education 110
    Moving to dual language 27–38

V

Valero, Wilma 14, 35–38, 46–47, 56–57, 75–77, 86–87, 99, 184
Vargas, Marcia 134–138, 184

W

Woodburn School District 111–114, 151–154

Y

Ysleta Independent School District 146–151

Contributing Authors

David Bautista

David Bautista is currently the Assistant Superintendent in the Oregon State Department of Education Equity Unit, where he and his staff support schools and  school districts in their work on equity. He also supports the Oregon state legislature's Strategic Investment initiatives to plan, design, and implement dual language education across the state. He has been a bilingual educator since 1989, completed graduate studies in education, and served as bilingual teacher and bilingual program coordinator in several school districts, as well as superintendent of one of the first K-12 districtwide dual language school systems, in Woodburn, Oregon. He is the proud father of two children who are fully bilingual and successful university students.

Emily Bivins

Dr. Emily Bivins, principal of Frank Porter Graham Bilingüe in Chapel Hill, North Carolina, has 10 years of experience as a principal of successful dual language schools and holds a doctoral degree in education. Her prior experience includes professional service as a primary teacher and central office administrator. She believes strongly that dual language schools are a valid and powerful means of closing student achievement gaps in the United States and very much wants to collaborate and network with other dual language programs to increase their visibility to other educators. In addition to strongly supporting dual language programs for others, Emily is gratified that her own three children have received the many benefits of a dual language education.

Nicolette Marie Grant

After receiving her elementary education degree in New York, Nicolette Grant served 13 years as an elementary school teacher and literacy facilitator in Charlotte, North  Carolina schools. Following the completion of her National Board Certification and receiving her master's degree in school administration, she served for four years as assistant principal of a long-running K-5 dual language school, Collinswood Language Academy, in Charlotte, North Carolina, and then became principal of this school, whose strong program she has expanded to grades K-8. The school has received many national and international awards and is proud of its International Spanish Academy Designation with Spain's Ministry of Education.

Wanda Hamilton

Wanda Hamilton, now retired, holds a master's degree in education administration. She was an elementary teacher and principal before moving to a succession of central office administration positions in testing, Title I, Language Arts, English as a Second Language, Foreign Languages, and English. She was instrumental in establishing newcomer programs for ESL students, as well as the first dual language program in central Virginia, in Harrisonburg City Public Schools. She served for 2 years as state president of the Virginia ESL Supervisors' Association.

Lisa Harmon-Martínez

Lisa Harmon-Martínez is a native New Mexican who returned home to complete her master's degree in secondary education at the University of New Mexico. She currently teaches AP English Literature, serves as language arts department chair, and co-coordinates the bilingual department, which includes the dual language program, at Albuquerque High School. Her professional focus is to support emergent bilingual students' English language development and align the English and Spanish language arts curricula in her high school dual language program.

Elena Izquierdo

Dr. Elena Izquierdo is currently Associate Professor and program chair of Literacy/Biliteracy/Bilingual/Early Childhood Education in the College of Education at the University of Texas at El Paso. In prior years, she has been principal of Oyster School in Washington, D.C., a nationally recognized two-way dual language school, and the director of Language Minority Affairs in the District of Columbia Public Schools. Currently, her research and professional publications focus on dual language, biliteracy, and leadership and schooling for English learners.

Mishelle L. Jurado

Mishelle L. Jurado is a Spanish language arts teacher and co-coordinator of the bilingual department, including the dual language program, at Albuquerque High School. The teaching of Spanish as a heritage language, in addition to Spanish language arts, has deeply influenced her instruction and advocacy over the last 12 years. As part of her Ph.D. studies, she is investigating topics in standards and curricula that meet the needs of secondary bilingual students and their families. Mishelle's son and daughter are currently in secondary dual language programs.

Contributing Authors

Patricia Makishima

Patricia Makishima has held many positions in Illinois School District U-46 during the past 15 years. She has taught at the middle and high school levels, has chaired the ESL/bilingual department at her high school, and for the last 8 years has worked in the district's ELL department, most recently as the district dual language coordinator. She is a passionate advocate for English learners who has committed her professional career to helping all students become bilingual and biliterate citizens of this global society.

Erin Bostick Mason

Erin Bostick Mason is an experienced dual language administrator, researcher, teacher and parent, with a master's degree in educational leadership. Over the past 20 years, her professional work has emphasized systemic reform through multilingual education from pre-school through university levels. After a decade of leadership, managing dual language/English learner services for the San Bernardino County Superintendent of Schools (a CA state education service center), she now focuses her energy on her role as an intervention coach at the Norton Space and Aeronautics Academy (a K-8 dual language school), an adjunct professor at California State University, San Bernardino, and a dual language parent.

Dee McMann

Dee McMann has worked in bilingual and dual language schools as a classroom and resource teacher, instructional coach, and as a district resource teacher and co-facilitator for collaborative professional development projects with the University of New Mexico. As materials development coordinator for DLeNM, she works with DLeNM staff and educators around the state and country to provide quality, credible resources; to highlight effective practices in classrooms, schools, and districts; and to support educators and families/communities working toward equitable instructional contexts.

Marjorie L. Myers

Dr. Marjorie Myers has served since 1995 as principal of Francis Scott Key Elementary School-Escuela Key in Arlington, Virginia, and the school has received international and state recognition. Her doctoral degree is in bilingual special education, with doctoral coursework in applied linguistics. She has taught and been a school administrator in Florida, Georgia, Venezuela, the District of Columbia, and Virginia. Her teaching experience spans kindergarten through higher education levels as a Spanish and ESOL teacher. In addition, she has previously served as a bilingual counselor, assistant principal, principal, and central office program manager for services for English learners.

Iris González Ornelas

Iris González Ornelas is an experienced program coordinator of bilingual/ESL/dual language programs in the San Antonio, Texas area. She holds a Master of Science in Education Administration and has previously worked in several school districts as a bilingual/ESL teacher, a curriculum coordinator, and a director of a newcomer center. She is currently the coordinator of a PK-12 dual language program in East Central Independent School District, having served in this position for 7 years. As a consultant, she has assisted school districts with needs in dual language program development, implementation, and teacher training.

Manuel Ornelas

Manuel Ornelas holds a master's degree in education administration and is specialized as a middle school principal. His professional assignments and consulting for school districts in the San Antonio, Texas, area and elsewhere have emphasized developing and implementing successful dual language programs. In prior years, he has served as an elementary school bilingual teacher, an elementary school assistant principal and principal, a middle school assistant principal, and as a bilingual education director who developed and implemented dual language schools.

Rony Ortega

Dr. Rony Ortega earned his doctorate in educational administration and he studied the long-term achievement of dual language and ESL students in his dissertation. He has served as a high school teacher, counselor, and middle school athletic director in the Omaha, Nebraska public schools. As a high school assistant principal, he administered the school's highly successful secondary dual language program. At present, he is an Omaha middle school principal who is passionate about promoting dual language schools. He has enrolled his own two children in the Omaha K-12 dual language program.

Gary Painter

Gary Painter is the principal of Smithland Elementary School in Harrisonburg, Virginia, and has been an educator for 24 years. He has been a primary supporter and developer of the first dual language immersion program in the Shenandoah Valley and has overseen the program at his school for the past 5 years. Gary received a master's degree in education administration from Shenandoah University in 1996. He served as an upper-grades classroom teacher and an elementary school assistant principal in two school divisions. In addition, he teaches education classes at James Madison University.

David Rogers

David Rogers received his Master of Arts in Bilingual/Bicultural Education in 1992 and completed his Education Specialist in Education Administration in 2000.

David has 20 years' experience as a dual language classroom teacher, program coordinator, school administrator, and director of an educational non-profit. He has taught in Paraguay, South America; South Bronx, New York; and Albuquerque, New Mexico. David presently serves as the Executive Director for Dual Language Education of New Mexico, a non-profit that is committed to promoting the effective design and implementation of dual language enrichment education. His daughters attend a dual language school.

Francisca Sánchez

Francisca Sánchez has recently retired as associate superintendent in the Hayward Unified School District in California. She has served in a variety of leadership positions at the district, county, regional, and state levels, including as chief academic officer for San Francisco USD and assistant superintendent for curriculum and instruction with the San Bernardino County Office of Education. She is a passionate advocate for equity and justice who first entered school as an English learner. Her professional work has been widely recognized by her colleagues in California, and she serves as president of the California Association for Bilingual Education. She has published on the topics of 21st century learning environments and notes proudly that her granddaughter is receiving the benefits of dual language education.

Cindy Sizemore

Cindy Sizemore is currently the assistant principal at Eastwood Knolls International School, Ysleta Independent School District (YISD), in El Paso, Texas. Deeply committed to dual and multilingual education, she was previously the YISD Dual Language Coordinator, as well as a K-12 German and Russian teacher, and high school dual language coordinator. Cindy is also the mother of two dual language students—Shea, who graduated with the dual language honor seal, and Devon, who is a dual language sophomore.

Shea Sizemore

Shea Sizemore is a dual language graduate from Bel Air High School in the Ysleta Independent School District in El Paso, Texas. She is currently a senior at the University of North Texas, earning her bachelor's degree in anthropology with minors in both Spanish and medical anthropology.

Tracy Spies

Dr. Tracy Spies is a faculty member teaching graduate TESOL courses at the University of Nevada, Las Vegas in the Department of Educational and Clinical Studies. She has prior experience as a teacher and instructional leader in transitional bilingual and dual language programs. She was one of the recipients of the national Milken Educator Award in 2010. Currently, she works extensively with public schools on designing and implementing bilingual programs that provide high quality instruction for English learners.

Edward Tabet-Cubero

Edward Tabet-Cubero is an experienced bilingual educator who is currently the deputy director of DLeNM, a non-profit organization that promotes dual language education nationwide and also provides professional development and advocacy resources to schools and school districts. He holds a master's degree in bilingual curriculum and instruction and has professional experience as a classroom teacher; as an elementary, secondary, and central office administrator; and as a university instructor. His professional focus is on the convergence of best practices in English learner education, instructional leadership, and public policy. He is proud to have four daughters who are dual language learners.

Contributing Authors

Dora Torres-Morón

Dora Torres-Morón is currently the Language and Literacy Executive Director for the Dallas Independent School District in Dallas, Texas, and oversees eight departments and the largest dual language program in Texas. She has served in a variety of leadership roles and on leadership advisory boards during her career, most currently working with the Department of Education in Guatemala. Several Texas and national groups have recognized her work as an advocate for students and as a leader in providing education opportunities for students.

Wilma Valero

Wilma Valero is a veteran educator who has worked in School District U-46, the second largest Illinois school district after Chicago, for the past 24 years. During that time, she has been a bilingual teacher, a reading specialist, and is currently director of the district's programs for more than 9,000 English learners, including a large dual language program. Her long-time goal has been to promote teaching and learning processes that emphasize language and culture as a means of attaining social justice and equity for all students. Wilma is the proud mother of two grown men—one fully bilingual (English/Spanish) and the other trilingual (English/Spanish/Japanese). Reflected in her family is her educational philosophy of validating language and culture as instrumental tools for success.

Marcia Vargas

Marcia Vargas is now retired as the executive director of 2-Way CABE, an affiliate of the California Association for Bilingual Education that promotes two-way dual language education. For more than 20 years, she has made it a priority to disseminate successful two-way dual language programs throughout the United States through conference presentations, professional development institutes, and direct assistance to school districts. She continues to be a national advocate for the development of dual language schools through her ongoing work with CABE.

Professors Virginia Collier and Wayne Thomas are internationally known for their research on long-term school effectiveness for linguistically and culturally diverse students. Dr. Collier is a professor emerita of bilingual/multicultural/ESL education, and Dr. Thomas is a professor emeritus of evaluation and research methodology, both of George Mason University. This is their third title in a series published by DLeNM and Fuente Press, following *Educating English Learners for a Transformed World* and *Dual Language Education for a Transformed World*. For other publications by Dr. Thomas and Dr. Collier, please visit their website at *www.thomasandcollier.com*.

About the Photographs

Our thanks to the following for the photographs in this book:

Academy of International Studies—Woodburn School District, Woodburn, Oregon

Albuquerque High School—Albuquerque Public Schools, Albuquerque, New Mexico

Carrboro Elementary School and Colegio Frank Porter Graham Bilingüe—Chapel Hill-Carrboro City School District, Chapel Hill, North Carolina

Collinswood Language Academy—Charlotte-Mecklenburg Schools, Charlotte, North Carolina

Corporation for Public Broadcasting: New Mexico PBS—American Graduate Day Champion, Gilberto Lobo, Truman Middle School, Albuquerque Public Schools, Albuquerque, New Mexico

Dallas Independent School District—Dallas, Texas

Dual Language Education of New Mexico—Albuquerque, New Mexico

Dr. Elena Izquierdo, Project LEAD Collection—University of Texas at El Paso

Key School-Escuela Key—Arlington Public Schools, Arlington, Virginia

Erin Bostick Mason, Personal Collection

Omaha South High Magnet School—Omaha Public Schools, Omaha, Nebraska

Francisca Sánchez, Personal Collection

School District U-46—Elgin, Illinois

Smithland Elementary School—Harrisonburg City Public Schools, Harrisonburg, Virginia (with special thanks to photographer Samantha Ritter)

Edward Tabet-Cubero, Personal Collection

Walnut Grove K–8 School & Dual Language Academy—Patterson Joint Unified School District, Patterson, California

—Special thanks to Moisés González, MarAbí Productions, Inc., for design and creation of the cover image—

DLeNM is grateful to Starline Printing in Albuquerque for their expertise and support in publishing *Creating Dual Language Schools for a Transformed World: Administrators Speak.*